True Stories

Of

Real Mines

Real Miners &

Real People

Written By
Harvey S. Bellm

Bisbee, Arizona
2010

FIRST EDITION
HAND BOUND

BISBEE, ARIZONA
2010

IN MEMORY OF ALL OF THE
REAL PEOPLE AND REAL PLACES
THAT HAVE INFLUENCED MY LIFE.

CONTENTS

PART TWO - GOLD MINING

PART THREE - URANIUM MINING

PART FOUR - COAL MINING

PART FIVE - "REAL PEOPLE"

PART SIX - SOUTHEASTERN UTAH

PART SEVEN - A FEW MORE STORIES

ACKNOWLEDGEMENTS

I would like to acknowledge the many people who made this book possible.

I am especially grateful to my wife, Freda, or Fritz (her endearing nickname) for her loving patience and never ending tolerance during the process of writing these stories and all of the other years we have been together. I love her dearly.

I am also grateful to my six children who I am very proud of. They have all done amazingly well and are all very talented and have acquired incredible common sense and work ethics. My hopes are that their children will care for them as they have cared for us in our older years.

Special thanks to Alan Prenty, for the time and effort he took to put together a number of the stories into book format which lit the fire that inspired the compilation of this book.

I would especially like to thank my daughter, Fritzie, whose fire was lit by the sight of the effort put forth in the initial attempt of making my stories into a book. She carefully edited each story without influencing my particular writing style and finally put it all into this first edition of my life stories.

Introduction

Seventy Eight Years Of Unbelievable Experiences Of Real People From The Time Of The Great Depression To The Turn Of The 21st Century.

I was born in 1931 in Glenwood Springs, Colorado. Being one of the "Bellm Boys" as were my father and all my uncles and it would also include my three sons plus three capable daughters. There are many experiences to be told.

My mining experiences started soon after I married Freda "Fritz" in December of 1950. In the spring of 1951 I hired out to the Placita Coal Company on the Crystal River in Colorado. This mine closed down after several months. Then in the fall of 1951 I hired out at the Empire Zinc Mine on the "bull gang". This was near Vail, Colorado. Soon with four feet of snow on the level I couldn't get to work.

In 1953 I staked uranium claims in Western Colorado and Utah. I staked eighty six claims in Red Canyon just east of what is now Lake Powel. I also staked one hundred and twenty five claims in Tabaguach Valley east of Naturita, Colorado. In 1957 I hired out at

Climax Molybdenum located at the top of Fremont Pass which was more than eleven thousand feet high. This mine was thirteen miles north of Leadville, Colorado. In the spring the miners went on strike so we moved to Placerville which is north of Telluride, Colorado. I cut timber for the Diamond Match Company until their existing contract was finished.

The next mine I worked at was the Mineral Joe 11 of Climax Uranium Company near Uravan, Colorado. After a year there I was offered a contract on Beaver Mesa just east of the LaSalle Mountains in Utah. The mine closed in 1960 and after that I was hired to produce ore from the old Rajah Mine on Rock Creek west of the Dolores River and north of Uravan. The boss went "bust" and then I hired out to Union Carbide of Uravan. I started out in the Paradox D "shaft" on Monogram Mesa and was then transferred to their 5&6 Incline. Next they had me producing ore in the Nil Mine until it was shut down.

I then produced uranium ore at the Dianna Mine and the John K. Mine far to the west of Carbide's mines on Wild Steer Mesa at the head of Bull Canyon for two leasers who were partners. I was then transferred to the American Eagle Mine in Big Gypsum Valley, to re-open and set up a mining operation which turned out to be a losing proposition.

The Mendisco Mining Company also on Wild Steer Mesa hired me as a miner. I re-opened the Babe Ruth Incline Mine. About that time I realized that too many of my mining friends were dead or dieing of radiation related sicknesses.

In 1964 I re-hired at Climax Molybdenum Company and stayed there for ten full years although after eight years they put me on the surface because of bad health. I left Climax and moved to Utah where it was warmer. I drove some drift and incline for private parties there and I had a clean-up lease on the Cottonwood 4 uranium mine. After the clean-up lease I quarried sand stone in the same area for building stone. Getting seriously injured while loading a large piece of sand stone put an end to the stone business.

I was hired by a promoter out of Aspen to open up a marble quarry that was in a questionable wilderness area and it proved to be impossible to do. Then I opened up several mines south of Aspen and even tried to open up a mine of my own. I worked some placer gold claims in the Bisbee area and then I produced gold from a claim near Virginia City, Montana.

From Virginia City, Montana we went to Jarbidge, Nevada and spent a year opening up gold mines and working there. All this is the tip of the ice burg.

Bellm Family History

I have always been fascinated by factual experiences of "REAL PEOPLE." That is, those who do not resort to exaggeration and outright falsehood. There is nothing more enlightening and interesting than the truth. I am not a fluent speaker or writer and have no reason to exaggerate or to be untruthful as you so will realize. Honest mistakes might be noted, but my word is my bond and my hand shake is my solemn guarantee. Any incident, any name or location of any mountain, mine or man is solid fact. Some of the stories may overlap but each one is a story in itself.

Continue along with me as I begin an almost unbelievable journey through the Great Depression, Uranium Boom, coal mines, uranium mines, molybdenum mines, gold mines and placers.

My father of a sixth grade education came from a family of German coal miners, lately of Illinois, just after the Turn of the Century (the 19th century that is). He was born in Glenwood

Springs. He and some of his brothers cowboyed in the Three and Four Mile Country south of Glenwood Springs. His father and the other brothers were coal miners. They were all hard workers who worked with their hands and used their heads.

My mother was a small delicate Swiss girl, born in the Alkali Creek area north of Glenwood Springs, New Castle and the Colorado River. Her family were ranchers. One uncle was a gun smith. I was told that he repaired a firing pin in a hunting rifle for Teddy Roosevelt. Teddy Roosevelt used to stay in the Hotel Colorado and hunt mountain lions in the mountains right behind the hotel. Many mountain lions were killed in that area, even within the city limits.

In 1928 or 1929 my father, Harvey, and his brother, Ray, were working on the big bridge that crossed the Colorado River. The big red sandstone Hotel Colorado was on the north side along with the largest outdoor natural hot springs pool. On the south side was the small town of Glenwood Springs which at that time was mostly farming and ranching community. The hot springs had originally been a gift from the Indian, Chief Ouray.

While my father and Uncle Ray were working on the bridge, the Glenwood Springs Light and Power Company saw how well they worked and hired them both. They both worked there until the start of the war. At that time their starting wage was under one hundred dollars a month and they worked a six day week. My father was married shortly after going to work for the Light Company and his wages were raised to one hundred dollars a month.

I was born in December 1931 in Glenwood Springs, Colorado, and sad to say my mother died as a result of a caesarian section. She was too small and delicate and couldn't have the baby on her own. The doctor tried to perform a caesarian section on her, but it was his first time and he made an honest mistake which caused her death. I was born with my intestines messed up and suffered with them for fourteen years. The same doctor operated on me and repaired the damage. He was Doctor Grenvil A. Hopkins and he was a good country doctor. I think, because of my mother dying, he never charged us for doctoring after that.

My Uncle Milton Bellm was noted for being a quick-draw artist with a pistol and managed to shoot himself through his holster and the bullet lodged in his knee cap. He was watching kids shooting sticks in the Colorado River with an old rifle and he told them he could do better than that with his pistol, but he had filed the trigger down and as he pulled the pistol out of the holster it went off and the bullet went down his leg bone and lodged in the knee cap. They were about a mile from town at Horseshoe Bend. They got him to Hopkins' Hospital but he died in three days of either shock or lead poisoning. This same uncle and his brother, Herman, recovered gold from around a rock just across the river from where he shot himself. Herman lost his life later in an explosion in the New Castle Coal Mine. Just as a matter of interest, that particular mine is still on fire to this day down underneath the Colorado River and up the other side.

My dad and two uncles were hunting grouse in the Four Mile country on horseback. My dad was using a brace of Russian 44's and he was a crack shot. He could shoot the head right off a grouse. He once got off his horse and began jumping from rock to rock in a lava bed. His pistol bounced out of his holster, went off and he got hit in the hip. The bullet went in his right hip and came out close to his tailbone. He was forced to ride his pony several miles to a horse drawn wagon and was hauled to the hospital another four miles. Doc Hopkins bent him over the operating table, pulled his britches down and ran a swab through the hole, both ways, that is. "Well, you better go upstairs and lay down a couple of days, Harvey," said Doc Hopkins. Then my dad told my Uncle Ray to get rid of those Russian 44's. I might add that I have only seen one old worn out Russian 44. These guns were mentioned many times in the stories of Louis L'Amour's and they were made exclusively for the Russian government.

These were the good old days, they were rough but people enjoyed them. Most every one was healthy and happy and mostly poor, I might add. One of my uncles lost part of his hand when a #6 blasting cap went off prematurely. Old Doc Hopkins bandaged it up and my uncle went back to work. That's the way real people were. Even the doctor himself amputated his own toes when they were frozen. There was no other doctor around. Later he got x-ray burns from steadying patients as he X-rayed them, not knowing how dangerous it was. He had to amputate his own hand with the assistance of an adopted son and a nurse and then later his arm above the elbow. He doctored until the day he died.

I had another uncle, Leo, who also got shot through the thigh and they made him walk to the wagon because they thought that it would be better for him to bleed than to get blood poisoning. He ended up back at good old Doc Hopkins' Hospital and he lived through that. Later he ended up working on the Alcan Highway and that's another story.

Now back to my dad and the Power Company. In about 1932 he was driving the Power Company's big old battery powered truck and he almost ran down my step-mother-to-be, Lorene. That truck was extremely heavy and it took two men to steer it. It had solid rubber tires and a big chain drive. It was a whining, screaming, clanking monster with no cab on it. So because of this incident, my dad became acquainted with Lorene and they later got married.

One of my first memories of that time was when I was standing on the toilet seat and my father and step-mother were wrapping gauze around my waist to keep my hernia in. Sometimes I would have to lie down on my back to put the rupture back in place, but it didn't stop me from getting into trouble just like all boys. All of us boys roamed the hills east of town and we all carried pocket knives, all of us. We played mumble peg, flipping our knifes at a drawn target in the dirt, lots of times between our feet. Another friend of mine, Severen Peterson, had bows and arrows that his father made us out of bamboo (his dad had been in the South Pacific before the war) which were soon taken away from us because they were just too dangerous.

It was about 1935 and I remember that we ate a lot of wild meat and fish. We had grouse almost every Sunday. Dad and Uncle Ray fished every other night at least three evenings a week and they carried me on their shoulders across and up and down the Roaring Fork River. I can remember that sometimes they would fall and go clear under the water and I would be screaming my head off. We actually ate pretty good, plain food, but we always had meat and potatoes and vegetables and fruits in season. I remember the Strawberry Day celebration where we could eat all the strawberries and ice cream we wanted. There still is a Strawberry Day celebration in Glenwood Springs, but it just isn't the same. I remember chili suppers and sleigh riding on the streets after dark and there would be several families involved. We had ice delivered several times a week for the ice boxes because there were not many refrigerators. All of us kids begged ice off of the wagon. It was probably like the ice cream trucks today—it was a great treat.

About 1938 or 1939 my dad's wages were raised to one hundred twenty five dollars a month and he bought a 1935 used black Dodge Touring Car. They used to drive down to Main Street on Saturday evening and park and watch the people walk by when we were too poor to go to the picture show. Dad and Uncle Ray managed to set aside a quarter-a-piece for each Saturday night so that they could go the Owl Café and Bar and get three raw oysters and a bottle of beer. Once in a while they had fifty cents each. It was about this time that I was told that I could go to the Glenwood Creamery and charge a nickel ice cream cone once in a while. I invited several of my friends to come with me and charged the ice cream cones to my folks and by the end of the month they got a bill for about a dollar and that was the end of that!

Keeping the proper sequence to seventy eight years of real life is quite challenging. There are so many things to relate and stories to tell I'm having trouble keeping them all straight, so bear with me.

We used to burn coal and stored it in a shed off the kitchen. Some times we had it hauled by a friend of ours named Winn Kyner. He had a homemade trailer made out of an old Model A car frame, pulled by a four door model A car. Anything over twenty miles an hour and the trailer was all over the road. Later my dad hauled the coal in an old 1918 Buick Touring Car that they stripped down for a fishing wagon to take in the High Country.

That old Buick's tires held sixty pounds of pressure and it took two men to hand pump them up. The tires were size thirty four by four. They were tall and mounted on wooden spoke rims. They managed to put an old flat head Dodge 6 cylinder in it with its three speed transmission and mounted the old 1918 transmission in the drive train backwards. With both transmissions in reverse it moved forward at about half a mile an hour. It had two seats made out of fifty gallon wooden whiskey barrels upholstered with horse hide. They used a wooden utility box on the back for a truck bed. There were three elliptical gas tanks on the rear with two or three spare tires fastened behind that. It had a thirty five pound mine rail for a front bumper. The hood and the fenders were made out of flat tin. There were several gallon cans with extra parts that were filled with oil and the lids soldered on and these were fastened on where ever they could find a space for them. On the right hand side just in front of the barrel seat was an offset platform built especially for our little pot bellied fox terrier dog. There was a low railing around it made out of plumber's tape and wrapped with friction tape to help hold him in. He used to jump off of it and just go end over end chasing ground hogs and sometimes they chased him. They carried a long one and a half inch rope that they used to winch them selves out of bad spots by wrapping the rope around a tree and then tying each end to a rear wheel. It was slow but effective.

This was the first motorized vehicle to travel the back roads in the area. Later there was a similar one to it that was an old Star Touring Car. In making the trip from Glenwood Springs to Deep Lake in the old Buick (they called it the "Jeep", it took fourteen hours, long hard hours, of digging through snow banks and fighting mud holes. The first twenty one miles were on the black top and then twenty more miles up over the mountain and across the flattops on the old abandoned stage coach road. We stopped at Coffee Pot Springs for water and made coffee and hunted arrow heads. From there we drove past the old county seat at

Carbonate. Then on to Grizzly Meadows where we would fly fish for twenty minutes and catch a dishpan full of little fish for our supper. From there on we listen for locust and picked them off the bushes and put them in tobacco cans for bait to catch the big fish in Deep Lake. Those fish went crazy over locust.

There was a Forest Service cabin on the north shore and a lean-to on the east side of the lake along with a couple of tables. There were snow banks nearby where we would put our wooden case of soda pop and a case of beer. It was usually late when we got up there and we unloaded as quickly as we could. The women took care of the camp chores and us boys headed for the lake.

There was an ancient old waterlogged wooden boat that we took out on the lake. Everyone sat on one side of the boat to balance it and it was my job to row the boat. I thought that was just great and they worked me to death. We would row out in the lake and fish back toward the bank until it got too dark. Still the fish had to be cleaned. We laid out a big heavy canvas tarp and we all slept on it. Sometimes both of the old vehicles would travel together. We camped together, ate together and all slept out on tarps in front of the fire. We all shared the outhouse with its Monkey Ward catalog. When there were two families the women did most of the work setting up camp and preparing meal, especially that first supper. Both families had dogs. There was one time when one of the women was pressured into making sandwiches for us fishermen. Out of spite she used canned dog food in the sandwiches and we didn't know the difference, the laugh was on us. We were up before daylight and we fished until dark every night.

P.S. This isn't the end of this story, but it's a good story and is more of a beginning to all the rest.

PART ONE
MY YOUNGER YEARS

The Great Depression
And The 1918 Buick

The 1930's were something to remember, and it wasn't all that bad. No one had any money, but we all had something to eat and a roof over our heads, of some sort. People were glad to be alive, even if they had to get by on bare necessities. My father and my Uncle Ray, referred to as the "Boys," fished in the Roaring Fork River almost every other evening so we ate fresh trout, three or four times a week. Saturday evening my dad went out to Three Mile or Four Mile Road and came home with grouse for Sunday dinner. The rifle he used was an old octagon barreled 22 rifle. This was also the gun that kept us in deer meat, which was the main meat that most of us had to eat. Gasoline was about fifteen cents a gallon and that was about the price of a box of 22 shells. We couldn't afford to go to the picture show on Saturday night, so my folks would park on the main street and watch the people go by. A lot of the folks that had cars, would park where they could watch the people walking by that had no car or no gas for their car and those walking on the street watched those in the cars. Everybody knew everybody and if someone was seen with a new hat, or a new pair of britches, it was talked about and people wondered if they were involved in something shady to be able to afford something new. Well, it was something to talk about, something to do, when there was no extra cash for amusement. Now, my dad and my Uncle Ray worked for the Glenwood Springs Light and Power Company for the exorbitant wages of one hundred dollars a month, with a one week vacation each year, and later the pay per month was raised to one hundred and twenty five dollars a month. With this raise in pay, we bought an almost new 1935 Dodge four door sedan and both Dad and Uncle Ray went to the Owl Café and Bar on a Saturday night to celebrate with a beer each and three raw oysters, which cost twenty five cents.

About this time, a 1918 Buick Touring Car came into our possession and Dad and Uncle Ray being avid fishermen, decided to make it into a car that would take them to Deep Lake on the Flat Tops. There had been a stage coach road at one time, perhaps thirty years before, that went up behind Iron Mountain to Transfer Springs, then to Hip-Roof Cabin, on to Blue Lake, Heart Lake, Bison Lake and finally, Deep Lake, but this road was entirely too steep for most vehicles. At this time the only four wheeled drive vehicle we had heard of, was one made for Antarctica. The 1918 Buick was stripped to the frame. A newer engine was installed with a three speed transmission and then the 1918 transmission was attached backwards, behind it. There were no welders to do the work, so the adaptation was done the hard way with the help of the only gas torch in town. The end result was a remarkable truck that had thirty by four inch tires mounted on wooden spoke wheels with utility boxes on each side of a wooden bed. There were three elliptical shaped gas tanks stacked on the back with two extra mounted tires behind them. The front and rear bumpers were made of thirty-five pound mine rail and the fenders and hood were just bent pieces of tin. There was the 1918 windshield above the old instrument panel and the two bucket seats were made out of old whiskey kegs, stuffed with horse hair and upholstered with horse hide. On the left side of the floor boards was a gallon paint can full of spare parts immerged in oil, and to the side of that was a place for the dog with a railing covered with plumber's tape and friction tape.

They got the idea that where the old stage road came down to the Colorado River, twenty five miles east of Glenwood Springs, was the place to begin the trip. It was twenty one miles up the Colorado River to Dot Zero, the turn off to Sweetwater, and another twenty to twenty five miles to Deep Lake, up over the mountains, by way of Coffee Pot Springs, the old ghost town of Carbonate, and then through Grizzly Meadows, a fourteen hour trip after the road was rebuilt. The first trip to the lake took two full days and most of the second night. On the washed out hillsides, the upper wheel was run in a dug out trench and where the mud was too slick, a rope was looped around a tree and tied to a wooden spoke on each wheel using the wheel hub for a winch drum. Streams were forded and snow drifts were crossed with tire chains and a great amount of shoveling. All of this was done for just one short week of fishing a year, and it was worth every bit of the effort that went into it. Trout under one and a half pounds were thrown back. There was at one time, a thirty six inch Rainbow Trout mounted and on display in the hardware store. It weighed one pound to the inch. It was caught in Deep Lake and hauled twenty one miles to town, packed in snow and brought out on a horse.

We had use of a rotten wood boat that was water logged on the left side so everyone had to sit close to the right side. We had a lean-to, a table, snow drifts for a refrigerator and even an out-house. That week we had a case of different kinds of pop in bottles and there was a case of beer in cans that had to be pried open with a special opener. It was always cold, so we all slept together with a tarp under us and another one over us. Fishing started at about four in the morning and lasted until way after dark.

There were oranges and a candy bar with our lunches of stew and sandwiches.

In the summer of 1939, we took a trip to the High Country in the "Jeep", as we started calling it. They started calling it that after the little Popeye character, Sweet Pea of the comic strip, because of the way that it could crawl over about anything. With both transmissions in reverse, the Jeep would creep along slower than a man usually walked, and it could do speeds up to forty miles per hour safely. On one trip, we were bundled up in coats and blankets and on the road up Glenwood Canyon before two a.m. in the open top Jeep. My dad and step-mother were up front in the bucket seats until she got too cold, and then she climbed into the back with us kids and Uncle Ray climbed up front. When we came to the cut-off up the mountain, the muffler was removed and hid in the sagebrush so we wouldn't lose it hanging it up on the rough road ahead. With the extra noise the truck made, just before daylight, we came down into a small park filled with elk. There was complete confusion in the herd as they tried to get away from the noisy monster with the two big shining eyes. Most of the animals ran away from us except for three of the bulls and they came right at us. Two of them veered off to the left, but one kept right on coming with its big antlers lowered to ram us head on! My dad killed the engine and turned off the headlights and the big bull jumped over the fender coming so close we could have reached out and touched it. Just a few seconds later, the lights were turned back on and the elk were all gone. Everyone was wide awake now and we continued on our way to Grizzly Meadows, where we fly fished for just twenty minutes and caught a dishpan full of small, pink-meat Brookes. We arrived at the lake about four in the afternoon. Dad and Uncle Ray were fishing within fifteen minutes. We had fish for supper, fish for breakfast and every meal after that. Fly fishing began at four in the morning and stopped at breakfast time. During the remainder of the day, we fished from the boat, cruising around the inlet and the outlet and even checking out the stream that flowed from the lake. We only kept the BIG ones.

Deep Lake is more than seven hundred feet deep, most likely an old extinct volcano crater. Most of the big fish caught there were Mackinaw trout, placed there many years before to upgrade the fishing. But because they ate all the small rainbow trout, their value is still questionable, however; large Rainbow trout and some large Brookies were caught there, weighing several pounds. The largest fish caught there were the ugly Mackinaw, except for a three foot rainbow, and that was the first and last that I know of that was that big.

The fishing was disturbed many times by two beavers that made a lot of splashing around the boat. One time, I remember, when the beavers were ruining the fishing in the lake. We started fishing down the outlet and one of them followed us, smacking his tail in the water. My dad pulled out his old 38-40 Navy Colt and let that beaver have it. Later, we went back to fishing in the lake and were catching nice fish again. My dad said, "If that other damn beaver comes around, the same goes for him." That evening, when I saw the beaver swimming around, I ran up to camp yelling, "Daddy, Daddy, get the gun, the other beaver is out!" As it happened, my dad and Uncle Ray were talking to the District Ranger and he had just asked the boys if they had seen the beaver. The ranger thought I was pretty cute and everyone laughed, but later I was taken aside and my hind end sure didn't feel too cute when proper emphasis was placed on the incident. The "Boys" took a friend with them once that got mad at one of the "tail smackers" and cast a spinner across its back and gave a yank. He set the treble hook and, boy! He got results! The angry beaver charged while he was standing up to his boot tops in the water. That was something to behold, a man half running and swimming to shore trying to outrun the beaver!!

The boys helped build another fishing rig for a friend. It was created from an old 1923

Starr Touring Car, and looked much the same as the Buick when they were through, except for the front seats and the gas tanks. It had wooden spoke wheels and the same narrow high tires, but only two fuel tanks. These two antiques pulled and pushed each other out of mud, snow banks and at times beaver dams, while fishing and hunting together all over the Flat Tops and the Glenwood and Aspen country. Later, one more of these fishing rigs was built out of a Model A Ford with a two speed differential. It was fitted with the rear tires covered with a band of spikes for better traction. It was the usual procedure to back up hills too steep for first gear, as reverse had more power. Everyone carried chains and ropes, and always had picks, shovels, a pole-axe and various steel bars. They also carried a full set of hand tools, along with extra parts and extra gas and oil. Those that went through the Great Depression learned to be self-sufficient and those of us who lived through it, continue to be that way today.

The direct drive steering gear required two good men to steer when the Jeep was moving at slow speeds over rough ground. When one of the tires was low, it was hand pumped back up to sixty pounds pressure, requiring two men on the pump. The remarkable old "Jeep" was the high-light of all the parades, loaded to the limit with adults and kids and a dog with everyone dressed up like Arkansas Hillbillies.

So to us, it wasn't so bad in the thirties, even with hand-me-down clothes and lots of beans, potatoes and wild game for a steady diet. Heck, for twenty five cents, if you had twenty five cents, you could buy a bottle of milk and a loaf of bread and have some change coming back. A big pie at the local bakery cost fifteen cents and a baker's dozen of cookies were ten cents. Ice was delivered to each home for ten cents and all the kids were given the chips that came off when the blocks were cut up. It was quite a luxury for us kids and we chased the truck as far as we could, and begged for more.

I will always have fond memories of all the trips we made in the Jeep. Whenever I smell potatoes or eggs being fried in bacon grease, or the wonderful smell of boiled coffee, or even peeling an orange, it brings back all the wonderful memories. Yes, I guess that is was a terrible depression and people did without a lot of things, but looking back to those times, we never realized just how bad we had it, because we were enjoying "Real Life" with "Real People" making new friends, having great experiences and were healthy and happy.

We made many, many fishing and hunting trips with the Jeep, and later, my folks bought a house that was built in 1919, with a garage, to park the Jeep in. People were beginning to prosper. The war in Europe began to change the whole economy. It changed our lives as money began to appear in people's pockets and our lives were made a little easier, or so it seemed at the time, and so it was the end of the Great Depression.

THE FOURTH OF JULY WEEKEND
ASPEN 1946

Aspen, Colorado was some town back in the 1940's. It came alive right after the war. Folks came from all over to be a part of the excitement. Aspen could not get enough builders, schemers, promoters and workers to satisfy its demands. Many were just after the money that flowed quite freely for a time and many were interested in seeing Walter Papki's ski lift climbing up over Aspen Mountain to the Sun Deck at the top of the mountain. The Aspen Construction Company just couldn't get enough men to rebuild the town. Workers took residence anywhere and everywhere. The crews lived in the old Vendome Hotel while it was in the process of restoration. They moved from room to room as work progressed and had to find water and electricity where they could for the time being.

The Prince Albert Hotel was open. The bedrooms on the second floor all had knotted ropes tied to the foot of each of the beds, to be thrown out the window in case of fire. The floor level of the building housed the carpenter shop with its big double fifty five gallon drum wood stove that heated most of the upstairs. Across the street was the electric shop, where my father was the Foreman. He later became the General Foreman of the entire crew. Across the street again to the Vendome, on the ground floor to the east was The Ice Cream Shop, much like they were before the war. The west corner of the hotel was the remodeled bar which was the only bar in town at that time. In the vacant lot next to the bar were the horse shoe pits which were always in use by the workers. There was, for a time, a volley ball court next to the horseshoe pits but it was moved across the street alongside the electric shop. Next to the horseshoe pits was, and is now, the Aspen Drugstore. Twenty five cents a person it cost to play and we could win or lose perhaps fifty cents a night betting. Horseshoe games were a little more serious when it came to betting sometimes it went as high as a dollar a game.

Baseball was popular and for a while there were only about five families in the town. Between two of the families there were enough people for a full team. There were several town teams that competed evenings and weekends. I remember a time when a player smacked the ball into the outer field and caught himself a charley-horse in the leg. Horns blared and spectators cheered as he jumped up and down trying to get to first base.

Aspen really opened itself up to the working men and all others that wished to get involved and enjoy the activity. For a time, there was one small narrow closet like room on the bottom floor of the Vendome that wasn't open to just anybody. It was lined with slot machines on both sides, but it didn't operate very long. The story was told that someone kept watch while others turned the machines upside down and tried to shake the money out of them.

Aspen was a real boom town again for a short while. Most of the people involved with the area at that time were "Real People," working with their hands and minds to accomplish a future for themselves and those about them. It was a little like the old mining days long past. True, there were no miners coming down off the mountains with their round lunch buckets and wearing the pompous looking black derbies which were the obvious indication of their line of work. There were very few hard rock miners in the area. One mine, the Midnight Mine, a mile up Queen's Gulch across Castle Creek, was still producing enough silver for some to make a living.

In 1946 there were still to be seen wet, black silver ore covered miners in wet suits and hard hats and rubber boots sloshing through the cold water running out of the portal of the mine to the cool mountain air on the back side of Aspen Mountain. These were the "Real Men" of the day just like the men driving the odd looking Aleutian Jeep dump trucks across the creek and up the narrow steep canyon road right by the mine, hauling the sand and gravel to the Sun Deck construction site far on up the very top of the mountain.

Most of the men worked hard, putting out an enormous amount of effort and energy into everything they did, their labor, their eating and drinking and when the work day was done even their recreation. The Forth of July was somewhat different there at that time, as many men went back to their homes for the holiday weekend, some over Independence Pass, and some just to the surrounding towns. It left a few of us to make the most of a few days off to our very own passions, and fishing was certainly one of them back then. Between the three Bellm Boys and Bob and several other fellows of authority, a well used Army Surplus 6x6 truck was borrowed from the usually drunk bricklayers and a fishing trip up the pass was to be undertaken, and that was the word for it, "Undertaken."

I backed the 1937 Chevy panel truck of the electrician's to the basement door of the Vendome and Bob began handing out the supplies for the three day trip. There was a huge hunk of beef from the freezer and gallons of canned goods, potatoes and other fresh foods. Several cases of beer and quite a few bottles of hard stuff and much more began to add up for all the men looking forward to the big event.

Before daylight the next morning, there we were, the whole bunch of us in and on the powerful old 6x6, traveling up Independence Pass to find two very high, High Country lakes that we had heard of. Up through the narrows in the cold Rocky Mountain air to the cut off to Lincoln Gulch, around the mountain and up a one lane trail, across an old rotten log bridge and we could see Grizzly Reservoir. There was a road of sorts seeming to go straight up the hill to the left, but we needed to go on up the valley, so my dad drove right into the reservoir camp and came to a halt just in front of the caretaker's house. That was the end of that road, but it was just the beginning of the obscenity and the screaming by the outraged pajama clad caretaker as he jumped up and down in front of the noisy old 6x6 truck with its load of eager fishermen. Screaming for us to get the hell out of his front yard and motioning for us to be on the trail like road above his place, the truck was backed up several lengths and aimed right up the hillside to the upper road. That didn't seem to please the old grouch at all and after tearing up the country side and forging a new path up the hill to continue up the road, his forceful encouraging comments could be heard for a quarter of a mile as we continued on.

Several miles up the gulch, we came to a wagon road aimed straight up the mountain.

We started in the lowest gear and speed to match. Creeping up the road with a cut bank on the left side above the wash, the outside duels hung over most of the time. We did quite well until we came to a cabin sitting a little too far out into the road and one of the rear wheels caught a bottom log and pulled it out from under the building. We just backed the truck up and forced it back into place as near as we could and continued on.

We were finally close to the lakes. The timberline was just above us and the sun was up over the mountains. Everyone was happy and nothing could stop us now. We made it! Locating a somewhat flat area, we stopped and set up camp, made coffee and took a minute to figure just what to do next. We were surrounded by snow banks and it was mighty cool, so the first order of the day was to lay in a supply of firewood. We chopped down and brought in the biggest tree we could carry. I think that there were seven of us at the time. We were all eager to fish but even with the sun up, it was still cold and so a big fire was started. The wood was damp and so several shots of gasoline were needed to get it going good and putting out some heat. Six of the seven had their cold backs to the fire, but one of the bunch was poking the fire around, so we thought. All of a sudden the cool mountain air was split with an enormous explosion and we all ran for cover as sparks and fire shot all around us. That fool had placed some pretty wicked fireworks in the fire. That, I suppose was the real beginning of the celebration on top of the snow capped mountains. By then everyone's blood was circulating quite well, and after some choice comments, we packed up our fishing gear and took off up to the first lake to fish.

At the Lake, we could see big fish close to the bank, some of them two and three feet long, but we couldn't get them to take a hook. Someone looked into the little stream flowing out of the lake and lowered a fly down to the water and BANG, he had a fish on his hook before it touched the water. All of us then hit the little brush choked water course and caught all the fish we could eat.

That night the air was filled with happy celebrating, with well fed men drinking and joking around the campfire under the bright night stars. The fire works really kept us on our feet most of the time and there was no shortage of them. After some of us crawled into our bedrolls the night finally became quiet and early the next morning we were up eating breakfast and getting started for the upper lake that was far above timberline. We waded snow banks, walked across snow slides and climbed to the lake and found that there was only a small pond surrounded by ice. We tied three fly lines together and tried dragging fish lures and flies

19

across the ice into the water and out the other side. It was a waste of time and so we started back. We slid down the snow slides sitting down, even joining several of us together, and holding our fly rods out to the side with our other gear in our laps. We were wet, but not too disappointed because we didn't catch any big fish. We had one more night under the stars with plenty to eat and drink and the finest fellowship any where.

The next morning, with our pan sized trout packed in snow, we loaded up, cleaned up our camp site, and started back down the steep narrow wagon road. We eased by the little old cabin, and reached the bottom of Lincoln Gulch and headed down the road above the caretaker's house to the rotten log bridge that spanned a ten foot wash. My dad shifted into high range and charged across the bridge and made a right turn against the cliff on the far side. We made it, but looking back, sad to say, the bridge didn't, it creaked and crunched and fell in behind us.

Aspen was a "Real Town" filled with "Real People", doing a "Real Man's" work in 1946. It was a little rough at times back them, more than fifty years ago. I remember the Chief of Police driving his old black pickup with City of Aspen painted in gold on the side, and the mayor rode a bicycle to his office-quite a change from today.

THE WILDERNESS TREK OF 1946

I was a fourteen year old boy with a nine shot H & R revolver, and a part wolf, part collie dog, climbing the high mountain trail above Dinkle Lake, looking for Thomas Lake that was only a spot on an old 1932 topographical map.

Beautiful, is the only way to describe the east side of the snow topped Mount Sopris, under a brilliant blue sky, with the view of a small clear water lake back behind me, through the green pine and the white aspen with the wake of a beaver crossing the quiet waters. Yes sir! Just a boy and his dog with a fly rod and a 22 pistol and an old 1932 C.C.C. bedroll and a few groceries secured to the home-made pack board. What more could you want? Clean, cool air to breath, cold, clear water to drink, fish and grouse and raspberries to eat, what could be better?

The sun was reflecting off of the bright white snow and the wet gray slide rock just where I figured Thomas Lake had to be, just a little ahead of me. Clouds were beginning to build up and I was expecting some great fishing, especially if a breeze came up to make riffles on the water.

Now that big dog was as eager as I was to make the most of the daylight hours, although he didn't realize that he had to share my fish or whatever the long barreled pistol would bring down. He did learn to like fried fish, he had to. For sure, the lake was there, and all the fish that I wanted to catch were there, and I sure caught them! Most of them seven or eight inch Brookies, all we could eat. Then the rains began and the fishing got better and my dog, Prince, and I got wetter. The rain turned into one of those High Country drizzles and it just wouldn't quit.

I put my bedroll and pack back under a sheltering pine, and made camp of sorts. Firewood was hard to come by and it was all wet by then, so I took off my boots and wrapped them in my coat and used them for a pillow and crawled into my well used army blanket in the heavy canvas bedroll. It rained and there was fog and mist and the water dripped down from the boughs on the tree above me until I was soaked and the dog was half drowned too and he climbed on top of the bedroll with me in it. We managed to make it through the night, uncomfortable and scared because we could hear the grinding noise of the enormous boulders rolling and sliding down the mountain just across the lake. It was dark and wet and cold and it sounded like the whole mountain was about to cover us up and we had nowhere to run.

Morning finally came, and the rain stopped and the mountain slide quieted down, but the sun didn't come out, there was only fog and dampness and a wet bedroll and pack and a half drowned big wet dog.

No warm breakfast for us, I ate a raw potato and had a drink of cold snow water and the dog nosed through the fish bones from the night before, that was it. I wadded up the wet bedding into somewhat of a lump and lashed it onto the pack board with the rest of the soggy gear and carrying the fly rod, we headed up over the mountain range to the south to the headwaters of Sopris Creek. One of my uncles was working on a cattle ranch some miles down the canyon. The fog was so thick that it was difficult to breath and the visibility was about as far as I could throw a rock. Finding the pole drift fence, that was built during the depression, I began following it south to what I believed to be Sopris Creek. It seemed like we had gone many miles before the fog began to lift. We had trudged for hours across the divide when finally the fog began to lift and there, across on the mountain side, were two cowboys, standing alongside their horses with their Winchesters aimed right at me and my dog. They were ready to shoot us, as the fog lifted. I began shouting and waving when I saw them and they just stared a while before taking their sights off of us. When we finally met up with them, they said that they thought that it was a bear and her cub. Well, that's what those two range riders said we looked like to them in the fog. It turned out that these were the Fender brothers, and they thought that we could use some help. Folks were like that, kind and helpful to a fault. They offered to ride to their camp and get me a horse to pack me and my wet gear, and they offered to feed me and the dog if we would stop in at their camp, but it was too far out of my way, so thanking them, we went on our way down into Sopris Creek Valley. Late that evening we came to a cow camp (back then, nobody passed a cow camp or a sheep camp without throwing in your hat), so we stopped and the puncher invited me in and offered to loan me a pack horse, but I refused. However, he wouldn't let me leave without eating. For supper he was going to fry a grouse that he had soaking in vinegar, but it had soaked too long and wasn't good, so instead he had venison steak, which is usual for cow camps. Early the next morning after a breakfast of steak and eggs and coffee with canned milk and sugar, the cowboy offered me a horse again, and I suppose that I should have taken him up on the offer, but I didn't and we left there and started the last of the trip down the trail.

I noticed that creek was full of nice big trout, bigger than the ones in Thomas lake, but we were getting close to the ranch now and there was a large bunch of range cattle in the field we were going through. We had no choice but to walk through them. Now, range cattle respect a man on a horse, but to have a two legged critter on the ground with a shaggy four legged critter close by was just too much. As I watched very carefully, most of them began to look my way and then began moving our way, slowly at first and then faster right at us. We had to run for the willows in the creek bottom and hide until they lost interest in us. This we did several times until we got through the field.

At the ranch, I met my Uncle Leo, and the new owner of the spread who offered me a ride to town in his Stinson Flying Station Wagon. It was my very first plane ride. What took four days, first by truck and then on foot, took twenty minutes by plane. My uncle brought my dog and my still wet gear back to the house the next week end.

Most likely I will never see the Thomas Lake and Mount Sopris country first hand again as I did more than fifty five years ago, but it's still there in my mind's eye, just as if it was yesterday.

DEEP LAKE
WINTER OF 1946

Twenty one miles of Colorado High Country, most of it around ten thousand feet, and in the frozen month of February, Deep Lake is an old volcanic crater filled with water and covered over with ice and snow. The lake is at least seven hundred fifty feet deep out in the center and the outlet drops in cascades down into the narrow rock-lined depths of Deep Creek. There is still evidence of the abandoned Stage Line Road that climbed up the back side of Iron Mountain that is north of the Colorado River and the town of Glenwood Springs, but I had found a shorter way this winter, or so I thought!

There was a freezing cold wind blowing down out of the dark depths of Canyon Creek that winter night. Three of us had been dropped off at the very end of that steep narrow road by my Dad in his 1937 panel truck, and he was headed back to town and a warm bed. There was just enough moonlight to see to strap on our eighty five pound packs and stomp into our snow shoes and secure them to our feet. The time was about eight p.m. and the snow on the steep trail was pretty well frozen so that we could walk on our "webs" with out sinking too deep. The snow slopes were solid enough for us to climb the seven miles of narrow trail to the top of the canyon.

All we knew of this trail and of Canyon Creek was what we had seen on the 1932 topographic map that I carried. The name Canyon Creek certainly did apply, especially in the cold moonlit winter night. We joked about the "snake tracks" that we saw going across the trail, dozens of them that soon became hundreds as we continued on. These were snow slide and avalanche areas and trails of various widths where snow that had fallen off of the trees began rolling down the mountain side. We were teenagers and healthy as horses, strong and eager and we were finally on our way to the Forest Service cabin at Deep Lake and we even had the key to the cabin.

My bedroll was the same vintage as my topographical map, a 1932 C.C.C. issue with the improvement of an Army Surplus mummy bag stuffed inside of that. I was packing a 9 shot H.&R. long barreled pistol and a steel hatchet, some vegetables (probably all frozen) and what canned goods I could scrape up and carry. We had coffee and odds and ends of G.I. rations salvaged from what was now the almost abandoned German P.O.W. camp at Camp Hale.

Camp Hale was where the 10th Army Ski Troops were trained during the Second World War. It was called Pando before that. I was wearing a Camp Hale ski parka and a pair of their G.I. ski boots. They were big oversized shoes that looked like they were discards from the Frankenstein Monster, but they were good ones. It was a good thing too, because as we gained altitude, the temperature dropped to twenty or thirty below zero and with the hard climb, all of us were sweating. We stopped in the wee hours of the morning and built a big fire, none of that "Injun" stuff for us! We sat on our packs and dried out our three pairs of socks that we each had on. We used socks and bread wrappers and socks for protection from freezing our feet. Just as it was getting light enough for us to see, we packed up and started out again.

We went right by Blue Lake and that cabin in the early morning light. After a mile or so, we saw the single phone wire that went from town to Deep Lake. Some of the telephone poles were just right to sit on and we could step across the wire when we needed to. Our backs and our feet hurt and the snow made a poor substitute for drinking water. When we rested, we rested with our packs on as they were too heavy to take off and put back on. All we had to do now was follow the wire and we did, hurting but happy and eager and we still had miles and miles to go.

Well, the snow got soft and it began to get dark. Black clouds were building up right in the direction that we were headed. We made camp, such as it was. We built us a fire on a raft of green wood on top of six feet of snow. We dug out for our beds and filled the hollow with nice soft pine boughs. We melted snow for water and made coffee and had a real meal out of some of the heavy cans of food. We climbed up the tree that we were under and cut off most of the limbs, both green and dry so we could keep the fire going. We got camped in advance of the real storm and it must have been close to forty below zero, but we were down out of the wind and had a nice warm fire. We talked and drank coffee and tea and settled in for the night.

Don Hysler, my neighbor, and Bud Donegan, my school buddy and I had hiked and fished and explored caves and had seen more beautiful High Country by then than anyone twice our age. Beautiful places just like this one with it's thousands of ice crystals gleaming at us in the smoky firelight. The moon disappeared behind the storm clouds. We could see the lights of a jet plane miles above us and watched it go out of sight. COLD-oh so very cold! Too cold to snow, but in the morning as we began again to follow that single piece of wire. It began to snow and blow until we could not see anything but the wire we were following.

We must have walked right across Bison Lake and had to be near Heart Lake or perhaps even beyond it. By now it was getting late and the wire went right up over a small hill and we just couldn't follow it. Then my cold brain told me that we were wading through the deep drifted snow down the inlet to the lake. Deep Lake, it had to be! So farther and farther we went down hill and all of a sudden the ground leveled off. It was almost flat for quite a ways to the lake so we kept going, but we were tired and cold and we were walking in a complete white-out, besides it was getting dark. The clouds broke and the moon came out for a few minutes and way back behind us on a hillside was a little triangle that was the top of Deep Lake Cabin. Back we went to that little triangle, pulled off our webs, and started digging the door out. We had to light a hand full of toilet paper under the lock to get the key to work, and then forced the frozen door open. It felt as if we got hit with a blast of hot air as we tumbled down into the cabin. We found the lamp and started a fire as we pulled out our gear. The blizzard hit us again, but who cared? We were inside where it was warm, but soon the room filled with smoke and ran us out of the cabin. We found that there was a gallon can on the top of the stove pipe to keep the snow out!

Back inside again, we found a big tin covered food box with instructions to use what we wanted, so we did, we really did! We got warm and ate a little as we were bushed. We sacked out and were warm all night, but when we got up in the morning, we saw that the snow had blown in through the key hole until it was piled back up to the hole. So there we were, snowed in at ten thousand feet, twenty miles from town and about the same from Trapper's Lake and the town of New Castle.

We had plenty of wood, already cut to size, plenty of food for the time being and almost a week to ride out the storm. Why, there was even a deck of playing cards, all fifty two of them.

Blizzard or not, we were going fishing even thought we hadn't seen any lake yet. Clear to the outlet side we went and there was close to five feet of snow, so we dug down and found about a foot of slush and water. Bud was down in the hole and one side of the bank caved in on him forcing him down in the wet slush. I snow shoed to the edge of the lake and cut a ten foot pole so we could get him out.

So, no fishing. We start back to the cabin because Bud was wet and it was still snowing. Don was in the lead when he suddenly sank four feet down in the snow and the snow closed back over his webs and he was trapped. Bud and I had to leave him there and we went back to the trees and cut two more ten foot poles, carrying them crossways before us. We rescued Don and he was wet and cold. We still needed to get back to the cabin, but the water must have flowed across the ice under the snow. We walked a ways and the entire area around us for twenty feet sank with us on it. Before we could get any distance between us, Bud went down and we had to dig him out. We eased back to the far side of the lake and had to go clear around it and that took care of that day.

The next day we dug out firewood and cleaned up the cabin, washed socks and played cards. We found a bottle of whiskey in the grub box. None of us were drinkers so I used some of it in the pancakes, but no one knew the difference or cared. We were sweet hungry, and the best we could find was pancakes with blackstrap molasses.

Bud was finicky about having coffee grounds in his coffee, so I suggested that he put the grounds in a clean cloth and tie it. That's not so difficult is it? Next pot of coffee, no grounds, Don had made it, and it was alright until Bud washed the pot and pulled out the grounds that were tied in a sock, one of Don's. No one had any really clean socks, least of all Don. Bud never complained about coffee grounds in his cup after that.

Cabin fever can cause all kinds of problems like, "Where did you get that snow for the coffee water?" "Not too close to the door, I hope!" "I sure hope those are raisins in the pancakes, I thought all the raisins were long gone." The cabin was beginning to get to us and those soggy pancakes and molasses just didn't have it. So the next day we planned to start for home. We all had to pack up and bring in wood and such. So early the next morning well before daylight we had coffee and pancakes and molasses. I fixed us each two skillet sized pancakes rolled up with molasses in the center, wrapped them in newspaper and that was our rations for the twenty one miles back home. We each wrote our name and the date on the steer head mounted inside above the door, then we locked up and put on our packs, strapped on our webs and started the long, cold trip back to our homes.

We went up over the ridge across Heart Lake and Bison, south to the Blue Lake cut-off and on to Hip Roof cabin. There we stopped and ate some of our frozen pancakes along with a portion of the newspaper it was wrapped in and washed it down with snow water. Home was still about thirteen miles away mostly down hill and a warm meal and a warm bed sounded mighty good. We were going to spend our last night at the Transfer Springs cabin, but there were a few hours of daylight and it was only seven miles to the bottom. One or two more bites of soggy molasses pancakes with the paper stuck on them and that was enough. We threw them as far as we could and took off for home with prospects of much better things to eat. We had seven miles of snow and ice on the steep trail down to the last mile or so of wet snow and soft mud. Wet, cold, muddy to the knees, tired and hungry, we made it to the highway. We sure attracted a lot of attention in that last mile and no one offered to pick us up, not even the local law. They knew all about us and our escapades especially mine.

We hadn't even gotten all our gear sorted out and packed away before we were planning another trip to the Flat Tops.

Winter Survival
In The Colorado High Country

Freezing to death is not painless as people have been lead to believe by some writers and even some so called "authorities" on the matter. I suggest you don't find out the hard way. Cold is a pain killer of sorts for a short while, if that is all that is available, but again, it is very dangerous.

In the early 1940's three of us boys loaded a pack horse with food and bedding and took off on foot to climb up and over the mountains to a cabin on the Windy Point Rim of No Name Canyon. Don and I were twelve years old and Calvin was fourteen. We had hiked and camped out many times, summer and fall, fishing, hunting and just exploring the hills. This time it was early spring and we had twelve miles to hike, climbing from five thousand feet to ten thousand feet, following the old stagecoach road that lead up out of the town of Glenwood Springs, Colorado. We continued on to the stage station at Transfer Springs, and then before we got to the way station at Hip Roof we turned right and went around the edge of the dangerous No Name Canyon.

We had left late in the morning and arrived at Transfer Springs in the afternoon, which was seven miles up the mountain. We made lunch there and took off on a path of mud and wet snow to Windy Point Cabin. Our leather boots soon became water soaked and we made poor time leading the pack animal. By then we were beginning to tire out. We found the trail around the point was buried in three feet of wet spring snow, except where the wind blew the narrow trail bare and there it was a stretch of ice. We drug and pushed the old mare through the drifts until she reached the bare ice. She got spooked and fell, rolling over down hill with her four feet up hill and her head down hill buried in the wet snow. Calvin ran a quarter of a mile across and down the hill to a small park to the cabin and brought back a scoop shovel so we could dig the horse out. Don and I shoveled a hole below the horse which was at the edge of No Name Canyon. There it was about two thousand feet to the bottom. It took all three of us to unload the horse. It was getting cold and the sun was almost down and we were on the east side of the mountain. We pulled and tried to lift the horse to no avail. We finally had to take a length of rope and whip the horse until she got mad enough to get up on her feet. She was wet, cold and shaking with fear.

We were young but with enough knowledge to know the horse would have died if we hadn't helped her. We dug a path back up to the trail and forced the horse back up to the trail. We loaded her back up with our wet and muddy gear and began digging a trench down to the cabin below us. She panicked and ran down the trail and fell again on an icy spot, but she was able to get up. We decided to tie her to a small tree in some brush to try to keep the wind off of her. We unloaded our gear and wiped her down with the pack saddle blanket. It was dark and below freezing, and we were wet with sweat and mud and snow, and still had to drag the panniers filled with our gear down through the snow in the moon light to the old cold cabin. It was a beautiful night. The moon and stars shining in the night sky and in the freezing cold the snow glistened.

We were twelve miles from town and there was complete silence except for the little sound we made building a fire and preparing supper. Like all cabins back then, it had a box full of wood beside the cast iron stove. It was supplied with a lantern and all we needed to be warm and comfortable. I lit the fire as Don dug out the food. Calvin found a case of, what he thought was beer, in a box and pried off the cap. He took a large swallow and threw it up on the floor along side the burning stove. It wasn't beer; it was white gas for the Coleman lamp. If it hadn't been so cold or if he had spit it on the stove, it would have caught on fire. It didn't seem to hurt him any, but his breath was very strange for a while. We ate supper and threw our bedrolls on the old bunk bed made from poles. I threw my old 1930 C.C.C. bed roll on the lower bunk and Don and I shared it along with some wool army blankets. Calvin took the upper bunk as he only had wool blankets and a ground cloth, but with the heat from the stove, he stayed warm.

The next morning we ate breakfast and dried out our boots and clothes and some wet spots in the bedding from when the horse rolled over. That horse was up and no worse for the experience. We had to dig away the snow to find some feed for her and then dug a trench to get her to the cabin, so we could care for her and she would be handy to load the next day.

We cleaned up the cabin and cut fire wood to replace what we used. Then the next day we packed our gear on the horse and struggled up the trench in the snow and mud and back across the bare icy spots. We got to the station at Transfer Springs by lunch and then started down the old road off the mountain, heading for home. This time we packed over Iron Mountain and went by Fairy Caves, as they were called at the time. We continued down the steep trail that turned off to the Cave of Chimes. We passed up that spectacle and went on home to unload and return the horse.

This was just a beginning of many snow shoe and ski trips into the High Country of Colorado in the early 1940's, some even in the dead of winter. Even with the lack of cold weather clothes and bed rolls like they have these days, we did real well and enjoyed every trip.

The Windy Point Cabin
"Loner"
On Halloween Night

Cold and black was the wintry November night beyond the bright campfire. The cold night air was brisk and clear at ten thousand feet and the sky was full of bright, sparkling stars that glowed through the snow covered limbs of the big old Spruce tree just beyond the fire. Ten, fifteen, maybe twenty degrees below zero? I really didn't know or even care as I sat there in the cold night air.

I was sitting on my homemade pack board on the frozen snow with my frozen boots next to the fire, thawing them out enough to get them off my feet. I realized how cold it was because the outer four pair of socks in my ancient rubber soled snow packs were frozen solid. At last the fire warmed my boots and my socks thawed out enough to continue on to the Windy Point Cabin, five miles up, over and around the cliff above No Name Canyon.

It was dark and cold and as I had already passed by the old Stagecoach Station at Transfer Springs just at dusk and the cabin ahead was my goal, I never thought of going back. Transfer Springs was the old relay station on the road north up out of Glenwood Springs at the mouth of Glenwood Canyon on the Colorado River, as there was no road up the river at that time.

Transfer had no appeal that cold winter night because looking down the frozen trail; I could still see the lights of town, just over the top of Iron Mountain. Twenty miles away, I could see the lights of the little coalmine town of Carbondale, just north of the big white Mt. Sopris. There I was sitting in the intense cold by myself in the dark cold night. All that could be seen were the stars in the heavens and all that could be heard was the whisper of the wind in the pines, the aspen trees moaning and occasionally the crack of frozen trees, exploding in the cold night air. Peaceful, quiet, nice, but the warmth of a snowbound cabin was drawing me up the dark winter trail miles ahead.

Struggling into my damp, cold socks and still partially frozen boots, I packed up my gear and kicked my packs into the harness on my Bear Paws and hoisted my old bedroll and my homemade pack board on my back and started out up the trail. Twice more I stopped to build a warming fire in the night before the narrow icy trail came into view on the high canyon rim. This short piece of trail is an experience in itself. In the dead of winter, the winds came up out of the depths of No Name Creek and kept the snow blown off the narrow trail. There was ice on the bare sections under the snow everywhere. Three of us boys had a pack horse slip and fall and almost go over the cliff the year before at Easter time.

Taking off my snowshoes and with a great deal of caution, I eased across the icy, snow free section to the deep drifts just above the cabin that was around and down below the crest of the mountain. I left the snow bound trail and crow-hopped almost straight down the drifts to the snug little one room cabin. I dropped my pack, stomped out of my webs and unwired the slab door. I could feel the heat hitting me as the door came open. Lighting a candle, I could see the packed dirt floor, a rough table and two benches, a small flat top stove with a big stack of wood behind it, an oil lamp and the bunk bed against the side wall. All the windows were intact. To top it all off, was that the only inhabitants for months had been pack rats and mice. First, I lit the lamp and then got a fire going and melted snow for coffee. I hung my webs and the pack board on the wall, set a wooden box next to the stove and began thawing out my feet. There's no place like home in the High Country!

I had coffee before the boots could come off. It was instant Nescafe that had been given me by a supply sergeant from Camp Hale. Much of the food I carried was the rations he didn't want and I fell heir to quite a bit of his leftovers. The few vegetables in my pack were frozen, so my supper consisted of K rations and coffee.

I threw my old bedroll on the top bunk where most of the heat was. Banking the fire and placing the eggs and potatoes and coffee pot of water on the back of the stove, I climbed up and into the sack. I wasn't alone without protection, I had a 9 shot H&R long barreled 22 caliber pistol under my rolled up Navy pea coat that I used as my pillow. The idea was to stay awake until what little heat there was soaked in and then get at least a few good hours of sleep. With a stub of a miner's candle on the bed post and one uncovered hand holding a book of Poe's ghost stories, I settled into bed. It was real quiet and difficult to read the small print in the cold with my breath making smoke in front of my eyes. Concentrating on the ghost story through the smoke of my breath, I heard a rustling close by. I held real still and listened. There it was again and the sound stopped. I thought it must have been an animal for sure! It couldn't have been a bear, they were in hibernation. It sounded more like a small animal-maybe a porcupine found its way in and was nosing around. Nobody but a fool jumps down in the dark with one of those on the floor. Then, there it was again! It was only about three feet from my head, but there couldn't be something there unless it was six feet tall. The candle was still burning, but I could see nothing. I grabbed for my pistol and aimed it at the direction of the sound and then there it was in the dim light. It was a big pack rat running along the side of the ridge pole on my side of the room. I began shooting out of spite? Fear? Relief? I didn't know, but every time I shot at that rat, it made me feel better. Satisfaction? Maybe. Every shot brought forth a cloud of smoke, like an old black powder gun. The rat kept running back and forth on the ridge pole and I kept shooting at him in the smoke and the dim light. I never did hit that rat, but I blasted him off of the ridge pole into the chipped enamel wash basin on a shelf. The last of the nine shots put a new hole in the basin as the rat slid around in a circle before jumping out to disappear. The smoke cleared and the noise of the gun died out and it got very still and quiet again. My heart was pounding and my blood circulating which warmed me right up and I slept real well the rest of the night.

A beautiful icy blue clear sunrise greeted me early the next morning. I started up a fire in the stove. The water in the coffee pot was almost frozen solid and the spuds and eggs were still frozen. I hated to take the time to thaw them out and cook them because I was in a hurry as always to climb back up the mountain and enjoy the quiet beauty of the Colorado High Country, besides it's easier to travel in the snow when it's still frozen solid on the surface.

Then, and even now, I still prefer being in the High Country, that to me is the "Real Life."

The Name High In The Aspen Tree
In The High Country

"Yes, at Transfer Springs-Hip Roof, ten feet up on an aspen tree, that's right! It's your nephew's name and it looks like it's been there forty years!" a man said. This was a dozen miles from town on the old stage coach road, just east from where those Oregon Smoke Jumpers lost their lives fighting the big fire on Storm King Mountain.

This was what a close friend of my Uncle Ray told him he saw while riding a snow machine on six or seven feet of snow. "Guilty! I told him." It must have been about 1944 when I put my name in that tree. That area was one of my escape places when town life got the best of me. Summer or winter, rain or shine, snow or cold, that was my country. Snowshoes, skis, shank's mare and later a good mountain horse by the name of Comet.

Now to get up there, a person has to go around Iron Mountain just north of Glenwood Springs or up behind the Colorado Hotel, where Teddy Roosevelt stayed several times while hunting mountain lions. The back side of Iron Mountain had the remains of the stage coach road that years ago went across the Flat Top to Trapper's Lake. It went across the upper end of No Name Creek and back along the rim of Glenwood Canyon above the then impassable Colorado River to Fort Defiance, which was to have been the county seat of Garfield County. It then continued to the town of Carbonate and the Sweet Water Country, where Diamond Jim, a Beer Baron of the prohibition days, had a ranch. The road then went on up the Colorado River to Bond and Burns and then on to Denver. That was sure some stage road, but my main stomping ground was just the first part of the route up onto the Flat Tops, the beautiful, lonely, quiet paradise that was almost mine alone back then.

As I remember, this was the winter of 1944 and there were three of us about the same age with the same frame of mind and little else as regards the winter survival gear and emergency rations not common to this modern generation. We had old bed rolls and 1918 scratchy wool army blankets with moth eaten holes here and there. Our food was just anything that we could get to cook. That trip, I managed to shoot an old skinny snowshoe rabbit with my new Marlin 22 long rifle and we boiled it with a few frozen carrots and potatoes and whatever else we had. We ate a lot of hot soup, but the rabbit was too tough to eat.

We gathered enough wood to burn to keep us warm and tried to play poker with a pinochle deck we found in the cabin. We read anything we could find, including the labels of the cans. After a time we all became sweet hungry to an extreme. "Hey! I know where some sugar and a can of cocoa are!" I said. It was only about five miles over on the No Name Rim beyond Windy Point to the cabin there. So off we went, up across the flats and through the drifts to the canyon rim where the wind was whistling and the snow was blowing. Easing around the icy wind blown cliff, overlooking the deep canyon, we took off down the mountain through drifts of powered snow four and five feet deep. When I lost my balance and sat down on my skis, I just kept going and my partners said that all they could see of me was the top of my rifle cutting through the snow.

We got to the cabin, dug out the door and got our "sweet reward". We found cocoa, a little lumpy sugar and a can of frozen condensed milk. Not enough, we decided, so up through the powdered snow to the treacherous trail around the point and then across the flats, through the trees where there was no trail even in the summer. We located the old stage road and we took off toward Blue Lake and the next source of candy making loot. This put us about half way to Deep Lake where we found the buried retreat. We dug into the building and carefully scrounged around for the badly needed candy making supplies. We found some more frozen canned milk and parts of bottles of white and brown Karo syrup, and what else, who knows? It was getting dark and the moon had not shown itself. We had five miles or so to go in the dark back to the lonely, cold cabin at about nine thousand feet altitude. The moon came out later and we chased a coyote and tried to kill it, but couldn't. We ended up eating more of that rabbit soup when we got back. The candy making would have to wait until the next morning.

We began the fudge by dumping everything we had gathered up into a chipped up old rusty dishpan and began cooking it on the stove, boiling and stirring for hours, it seemed to us. It looked and tasted more like chocolate syrup, which is about all it was, but it was sweet and we didn't want to wait any longer to eat it, so we took the dishpan out and poured it on the snow and started eating. Now a dish pan about half full of our sweet concoction was a lot of candy even for three of us. We couldn't keep it so we managed to eat every bit of it. We seemed to live through it, even thrived on it, and looked forward to the next time and there were many "next times," never a dull moment.

So down the mountain trail we went, as far as we could on skis until the mud stopped us. We went the rest of the way on foot, down the mountain and across the big bridge into down town Glenwood Springs with people looking at us like we were crazy. Crazy? Well, perhaps we were a little, but back then close to sixty years ago, we were the "Real People," and we would do it again.

SNOWSHOEING
ON A WINTER NIGHT

Cold the night air was in the Colorado High Country. It was pitch dark on the narrow steep trail above the depths of Canyon Creek. Three of us boys on webs with eighty pound packs on our backs were headed to Deep Lake on the Flat Tops some twenty miles from Glenwood Springs.

It was about ten p.m. when the moon came up and the whole valley was as bright as day. There was no way to describe the bright snow covered trees and the cliffs on both sides of us in contrast with the dark shadows. Well, why at night? It was the only safe time to walk on frozen snow instead of slush and there was less chance of the ever threatening avalanches. We crossed several small slides and there was evidence of more to come especially in the late afternoons when the sun warmed the steep slopes. The trails of snow snakes crossed our path in dozens of places, made by pieces of snow falling from trees and overhanging ledges and rolling down hill looking like white wheels going until they fell over or started snow slides. Even in the frozen night we made no more noise than necessary and watched and listened carefully.

We were beginning to tire out and all of us were beginning to sweat which could become a real killer when sleeping in the snow. We were close to the end of the steep canyon trail and stopped on a fair sized bench for the night. Using green wood for a raft, we built a small fire on top of the snow, stood our packs next to a tree and set up a sleeping camp. We gathered enough firewood for the remainder of the night, and made coffee from snow water. I dug a shallow trench to get below the cold wind, then lined the bottom with pine boughs and laid out my old 1932 C.C.C. bedroll with its one piece mummy bag liner. I placed more pine boughs on top for more protection from the wind and cold. Bud was so tired that he placed his bed right on top of the snow. Bob, who was the District Ranger's son, looked at my bed and decided that it could be improved on so he went off to the side and dug a deep trench three feet wide and almost six feet deep. He dropped his gear down the hole and crawled into his sack shouting up out of the hole just how nice it was and how warm he was. Bud and I sacked out and the fire died down and the wind came up covering my pine bough covered bedroll with a cushion of snow-maybe it could have been little warmer but I can sleep and I do.

Then in the wee morning hours, Bud and I began hearing strange noises, something like a person shouting for help. It was muffled and sounded like someone far away and in grave danger. Well, that was exactly what it was; Bob was quite literally in grave danger. The wind had blown his "grave" about half full of powered snow and he was trying to come up for air. We pulled him out with only his socks on his feet. As we sleep in part of our clothes, we loosen our belts and pull our britches down some so as not to sweat. So there was Bob with his pants full of snow, no boots and the fire was out. His parka, boots and everything else were down the hole covered with snow, fine, dry snow and it was perhaps ten to twenty below zero. Bud built a big fire, and I gave Bob my parka, as I sleep with my snow pack boots wrapped up in my jacket for a pillow. Then using one of my webs, I dug out the hole and rescued his bedroll, boots, parka and even his snowshoes. Before long Bob had his boots and his parka on and threw his bed along side mine and crawled in, clothes and all, with the daylight not far away. We survived that stint, but the next one was coming up.

Up at first light, I placed firewood on the low fire and found that one of my bear paws got kicked into the fire during the night and about eight inches of the end was burned off. It took me about an hour to fit a green spruce tip on the burned place and lace it on with silk fishing line. The sun was coming up over the far mountain and we had hoped to make it to Blue Lake before the snow slushed up. We made it to Jolly's sheep camp and the cabin was unlocked as all of them used to be. We went in and fixed some lunch on a wood stove and found a frozen, partly filled, bottle of wine. Bud and I finished it off except for the frozen slush left in the bottle. It was pretty potent stuff! Bob wouldn't touch it. After our lunch, we headed off up the trail and the snow was getting soft. We were all chewing on dried fruit and getting thirsty. We found an open hole in the creek and we drank, and drank and drank. Snow water is not very thirst quenching.

This was my first trip up Canyon Creek, but I knew the top country well. We only had about three miles to go to Blue Lake. The snow turned to slush and our webs sunk down about two inches. We sloshed along, dragging the weight of the snow building up on our snowshoes and sinking deeper until we were dragging about five inches of wet snow every step we took. We began to sweat and the webs and the harness became loose and we were making little headway. The winter sun was dropping behind the mountain and the slush began to freeze. We began to feel the cold and worse yet Bud and I had drunk that wine and too much water. All that dried fruit we ate began to swell and we were hurting. This slowed Bud and me up while Bob began to go faster because he was cold and worse yet, he was wearing ski boots instead of packs and the boots were too tight. His feet were wet and freezing. Bob reached the cabin at the lake half and hour before we did and we found him standing along side it. His feet were frozen and he could not even get the webs or his pack off. He was literally frozen stiff.

We couldn't find the key to the cabin and the lock would have to be thawed out anyway, so I knocked a small window in with my fist. Bud crawled in as I cut the webs off of Bob's feet. He never said a thing, or even attempted to drop his pack. He never moved, he never even tried to. I picked him up and handed him through the window to Bud who dropped him on a bed with his feet to the stove. He was stiff as a dead man and stayed that way until we got a fire going. All three of us were cold and sweaty. It was dark and we were nearly twelve or more miles from town. We had to put Bob's boots in the warm oven to thaw them out enough to remove them and then the sock on one foot was still frozen to his big toe where there had been a blister that had formed and broken from the tight boots.

Bob was trying to move now and could talk, and as his feet began to warm up, we rubbed them with our still cold hands to restore his circulation. In this situation, cold hands were better than using frozen snow because the ice crystals would cut his feet like hundreds of sharp knives. He soon began to feel the pain and his face was white as the snow, and he was not quite screaming with the pain. We had to just let him suffer for a while as we made coffee and stew and tried to figure out just what to do next. All we could find at the time was a box of tea and part of a jar of mentholatum. Making a strong batch of tea and soaking his feet in it seemed to help. The mentholatum gave some small relief, but he was hurting and the situation was serious. The warm cabin was a blessing. In the morning we wrapped his frozen foot in mentholatum soaked rags, put his socks back on and into those same wet ski boots and we started our hike back to town. I carried my pack and most of Bob's and Bud carried his and some of Bob's. We helped Bob the best he could. I broke trail and we all had to wear snowshoes. Going down hill toes tend to slide up against the end of the boots so it had to be hard on Bob.

We were in the shade of trees and on the north slopes much of the way. The snow remained frozen which was a help as Bob's feet were causing him so much pain. The extra weight of the packs was taking its toll on Bud and me and we were getting snow blind. We rubbed mentholatum and charcoal on our cheeks and kept on struggling down the trail.

It took us all day to get to the cabin at Transfer Springs and Bob had walked all the way on snowshoes going downhill much of the way. We stayed the night there and the next morning started down the steep old stage coach road seven more miles to town. As we neared the end of our trip, the snow had turned to a mixture of snow and mud and Bob was still plodding along. Bud and I had left our packs at the last cabin to lighten the load and I ran down the last few miles to contact Bob's parents and get some transportation. It seemed like a very long time before we finally saw them coming. Bud was practically carrying Bob.

Well, we made it--Bob went to the doctor who told him that his foot hadn't been frozen and who were we--three young fellows--to know anything anyway? I knew! And so did Bud and most of all--Bob! After that Bob was welcome to come along with us anytime, summer or winter, but, sad to say, his feet caused him problems from that time on.

We spent many enjoyable outings on the south side of the Flat Tops with skis and snowshoes, looking at the lights of Carbondale and Basalt and even Aspen at times. We were there.

Summer Job At Billing's Springs And The Trip Home

Beautiful it was and it's still there, a small open park on the top of the Continental Divide between the Frying Pan River at Thomasville and the Eagle River at Eagle, Colorado. It is fifty three miles north and fifty three miles south to get to Glenwood Springs to the west. To see it even now, I remember it as it was back then with four slab cabins a horse barn and the icy cold crystal spring water running to the cabins through a one by four inch rough wooden trough. There were Aspen trees and big

Engelmann Spruce trees, Columbines of several different colors and Monks head, and always the Bluebells and even some of the deadly Larkspur plus so much more. This is also Gold Country where the stories of Buck Rogers and the lost Slate Mine that disappeared in a rock slide only about seven miles from our logging camp. It was only four miles from here where I finally located the Lost Van Dyke Mine, which took me eight years of searching in mud and snow, climbing most of the mountains and valleys in the area. I will leave that story for another time.

There are still remains of the ancient Stamp Mill just below Fool's Peak, an area where prospectors found pockets of rich gold but couldn't make it pay because of the short seasons at the altitudes of ten to thirteen thousand feet. This area is also filled with streams and lakes that are full of trout for the catching. It was eighteen miles to the closest town, down either side of the pass. We mostly went in to Thomasville because my boss lived there and had relatives there. Down the road a few miles was Deerhammer's Store with its old hand cranked gas pump and the only Post Office for the entire community.

It was there at Billing's Spring where I had my first summer job. I was just a punk kid, skidding logs with two big, and I mean BIG, Percheron horses by the names of Sam and

Bess. I still remember the smell of sawdust and fresh cut lumber, the aroma of bacon, venison, and elk cooking in great amounts for the hard working, big eating logging crew. We ate like we worked and we worked just as hard as Sam and Bess, the two big draft animals.

We logged five days a week and if we lost a day because of rain, we worked on the weekend. The "bad days", as we called them, were the times that we hunted for meat for the table and fished and prospected and had fun at each other's expense. Hard work brings about hard play and we put a lot of effort into both. That was a good summer. It was the year that I bought a young half broken bronco that I used for wrangling horses.

The last week of the summer, on a Friday night just before dark, with a pay check in my pocket, a bag of cooked venison, lots of biscuits, my 1932 C.C.C. bedroll and my horse, Comet, I started up the trail on Mt. Thomas to head the seventy five miles back to Glenwood Springs. I had never been up that trail very far and after it got dark, the horse began acting up. I was told that there was no way to miss the trail or get off of it and that proved to be true. This section of the trail was just a trench dug through the rocks to the very top. I had to walk and lead the horse and neither of us could stand up in it. It topped out above eleven thousand feet in snow drifts under a beautiful black sky filled with a million stars and it was about midnight. It was COLD, and car lights could be seen coming over the high mountain passes fifty miles away. Just flashes of light up, over and down again, out of sight. Making camp under some stunted pines and building a small fire, as wood was scarce, I melted snow for coffee and Comet had to eat snow.

Morning came and I threw more coffee grounds and snow in the frozen pot, soon I had very hot, black coffee. The coffee, cold venison and dry biscuits were breakfast. We set out again just as the sun was coming over the Continental Divide. The early morning sun began to feel good and many of the far mountains became visible. I could see the back side of the Holy Cross Mountain, Basalt Mountain, Capital Mountain, Sopris Mountain, Grand Mesa, the Flat Tops, White House Mountain, and Treasure Mountain near Marble and they were many miles away. This high mesa was named the Red Table Mountain. The Eagle River on the north and the Frying Pan on the south could be seen at the same time on this high wind blown trail.

We traveled twenty five or thirty miles that day with only dirty snow water for both of us to drink. I shot a Ptarmigan about noon to eat for supper. The bird, roasted over a fire using Aspen twigs, with the white ashes sprinkled on for salt, a can of peaches and some soda crackers that I found in my pack made my supper. That cold night my horse tried to get in my bedroll with me. In the morning I knew why. We woke up to a cold High Country drizzle that lasted all day and all night.

We had water and miles of muddy trail leading down off the mountain. My big wet navy pea-coat weighed a ton and the both of us were wet as drowned rats, tired, hungry and cold. Bottoming out on Cattle Creek road on the west side of Cottonwood Pass, in the far distance down the muddy wet road in the dark and the rain, we saw headlights coming at us. It was a 1935 Chevy four door touring car with a broken windshield and the right side smashed in. Other than that, it was a beautiful car. It slid around and stopped, blocking the road right in front my horse and me. Two men jumped out, or rather fell out, and staggered out to me. One man had his head covered with a bloody bandage and his right arm in a sling. I wondered what was going on. One of them offered me a drink, handing me a bottle of what ever they were drinking at the time. I took a big swig and it hit my empty stomach like a lead balloon. Comet needed it worse than I did, as he was standing there spraddle-legged with his head down. They told me to turn my horse around and head up to the cow camp just a little way up the road. They then stripped my horse of all the gear but the saddle and halter, and threw the wet gear in the back seat with another fellow who was too drunk to know what was going on. There was a little dog back there too. With a broken front leg all bandaged up the little dog kind of looked like the guy with the bandaged arm.

We got to the cow camp, about three hours later it seemed to me, but it was only five miles back up the road in the rain and the mud. Someone pulled me off my horse and put him in the barn. They rubbed him down, watered and fed him while I was dragged into the cabin and given a glass of whisky which I drank right down. They sat me at the table and put one skillet filled with chili and another with bacon and about a dozen eggs in front of me. They handed me a quart of coffee and we began swapping stories. I told them where I was going and that I was coming back from Billing Springs. They explained that they were heading for town going through Gypsum. While they were trying to sneak by one fellow's house, not wanting to be seen, they had the lights off and ran right into a loaded logging truck. They then had to go all the way to Glenwood Springs that night to find a doctor. The doctor fixed the dog up too. Doctors would sometimes do that back then. They figured that was a good reason to get drunk. That is when I met them, on their way home through Spring Valley to their camp at Cattle Creek.

They had me spend the night and in the morning it was still raining. They were still too hung over to wrangle their horses in the wet brush, so I saddled up Comet and ran them in about daybreak. I tried to tell them how much I appreciated their assistance but I must have expressed too much gratitude. They wanted me to ride the rough off of some of their horses. I had to make excuses as I was still eighteen miles from home down a muddy road and had to be in school the next morning.

So down the road I went as quickly as possible with no coffee, no food and a long way to go. All the excitement wasn't over, as I was crossing a barb wire fence, taking the first two strands loose and making my tired horse jump the lower two, apparently the fence must have been hit with lightning somewhere along the line. Both of us were zapped, not enough to do any damage, but it took me thirty minutes to catch my horse. By then he was rested and had a lot more life in him. All I found to eat that day was some green potatoes in a field and so Comet and I shared and shared alike.

We got home late that night and Comet went to his pasture and I went on home for my last year of high school with fond thoughts of returning to the High Country again in the spring.

THE TRUE LOVES OF A
MOUNTAIN MAN

Sixty years ago I found my first love on a hillside, high in the logging woods of Colorado. Oh how I loved the high mountains and the fast running cold streams that were fed from a snow bank, the trees, the cliffs, the blue skies, and the clouds and even the countless stars on a clear night, both in summer and in the cold winter nights. These things have been a part of me since I was about five years old and many times it was just me all alone, but never was I really lonely. There was something there and there still is and always will be, but then there came the realization that something was missing, but what?

At fifteen years of age I was ask to help skid logs that summer. I took the essential things with me, you know, a 22 rifle and my fly rod, and an old 1932 bedroll, and boots and gloves and clothes and back then, always my harmonica. At the logging camp, I was introduced to one of my first real loves, her name was Bess and her partner was Sam. They were two big Percheron skid horses and the largest animals I was ever to become acquainted with. I surely did learn to love them and they learned to show affection to me as they became a part of my young life.

It took two of us, standing on bails of hay, just to be able to throw the harness over their backs. Bess was my skid horse and she taught me how to skid logs. She had female feelings, much like a good wife. Treated with respect and never abused, that enormous, almost one ton of horse, would pull her heart out for me, and I loved her for it. She knew when lunch time was near as we fed and watered the horses at the same time each day. Both horses did not like to work overtime, even though they had to at times, their feelings about it were very apparent. We moved monstrous logs down to the skid way, some so large that it took both horses to drag just one log. Those big horses would go down almost to their knees when starting to pull out a heavy load. We didn't use lines on them, but we talked to them and they understood. We yelled at them as far away as they could hear us, and they responded. They had feelings, and as big and powerful as they were, they responded to our love and care for them. They also showed their love for each other. One time, Bess miss stepped or slipped and fell while tied on to a log and she ended up lying with her back lower than her legs (a bad situation for a horse to be in) and she had a hayme stuck in a rotten log. Sam seemed to know or to feel her pain and frustration and he pulled the tree that was holding her into two pieces getting her out. There are feelings between horses and even between horses and man, if we just allow it to happen.

It was at this same time that I bought a young pony, he was almost four years old and his name was Comet. He was not yet broken and as I later found out, had been much neglected and abused. He was to become my second real love. It took time and much effort to combat the wrongs done to him. He was referred to as an "Outlaw", a horse that couldn't be broken for any good use. The outfit that sold him to me thought that they pulled a good one on a fool kid. Thirty five dollars he cost me and I was offered three hundred for him in just two months.

I didn't dare use a saddle to break him so I spent a lot of time in the dirt. I got on and off, time and time again until the last fall and I got up with a big fistful of hair torn right out of his mane. He would buck me off and then wait for me to get up and get back on. He was enjoying all the attention he was receiving. We finally came to an understanding, but on a cold morning, he would always hump just three times to make sure we both were ready.

I had Comet with me that summer I was logging and I used him to wrangle the skid horses every morning, besides Bess and Sam there were two more. The wet grass was three feet tall and even riding my horse I still got my feet wet. If I'd had to do it on foot, I'd been wet to my waist. Truthfully, up until that time, all I cared about was the mountains, both in summer and winter, and of course now logging and those big horses and then my horse, Comet.

It was a great summer, but soon over and I was back in high school and I met another love. Oh, it took quite a period of time for this girl to grow on me. We went to school together for three years and I worked for her father in a logging camp one summer. We graduated from high school and were going together and even thinking of getting married, but her mother wanted her to go to college for a year first and so we were married the next year. Then I began to love and be loved by a very special woman.

Neither of us understood the meaning of love like we do now, it took many years, but early in our marriage, we began applying bible principles, and we associated with other couples and families that lived by righteous principles and actually were able to see the fine results. Both my wife and I were shown just what was written in the bible, and then we discussed it with others and began to seriously apply it in our lives. We found our love growing stronger with each year. We have been together over fifty five years and our love is stronger and more secure that it has ever been. It was never easy raising six children and living in and around hard rock mines, uranium mines, and logging camps and sawmills. The work was always hard and the living conditions extremely difficult for any woman, let alone one with a large family, but we made it this far and our love seems to grow better with each year.

We also had to learn to hate what is bad and love what is good and righteous and live by it. No double standards, always putting forth an effort to display principled love, not by just works but by our everyday actions. We determined that we could be better husbands and wives and neighbors and even citizens by applying what is written in the scriptures, such as staying neutral in political and military matters, by respecting the sanctity of life and keeping a high moral code. It has worked for us and our love is strong, but I have another love that I found was necessary, too, and that is love for Jehovah God and his word, the Bible.

PART TWO
GOLD MINING

THE OLD VAN DYKE MINE

It was October, 1901 in the Colorado High Country. Cold wet snow was falling, creating slush and mud on the trails, making them impassable except to go down country with the pack string. There was no chance of getting to the stamp mill. It was just three miles up from the mine through the bog, but that was impossible with the snow. Going around the bog was about seven miles and there wasn't time. The mill would be shutting down with the snow, and everyone would be heading off the mountain, laying out the winter in snug warm cabins. The mill would be closed till next spring, which was about the Forth of July at this altitude. Each year as the season started to change, it was the same gamble. How long could he continue to mine the gold and still get it to the mill without getting caught by the snow?

The mine sat at more than ten thousand feet, the miner knew that he had no choice now. Leaving his burrows, as always, with Mrs. Irons at the boarding house, he caught the Colorado Midland train to Leadville and then headed back to the Old Country. His luck wasn't all bad; it was too early for the snow to block Hagerman Pass and the tunnel through the mountain above Ivanhoe Lake. The miner knew the gold was just sitting there to be taken to the mill.

He'd be back in June, God willing, barring accidents in steam trains and ships and sickness and the unforeseen. He was gone from October till June of the next year. Yes, he'd get his gold, if the snow stayed deep so no one could find the mine, if the train didn't go off the track pulling through Hell's Gate below Ivanhoe Lake and if the ship didn't sink.

This is the story of Old Van Dyke, the Dutchman, and his gold. I don't know anybody that doesn't like a good lost gold mine story. So, just think, gold already mined, sacked and just laying in the High Country of Colorado in an old mine waiting for you. No one knows what really happened to the miner and why he never returned, just that he never came back to claim his gold or pack animals. It could have been illness, family problems, or a traveling accident. I have personally seen the old coal tender and some wheels down in the canyon among the granite boulders below Ivanhoe Lake, so who knows what happed.

Most stories are just for the telling. Sure, there seems to be some facts that started the story someone saw some gold or heard of it. Well, this account is factual as to the man, the mine, and the incident, I know because I saw the mine in 1938 or 1939, but I was still too young to really know what it was all about.

I was only six or seven, but I remember it well. My folks drove up the Frying Pan River from Glenwood Springs, then on to Woods Lake. The 1935 Dodge got as far as the corduroy road on the hog-back above the lake. For you who don't know what a corduroy road is, it is a road made by laying logs together side by side and filled in with dirt or mud to make it as level as possible. It ends up looking like corduroy cloth and no matter how much mud and dirt is used to fill it in and a corduroy road is very rough. My father didn't want to take a chance with the car, so we walked about three miles up the road, down into the valley, through the muskeg and up the Little Crooked River to the mine site following the directions given to us by Mrs. Irons. I was pretty young, but I remember that trip very well. There was my father, stepmother, stepsister, who was about ten or eleven, Mrs. Iron's sister, Iva Faletti and her daughter, who was the same age as my stepsister, and my Uncle Ray. We all hiked to the mine together. They drug me by my arm a good portion of the way, because the excess starch that my stepmother used on my bib overalls rubbed the insides of my legs raw. Funny how some memories stick with you for a lifetime.

Van Dyke's cabin was still standing and the door remained locked on the cabin as well as the mine. The mine had caved in behind the locked door and water was running from under the door of the mine down the track to the creek. In the small shed, still standing, were the burro harnesses hanging from wooded pegs. In the cabin, bedding and clothing hung from the ceiling, and dry goods were stored in fruit jars on the shelves. Personal possessions remained, just as if waiting for him to come back and start mining again. We ate our picnic lunch, and my dad and uncle picked up some white quartz that was filled with some kind of faceted nuggets. It looked like gold nuggets to us, two electricians, a school teacher, a house wife, and three kids.

Mrs. Irons told us that she had fed and cared for old Van Dyke's burros for three more seasons after he left. She had not heard a word from Van Dyke in all that time, so she finally sold the animals for the feed bill. Now, Mrs. Irons is a story by herself. She was well known on the "Pan" (The Frying Pan River). We knew her because she was a distant relative and my father took groceries up the "Pan" to Mrs. Irons early in the spring each year. It was always fifty dollars worth of flour, sugar, coffee, and dry goods which was enough to last her many months. If it was too early and there was too much mud or snow, my father would have to come back and then try again later when the conditions were better.

Mrs. Irons ran a boarding house for the miners, and later, for the men that worked at the lime kiln. She had also run a boarding house at Marble, Colorado, up the Crystal River, until the quarries closed down because of mud and snow slides.

She picked up the mail and cared for pack animals left at Thomasville in the winter months. Nellie was her first name, and as I remember, she had five cabins on the North Fork of the Frying Pan River. She rented them out to fishermen through the summer and to hunters in the fall. She lived in one cabin next to the road and stayed snowed in all winter. She was alone sometimes for five months at a time. Alone? Well--not really, because along with the animals she boarded, she had a few milk goats, an old hand crank Victrola with dozens of phonograph records, and a rosewood Baby Grand Steinway piano in the living room that she played to keep herself company. The piano was originally used in the school house on the Frying Pan River and Nellie ended up with it. The piano was brought in by freight wagon even before the narrow gauge Colorado Midland Railroad existed. Many was the times that Nellie would play the piano after dinner and the people would stand around and sing songs from the twenties and the Turn of the Century.

She was a tall, dignified, old woman, wearing her knee length hair up in a bun on her head. She certainly impressed me as a youngster. I can still remember the meals she prepared for the boarders and for us when we came to visit. They were made from home grown and canned fruits and vegetables, canned meat and game. I especially remember the onions she grew. They were sweet as apples. It was not unusual to find fish, grouse or deer meat on her table. The meals were always well prepared and there was plenty to eat. The hardy soul never saw a doctor until she moved in with my folks in Glenwood Springs, just before she died. When she was snowed in and she had a cold, she stuck her finger in a jar of mentholatum and then stuck it down her throat. She sure wasn't sick much. She died at around ninety years old in 1939 or 1940, as I remember. My stepmother ended up with the rosewood Baby Grand Steinway after Mrs. Irons died.

But back to the mine--after our one trip up there and finding it caved in there was not much interest in it. In 1942, my dad joined the navy, too old really, but wanting to be involved. He ended up as an Electrician's Mate, First Class. Not bad with only a sixth grade education. While he was away from home, I went down in the basement with a neighbor kid and we found the sack of "gold nuggets" still in the quartz. We broke some out and asked my Uncle Ray what they were and where they came from. He told us where they came from. We hammered some of the metal out, and into gold colored powder, dreaming of gold, but we were too young to do anything about it.

In 1947, still in high school, I spent the summer skidding logs at the base of Mount Thomas in the "Pan" area. We still used horses back then. The sawmill sat at the top of the divide between Crooked Creek and Brush Creek. I bought a saddle horse that summer for thirty five dollars, and roamed the hills, hunting and fishing. The thought had surfaced about the old gold mine, but at sixteen years old, fishing was a much bigger lure. The next summer I went back to old Bert Billing's sawmill and took over the skidding, using two big Percheron horses, Sam and Bess. Those two horses together weighed about two tons and I had to stand on a bale of hay to be able to harness them. They were so wide it was impossible to ride on their backs, so I would have to sit between the haymes on their collars. Soon after that, I was offered a contract on Basalt Mountain by my father-in-law to be skidding logs, and so I moved out of the lost gold mine country. A year later, after getting married to the old Cripple Creek gold miner's daughter, I told him the story, and he and I went looking for the mine together, but we got distracted much too often by fly fishing in the upper meadows of the creek.

In 1953 I was married three years and working for one dollar and twenty five cents an hour and the idea of that old gold mine looked good. The fishing, too, of course! My wife's dad, Gus, and I looked some more, but we still didn't find it. Then, one day, I woke up and it hit me out of the blue, there was one small area in the High Country that we really hadn't looked at. I called Gus and we went right to it. Gus, being knowledgeable, cut samples of the rotten quartz vein filled with nuggets of iron resembling garnets, with blue limestone on one side and gray limestone on the other, all cutting through a porphyry dike. Then we went down the creek to the meadows and caught our limit of Brook trout. Not necessarily the "legal" limit, but all we could carry out and eat. We must have had fifty fish between us and all no more than eight inches long. Good eating! We never wasted one.

The mine was too much for Gus, but his brother, John, who was also an old Cripple Creek miner, saw the samples and said he would back me to open the mine clear to the face. He had the money and time, but the deal was, I would have to pack everything in and do all the work. I had a wife and kids to take care of, so I decided to open it up by myself, at my own expense. If I had to do all the work, then I sure wanted all the profit.

I took an extra day off work and drove the seventy five miles to the mine, taking a wheelbarrow, bed roll, coffee pot and some food.

I left the fishing pole in the car, as it was much too tempting. I also took a bottle of Old Kentucky snake bite medicine to ward off the cold, along with twenty sticks of thirty percent DuPont powder with caps and fuse. I pushed the wheelbarrow loaded with supplies three miles through swamp, over dead falls and washed out trail in the pouring rain. I wasn't surprised to find the cabin and shed had fallen in and everything of value had disappeared. I did find old Van Dyke's anvil, a Fisher 1885 Number Five, and hid it under a tree, covering it with pine needles, because I wanted to take it back with me whenever I could.

I set up camp. First making a fire to dry out a little, then a shot of whiskey to warm me up and a cup of camp coffee made by dumping the coffee grounds directly into the boiling water and letting them settle a little before pouring. That coffee was hot, thick, and black and tasted wonderful even if I did have to pick grounds out of my teeth. I stashed the whiskey bottle behind a slab of rock in the creek for safe keeping. I only had three days, so I immediately started digging out the caved in portal.

There was wet clay, porphyry and thirty feet of cave in, so I went above the cave in and started digging. I dug in the rain till I was drowned from the outside in, took a swallow of whiskey, a shot of black coffee and went back to work. I had three days of water running off my hat and down my back and into my pants, wet clothes, mud, whiskey and coffee and three nights of a wet cold bed roll. The morning of the third day, I dug down to the rotten timbers, and uncovered a cap (the top brace on the timbers) still sitting on the big posts. The trench I had dug to the rotten timbers was ten feet deep. Lying in the mud, so excited I forgot about the rain for a few minutes, I started digging under the cap trying to see into the mine. Maybe this was it! Could I have found the gold so soon? I opened the hole up very carefully, being sure not to bump the rotten timber. After lighting my light, I flopped back down in the mud and slid on my belly half way into the old mine to get a better look.

Excitement soon changed to disappointment. Just ahead several feet, another cave in, and it was filled in solid. As if that wasn't enough, just then the side of the trench gave way and buried my backside and what was left of me hanging out in the rain. Wet cold mud and clay covered most of my body, but I had my head and shoulders in the dry, more or less. I didn't dare disturb the rotten timbers. Pinned by hundreds of pounds of rock and mud, I swore, and started wriggling and pushing backwards, not touching the rotten wood. It kept raining and I kept pushing and twisting. Soon, wriggling and pounding with my behind, with some help from the heavy rain, the muck began to give. Using my panic and a good deal of effort, I finally emerged into the day light. Looking up, I saw beautiful gray sky and let the nice clean rain wash some of the mud off my face. It was quite a lesson for a young man, alone. The only person who knew exactly where I was lived seven hundred miles away, in Bisbee, Arizona. Occasionally a government trapper or a range rider might happen along, but at that time, I don't imagine more than three or four people traveled that whole area in a year.

My adrenaline was still running pretty high, and I was feeling a little shaky so I had a shot of whiskey, and fixed myself a cup of hot coffee and something to eat. At first I felt sick, and then disappointed and finally just plain mad. I hadn't opened the mine, there were no bags of gold, I lost a day's work and wasted money on explosives and groceries and gas, and could very likely have dug my own grave in the process! Well, what now? I figured it was time to go home while my skin was still intact. I loaded up the Irish dump truck with pick, shovel, ax and camp gear, but the twenty sticks of powder and thirty feet of fuse I threw in the caved in hole, spit the fuse and started home in the rain. A half mile down the trail I heard a muffled "woof!" That's all, no hole, no mine and no gold!

In 1959, I was working in a uranium mine on Beaver Mesa, up on top of John Brown Hill, right on the Colorado-Utah border. The Van Dyke Mine story came up as we were eating in the lunchroom. By then, after talking to the range rider for the cattle association on the "Pan" and other old timers, more facts had come to light. The name of the mine was "The Green Monster," named after the huge Engelmann spruce tree in the front of the mine. The mine had not been recorded at the courthouse at Eagle, Colorado. I had already checked the record books and found the mine was not patented and was subject to re-location. It was very possible the mine had been recorded at Aspen in Pitkin County, Colorado, as the mine could have been in Pitkin County at that time or what is now Eagle County. Someone mentioned old miners from the Frying Pan area crossed the mountains to Aspen, and that it was a thriving town with supplies and banks, and the town of Eagle to the north was really a tiny cow town at that time. I had also found out that his name wasn't Van Dyke that was just a moniker because he wore a Van Dyke beard. When hearing talk about the mine, some older person remembered his name as either Henderson or Richardson.

A lot of time had passed since that old miner had left that fateful winter. There had been the First World War, the depression and the Second World War. The stamp mill had been torn down many years before for scrap metal due to not enough ore to process. Much gold was found, but as usual, much more money went into mining than ever came out as bullion. They even named the peak east of the mill "Fool's Peak".

My partner and I were making top wages as uranium miners, about two dollars and forty cents per hour and living at a mining camp with our families. The company furnished a place to park our trailers, providing water and electricity (at least at night). The nearest town was one hundred miles away down John Brown Hill which was a challenge even when dry. From John Brown it was up over the Uncompagre Range, though Unaweep Canyon and down Nine Mile Hill, across the Gunnison River to White Water and north to Grand Junction.

We were both in good health and story of the mine, "The Green Monster," with its sacked gold just waiting in that mine, had started my partner dreaming. He said he could just see the gold and taste the fish and wild game the country was filled with. So we decided to try once again to open the mine back up. We would leave the uranium mine on a Saturday night after work because we worked Tuesday through Saturday, while some of the crew worked Monday through Friday. That way the company could operate the mine six days a week and not pay anyone overtime.

Down the hill we went in my old Plymouth, leaving our families at the uranium camp. Gene had a late model Ford Fairlane at the bottom of John Brown Hill and we drove the speed limit through to Grand Junction, one hundred miles away. Then up the Colorado River, through Glenwood Springs to the town of Eagle, now the county seat, and then eighteen miles up Brush Creek over the top to Billing's Springs, formerly the logging camp where I'd worked. Then we went up Crooked Creek, around the new man made lake where we would park off the road just east of the Wood's Lake hogback. It was close to three hundred miles one way and probably forty of it dirt road. We slept alongside the car.

The next morning we loaded up tools, powder, bedrolls, and food and packed into the mine which was another three miles or so. We crossed the creek and climbed over dead falls to get to the mine. We arrived tired and our backs were already sore. We built a fire and made coffee and started looking. The cabin site was much the same as I had left it, except now it was used as a hunting camp. We found a hollow stump filled with canned goods and utensils. We went to the hole I had blasted on my last visit and dug, and dug, and dug. I threw the muck to Gene and he moved it back down the dump as far as he could sling it.

Sunday we dug till way after dark using carbide lights. We were after the gold and nothing was going to stop us. Rising Monday morning at daylight, we were still tired, and just plain bone weary, but we started digging again, stopping only to drink water from the creek. We thought we might drink it dry that day. As luck would have it, I found my old bottle of whiskey still in the water behind the flat rock just where I left it. Beautiful amber energizer, much needed right now. I popped the top, took a healthy sniff, and gagged. It was rotten, but we kept it for antiseptic. I've always believed that whiskey, used reasonably as a stimulant and germ killer, is a whole medicine chest in itself. Of course, people that never subject themselves to a great deal of hard work, cold, mud, snow, lack of sleep and food, will say this isn't true. To those lace-bottomed panty-waists it might be true, but then again they are the big talkers, not the "Real People."

By Monday afternoon, we stashed what we didn't take back with us, like the explosives some tools and canned goods, and we packed out the three miles to the car. We drove the three hundred miles back to the camp on Beaver Mesa to go to work in the morning. Tuesday through Saturday, we broke and shipped uranium ore, but when putting the

"Monkey Ward" hitches in place, timbering, and eating lunch, all we talked of was the gold at "The Green Monster."

Our wives took it pretty good, come Saturday after work, when we headed back to Eagle and Brush Creek for weekend number two. Once again, we packed in supplies, and dug. Sunday night by the fire we talked of getting through the cave-in, and digging down through the muck to the rotten caps. Monday we dug into rotten moldy wood, and saw that the drift was caved in clear to the top. So, what! We had nothing to do, but dig it out. When we left late that afternoon, we had a nice looking trench, much like the one that caved in on me in 1953, the difference being, there were two of us now, and it wasn't raining!

Weekend number three. Same scenario (just like the first two trips) drive, pack in up the creek and dig. In digging out the trench over the old rotten timbers, I found a Prince Albert Tobacco can. I picked it up, wiped it off, and pried it open and out fell a folded up location discovery notice. That was all we needed. Scared of losing the gold? You bet! We had talked to too many people and hadn't bothered to recheck the court house. Anyone could have found the mine and recorded the claim. Unfolding the old paper, with Gene looking on sad faced, I read the certificate, "Sunshine #1 recorded and dated 1953 by one

H.S. Bellm." Slowly it dawned on me, "That's me!" Tired and befuddled, I had forgotten. It was years ago, and the claim was invalid anyway. There was no record of assessment work for the past years. Laughing and relieved, we started digging again. Digging? You bet! We dug and dug and dug. I was still pulling the cave-in down into the trench and Gene threw the muck back out of the way. We supported the ribs with slabs from the cabin and shed, with stulls, and posts. It was just enough, we hoped, to hold it. The trench was longer, the face became steeper and higher, and there was still more cave-in, with clay, rock and no stable ground to tunnel through. So we packed out and drove back to the uranium mine.

We had gone to Grand Junction during the week, after our shift, to pick up groceries and supplies for our families because both of our wives were pregnant. That next Saturday was weekend number four and although our families were not so pleased with the gold prospecting anymore, we were on our way back to our glory hole. Saturday night, Gene and I were getting tired of the driving, the hard work, and the stress of family but we were on a mission. That weekend we began to tunnel under the brow. We put posts up at the face and propped stulls against the uprights. We were just underground above the cave-in and hoped that the face held up and the ribs didn't cave-in on us. Our waist lines were looking pretty good, with all the hard work, and our enthusiasm was strong. So back to Beaver Mesa we went.

Weekend number five and my wife was getting pretty far along and stayed home with both our kids and Gene's, because Marlene, Gene's wife, insisted on going with us, pregnant and all. My back was strong, so I packed in a mattress for her to sleep on and of course, Gene got to take advantage of it too, which didn't hurt his feelings. We both must have packed in about a hundred and fifty pounds each that time. The loads were too heavy for us to set down and get back up without helping each other.

Now with Marlene along, we ate better, but had to pack in more food, bedding, and make a lean-to from the fallen down cabin. It rained a little or a lot each afternoon, and it was getting cold at night. Marlene being pregnant and in her bare feet, still drug what poles she could handle up to the trench. She did the cooking and we ate well. It made the work go faster as we didn't have to stop to fix food. We were underground in a three by four foot hole, at least I was. We were still above the rotten timber, but they were less rotten now. The drift was still filled in solid. Down on my knees, I worked on in, throwing out rocks and dirt with a G.I. shovel. I was far enough in to have to use my carbide light. We had to leave early to get

Gene's wife to the car and that woman walked all the way out in her bare feet.

Week six, sixth verse, was once again just like the first. "And bang went the hammer on the out house door!" or so the song went. No Marlene this time. We must have dug until the brow shored up six to eight feet after digging out the sloughed in trench. Our mining game looked serious, a little dog-hole and a great big pile of muck on the elevated dump. That morning as I dug deeper into the hole, Gene got my attention. We had company. There were seven or eight horses with a wrangler and dudes from the city. Gene and I were in ragged, dirty clothes with several days' growth of beard, but we took the time to talk to them. They wanted to know what we were doing. Was there really gold there? All the usual stuff, but it was just slowing up our mining. We talked to them and tried to be as polite as possible. They were on a trail ride from Woods Lake Resort and they wondered if we had seen the mine up the valley three or four miles. Well, NO, we hadn't. They offered us some apples and a few sandwiches, somewhat soggy, as a peace offering, we thanked them and they finally left. We decided, after our curiosity getting the best of us, and digging being such hard work, that we would take a walk up the trail and check out that mining. We found lots of digging, mostly short prospect holes, nothing to get excited about.

On the way back, the sole came off of my logger boot and I tied it back on with the laces of both boots. We went back to our diggings, me with my boots flapping around my ankles, and it was time to pack up and hike back to the car and get back to our wives.

It was now week seven. We were now a tourist attraction for the Woods Lake Resort. They came by to talk and brought us all sorts of food and goodies. Some eager to watch us and hear about the project, and some to snicker behind our backs at two fools moving tons of dirt and risking their lives--for what? But they weren't "Real People," not even the horse wrangler, who just looked the part. So after the side show, they would go back over to the lodge and their steaks and ice cream and soft chairs.

Gene and I had hit solid rock, or at least a mighty big rock. I shored up the ribs next to the face so it wouldn't cave in and so the big rock, that we hoped was solid, would not move. Now we dug down, benched off, and dug down again against the rock. It was Monday afternoon, already late, and our jobs weren't too secure at Beaver Mesa. There was talk of closing down the whole camp. "Poor ore, bad roads, too much expense," so we were told. We had to give up and head home for another week.

Week number eight. We were worn out, tired, and had spent too much hard-earned money on our "mining enterprise". Our wives were more pregnant than ever, and I don't know about you, but I never saw a really happy pregnant woman. Each of us with several small children and the only real prospect we could see that might pay off in our lives was to get that gold. We wanted that gold for our families. Gene was having nightmares about it. We even quit playing pinochle games at night. We worked eight hours and then got our rest, trying to conserve our energy for the big push on the week end.

Determined that we were going to make it this time, we packed up and took off again. Gene didn't drink hard stuff as he was badly hooked on it once. He used to be a whisky runner back in the south east somewhere. He drove a Packard with bullet-proof tires and a sheet of iron plate that came up the back seat. During that time, Gene had to have a half-pint of the good stuff just to get out of bed in the morning, but marrying Marlene sure put a stop to that. Gene was now a teetotaler, of the hard stuff that is, but he drank cold beer to stay awake, while I drank black coffee. We were both running without enough sleep, too much traveling, too much work and too much worry. Early Sunday morning, we started under the big overhang, going deeper and deeper, digging a shaft, not quite vertical, but just off by six or seven degrees. Gene had a rope tied to my feet, and he was straddling me, reaching down the hole on either side, pulling up lard buckets full of muck. I got deeper, and he tied the rope on my feet to the stull across the roof and put ropes on the buckets. The hole was getting deeper, three feet wide, almost twenty four inches across, and the rope on my feet getting longer as I went deeper headfirst. Gene was lifting out the buckets filled with loose dirt, and then he had to get it outside. Down the trench and over the dump, and I could tell that he was about beat from crawling, hanging over me, and moving muck. Here I was, hanging by my feet at the edge of the hole, upside down in the dark. Carbide lights aren't too dependable under these conditions, and they sure don't stay lit upside down. They fall over and go out, or start a fire, burn your arms or the hair off your head. Freda, my wife, found that out the hard way. She was helping me work a mine in Cotton Wood Canyon out of Blanding Utah. I moved too close to her and caught her hair on fire. We put it out, and she was okay, just a little singed. We both learned a little more about carbide lamps and she didn't run me off over it. It worked out all right in the end. She's much more knowledgeable about the old ways of mining than a lot of the so called "experts" of today. She was the best overall partner I ever had and still is!

Back to the mining...Soon the dirt started falling down the hole, so I shouted up to Gene to lower me a little more. With fists and a prospecting pick, I pounded the rocks and mud down into the open tunnel. Then I got stuck! I couldn't get into the drift, the rocks and dirt caved in and came down on my legs and behind. Gene finally got me back out by pulling me up with the rope tied on my ankles, getting my eyes, ears and nose full of dirt in the process. After a nip of whisky and a cup of coffee, I tied the rope under my arms and slid back into the shaft, this time feet first. We were both hoping the gold was just waiting for us, and that the tunnel would be open to the sacked gold. I yelled at Gene for a little more rope, and then I was sliding on loosely packed dirt. I stomped, tried to jump up and down, pushed, wriggled, and called for more rope. My feet and legs were finally hanging in the void of the tunnel, but I couldn't see in yet. I yelled for still more rope, and my butt got hung up. I wriggled, pushed and poked down the dirt and finally, after twenty years of being so close, I slid down where I could see into the old mine. With my head bent down and using carbide light, I finally got to look around. And what did I see, gold? No! An open drift leading to the gold? No! Just another damned cave-in clear to the back not ten feet ahead. I had Gene pull me up. Disgusted and tired, we packed up and went back to our families. That was the last trip Gene and I made to the mine together. We both rustled new jobs in different mines, later, and lost track of each other.

In 1967 or 1968, I was stope mining for the Climax Molybdenum Company at eleven thousand feet on the top of Fremont Pass in Colorado. Three quarters of a mile underground, we talked of gold at dinner time in the lunch room. My new mining partner wanted to go and try to open the gold mine back up. Well, why not? Someone really should find the gold.

Living now below Leadville, my partner, his wife and myself and our oldest son headed for Twin Lakes. We crossed Independence Pass and dropped down into Aspen and drove to Basalt, then up the Frying Pan River to Thomasville, traveling up Lime Creek and Crooked Creek and packed into the old mine. This time we came in from the Frying Pan just like Van Dyke did, hoping again to find the sacked gold.

Before Gene and I had left the last time, we had framed in the dog hole, and made a pretty good door on it, placing tools and carbide lights and such behind the door. We had shot down enough of the brow above the door to cover it. We now had to dig that out to get started. It took us the best part of two days to dig out the caved-in trench and open the door. Behind the door was a solid wall of porphyry packed in so solid it didn't look like we had spent any eight weekends digging there. We sat back for a rest, and then began to look around. We found an old pottery inkwell, a two sided hard rubber comb, and parts of some pretty china cups and saucers. I looked for the old 1885 Fisher Number Five anvil where I stashed it ten or twelve years before. Instead of the anvil, there was a bottle of strychnine about half full in its place. The trapper up there must have been using the poison and didn't want to carry it around for some reason. Using strychnine may have been against the law even then. The anvil turned up more than ten years later buried in the rubble of the old burro shed and my oldest son packed it out for me in the 1980's. I wonder if it is still setting at the portal of the Silt Silver Mine in Aspen, Colorado, because that is where we left it.

I worked ten years for Climax the second time, until the cold and years started to tell on me. We sold out and moved to the four corners area, where my health improved, but not enough to go back to "The Green Monster" mine.

My oldest son, Gus, got the bug and went back up there to try to open it up with a little cash, a lot of hard work and a group of his friends. They dug out the drift, timbered up the portal, drained the water, and got inside. This involved weeks of traveling back and forth from Leadville, digging and dragging heavy porphyry and wet blue green clay out of the drift. The quartz veins inside assayed a little gold everywhere, but Van Dyke had taken only the richest ore. Gus and my youngest son, Donald, finally cleaned out the hole. They opened up a raise that was still shored up with rotten timber, and crawled in with their last remaining light, and once again the mine caved in. Their light quit, and they clawed their way out, bruised and dirty, but still alive. Enough was enough! They packed out and went back to their jobs six hundred miles away.

It's still there. That old mine must be completely caved in again. Porphyry, when exposed to air and water, swells up, and exerts great pressure as it expands. It's evident the old man had lost the portal at least two times. Men were men back then and there are not many of us left, and I'm sure not the man I was back then.

My oldest son, Gus, talked to an old timer, over the mountain several miles north of "The Green Monster," at a place called Fulford. Gus was told that a man by the name of Buck Rogers packed several leather bags of gold ore out of the Woods Lake country sometime after the First World War. He said it came from and old caved-in mine. It's possible he dug down behind the old locked door with its big brass lock, and made it inside years before we ever got there. Possible! But who's to say for sure. The mine is still there; the quartz vein can't be seen as it has weathered away. The access is about the same, not quite as much dirt road. I heard one of the environmental whining singers with a nasal twang from Aspen bought out the old Bowles place at Woods Lake. It seems the self-righteous rich, after they have plundered their share of the country, become quite stiff-necked about anyone else possibly digging a hole or cutting a tree for any reason.

But I'll tell you this for sure, even though I'm not able to work underground much any more, digging placer gold is what kept me alive. If I was younger, with the knowledge and experience I have now, I'd tackle the gold mine, the cold, the mud and the High Country, again. I would build a small cabin and open the mine back up. My wife and my family would help me. We'd replace the timbers, clean and dress up the entrance of the mine. We would dig it out, lay new ties and number eight rails, and have a piece of rolling stock to push up and down the track. There is a lot of dry, good timber there, with fresh air, and clean cold water coming from the ground and the limestone ledges. There are still a few elk left, lots of deer, and grouse, and just down around the old porphyry dike, the beaver ponds must still be full of little Brook trout with pink meat and the best of eating.

Gold is still the thing our dreams are made of, and the old Van Dyke mine is still there, sitting quietly in the Colorado High Country, just waiting for another prospector with gold fever to open it back up and find the gold. I have no regrets. I'd do it again, and so would my sons. And it's a fact, age and circumstances won't ever stop some of us from being the "Real People."

RUSTLER GULCH &
THE LOST BENNET SILVER MINE

It was cold and wet in the early fall of 1920. Old man Bennet and his partner had a load of galena heaped next to the cab, in the bed of their almost new Dodge one ton truck. As most trucks then, like the Graham and the Rio, there was only a half cab with windshield and no side doors. This was the last of the high grade ore to come out of Rustler Gulch in the bed of the rough riding solid rubber tire truck.

There were fifty seven switchbacks in the last quarter of a mile up to the Eagle Mine, on the steep side of the mountain, thirteen thousand feet high.

It was the summer of 1957 when I opened up the Lost Bennet Silver Mine, high on the steep slope of the back side of Emerald Mountain. I was hired to pack in and dig out the caved in mine and have it in operating condition by the time the road was put in at bottom of the mountain, just under the mine. The new owner of the mine, Billy, my boss at the time, led me up Muddy Creek and over the top of Kebler Pass to Crested Butte and then east up Rustlers Gulch. I was driving his Jeep, fully loaded with tools and supplies. Billy drove his pickup pulling a horse trailer. The horse had the name of "Tall Enough" and he was. The last few miles up the creek were by horse and Jeep only.

We arrived at timber line just before dark. Billy pointed up to where the mine was supposed to be. We had our heads tilted back and were looking almost straight up the mountain and there was no mine to be seen. There was only a long slide that was part mine dump and a few boards and an old weathered wash tub way up the slide. We sat up our camp in the last clump of stunted trees next to a small stream right below the mine dump slide.

Before day light, the next morning, we lashed all the tools and equipment we could on Tall Enough and started up the switchbacks. I packed the dynamite, caps, fuse, carbide and Coleman lamps. Billy led the horse and I hung on the horse's tail, careful not to pull back on it because it was steep and just as tough on the horse as it was for us.

We finally made it to the top of the dump and unloaded. We located the remains of the small cabin that was once perched in the wind and snow on the edge of a cliff at twelve thousand feet. All the building material for the small cabin was packed and drug up the hill with horses and by hand. We also found an old wheelbarrow rusted beyond use. Next we checked out the mine and found we could still work our way over the rubble into the haulage level. We found a one ton mine car in fairly good shape except the wheel bushings were dry. We saw silver ore everywhere, on both sides of the track and all over the twelve pound rails. We noticed about a dozen very old World War I tent poles all joined together to make one very long pole. It took just a short time for us to realize that it was just long enough to reach up to the vein and was then used to poke and pry out the silver ore. We tried it and it worked. The air became full of gray silver particles of all sizes from walnut size to fly ash. We ran out to the entry to escape the downpour.

We continued climbing another thousand feet or so to the top of the mountain. We could look out across the country and see down the Crystal River clear to the quarries in Marble, and all the Muddy Country. We could see Mt. Gunnison, and even Independence Pass beyond Aspen. There was absolutely no end to the view we took in, on the thirteen thousand feet plus mountain top. We had examined yet more silver mines on the climb, and found another tunnel with another wheelbarrow sitting in it, just as pretty as can be. I figured it was probably forty years old.

We started back down the mountain, taking our newly found wheelbarrow. Down we went, slipping and sliding. I fought the wheelbarrow all the way. The wheel didn't turn very easily. I even tried to wire it solid and push it like it was a sled runner until it hung up and I went right over the top, ass over tea cup, and down the slope without it. Once I got up and came to my senses, I tried dragging it backwards and even turned it upside down and drug it. We finally made it back to the Bennet Mine.

I had found a can of Crisco cooking fat in the ruins of the broken down cabin and we used that to grease the wheelbarrow bushings, leaving enough for the mine car back in the mine. By then it was late, so we went back down the mountain to our camp. Billy rode the horse and I slid down the slide of loose gravel, getting to camp before Billy did. We fixed supper and ate, climbed into our blankets and slept the sleep of the dead.

Before daylight, I had coffee made and shook Billy out of his deathlike state. We ate breakfast, saddled up and then took turns riding and tagging Tall Enough up the fifty seven switchbacks to the mine. I loaded the wheelbarrow and dumped the waste over the hill while Billy checked out the small upper drift. With much enthusiasm I shoveled, moved and dumped loads of the waste until I felt as if my heart was going to give out. I fell over backwards on the ground like a lump of lead for half an hour. My eyeballs were all I could move. I thought that I was strong as an ox then, and I began to realize, just about as smart as one, too. It was the altitude that got me. After a short while, most of the pain went away and I went back to work, but I only moved half as fast and half as much as before.

It took two days to dig out the mine car, then I greased the wheels and repaired the rails, so cleaning up both ribs (sides) and mucking up the waste was much easier. We packed out three loads of silver ore on Tall Enough. Two hundred pounds at a time was all he could handle going down the steep trail.

By standing out on the waste dump using a hand mirror to reflect the sunlight back into the mine, we could see where the old miner had mined into a horse of waste, (a non producing quartz vein) that cut off his silver bonanza. He blasted through this barren section, but misjudged and missed his vein of silver ore. It was easy to see with the mirror. Old man Bennet missed the vein by only a few feet. We had seen a similar bull quartz vein on the Crystal River side of Emerald Mountain, stretching as far as we could see, extending toward Aspen, until it went out of our sight.

He had five mineral locations in that area that produced either silver or gold. Billy assayed the galena and it was rich in both silver and gold, but the galena from the Eagle mine was formed into countless small cubes of silver and lead and each little square cube had a crystal coating of zinc around it and the Guggenheim Smelter at Leadville which was more than a hundred miles away could not separate the precious metals from the lead and zinc. It was too complex for them at the time. It assayed at more than one thousand dollars per ton, at that time, and today it would probably go for more than two thousand dollars per ton.

This was the fifth year Billy had done the assessment work and had it recorded. The claim was up for patent as soon as he had it surveyed. Billy had found a partner to build a road and help finance the operation. The partner was an old Swedish miner. Together they checked the court house records, and found the mine to be legally recorded, and the assessment work properly recorded, but it was in the wrong township and range. Five years of effort was wasted because Billy had copied the original recorded paper that Bennet placed on record in Gunnison. Billy discovered three more of Bennet's Mines, all recorded properly. The other hard rock mine down in the valley, which had easy access, had poor ore and the two placer claims were in clay banks and at that time could not be worked at a profit.

Years later when I was working in a uranium mine on Monogram Mesa, I met two brothers that had attempted to open a galena prospect about a mile up the valley from the Eagle Mine at about the same altitude. They went broke because of the complex ore and ended up going back to work mining for a big company.

The rich deposits of minerals in the beautiful mountains of Colorado opened up the state and paid for the development of everything from the roads to its public schools. This, in turn, led to the logging, the cattle, the sheep and the farming. It was then that the criminal element and the parasites crowded in around the mines and began to edge out the hard working people. Today it is still the criminal element with a lot of money and great political influence and the non-productive inexperienced parasites that are destroying the ecology with their greed and stupidity. It is not us, as miners and loggers and ranchers. You see most of us are "Real People" and the "Real Ecologists", because we choose to live and work and care for all the earth.

THE MOHAVE DESERT GOLD OF OLD PEG LEG PETE

It's there, no doubt about it! It was found again, the Peg Leg Pete Mine. It was discovered by two men in the latter 1940's, not long after the end of World War II. Although this is one gold mine that I have not looked for personally, I did re-open one of the old Bennet Mines up Rustler's Gulch. I also located and attempted to dig open the lost Van Dyke mine up the Frying Pan River in Colorado.

Now my involvement in this started in the late summer of 1954 while working on a cattle ranch near the town of Hotchkiss on the North Fork of the Gunnison River. Billy, my boss, a cattle rancher then, had been a prospector, ex-government trapper and was a G.I. He told me first hand of his experiences checking out treasure stories.

This is what took place at that time; Billy reached down and picked up two small river stones and asked me what the reddish marks were that were on them. I did know that much, and told him so. The marks were just old rust stains from iron of some sort and they were mostly man made, so what? He then tells me to take them in at lunch time, for what reason, only he knew. After finishing our lunch and enjoying a last cup of coffee, Billy picked up one stone and asked me if I could tell him when the marks were made. Then, after a long pause, he went on to explain the importance of the rust marks on the rocks and the importance of examining them. He figured that a person could follow the older rust marks on the trails in the Superstition Mountains and it would be logical to locate the mine. "Let's go find the Lost Dutchman!" was his next remark. "Both of us have packed and used hand guns since we were knee high and could shoot a grouse in the head," he said, "We will get us a couple of mean dogs and with our rifles and pistols we stand a good chance of getting in and back out without loosing our heads to whoever or whatever it is, that chops them off. So when the work's all done this fall, as the old cowboy song says, we head for Arizona."

The two of us had returned just recently from opening up one of the old Lost Bennet Galena Mines near Crested Butte, which were abandoned and forgotten after World War I. The mine was near thirteen thousand feet and there were fifty seven switchbacks in the last quarter mile of the road. We had sort of slipped off at an opportune "slack" time.

But to get back to the Peg Leg Pete story, Billy was part of the Military Police that patrolled in and around the Mohave Desert during World War II. They used both military

Jeeps and motorcycles to cover roads and desert. It was so dull and boring that he and his partner played games on the bikes on the blacktop and even slipped off to visit their wives sometimes. They began to pick up information about the gold mine of Peg Leg Pete. It was supposed to be near three mounds or mountains and a pond of water with a stand of bamboo around it. On the left side of the pond was a trail. Above the trail, leading to the gold there was supposed to be an old canteen left on a ledge.

Billy and his partner hunted as time permitted, in fact until they were discharged at the end of the war. Billy went home to the Paonia Valley with his wife to work on his dad's cattle ranches and his partner went home to Texas and whatever he did in Texas.

In time, the "Gold Bug" bit them both again. This time it was several years later and they were equipped with a pack horse named Shorty, plenty of food and plenty to drink and enough energy and determination for a dozen men. After several long, hot days, they found the three mounds at the edge of the mountains and the pond with its bamboo and even found the trail and the canteen on the ledge above the trail. NICE! GREAT! But this was only the beginning, they still had to hunt the hills and valleys and find the gold!

There is an old Scottish saying, "Nothing comes easy the first time." Billy said that was true, but it didn't come easy even after the fortieth time either! So up one mountain and down the other, packing picks and shovels and all the water they could carry. No shade and just one prospect hole after another, one black iron dump to another, one mountain to another. They would be checking one old prospect hole and look back to the hill that they were just on and see more there that they had missed. Back and forth and up and down, packing out samples to crush and pan out at night by lantern light. Heat of day and cold of night, sweaty and then freezing, tired and hungry, stiff and sore and there was never a speck of gold to be seen. Days became a week and one week became two, and they couldn't take any more and were about out of food, so they packed up and headed for home, depressed and give out.

Now the important point here is that when the two worn out prospectors headed for home, Billy loaded up a quantity of black ore samples and took them home for "show and tell" so Ruth, his wife, could see them. Sometime later, Billy picked up some of the ore and crushed it on the anvil at the smithy shop, and of course, you guessed it, one piece contained nice pieces of pretty yellow gold! But, just which prospect hole did it come from and was that all there was or was there a real bonanza there? Ruth told him to write it off as experience, good or bad such as it was. Then the final blow came when Billy received an Argosy Magazine in the mail, along with a letter from his partner, telling him that he had written up the whole story and had it published in the magazine, giving the location and directions and all the facts about their trip.

So it goes, really just an episode in the life of a prospector searching for gold, or silver or uranium or any other valuable mineral. But the fun is in the "looking" because after the "finding" then it's all hard work. There's not many of us left that have actually found and produced gold and can prove it. All those mines are still there; The Peg Leg Pete, The Dutchman, The Adam's Diggings, The Bennet Mines, Potato Bill's Claim, The Van Dyke Mine and many more--all proof that there is lots of gold to be found. There is nothing easy to any of it, however the rewards are many and gold is the stuff that dreams are made of, I know.

\

GROVER'S GOLD

Telluride, Keystone Hill, Opher, Placerville, Norwood Canyon, through to Naturita and Uravan, then down the San Miguel River which carries gold on down into the Delores River, which in turn carries it's own fine gold from Delores and Rico and the mountains beyond.

Well, now, what got us started on this trail of gold was a bad case of monoxide poisoning from using diesel loaders underground in the Nil Mine on Monogram Mesa, on the Colorado Plateau in about 1963. I had been given two weeks off to try to get rid of the monoxide build up in my system. Breathing in and out of a brown paper bag was the doctor's prescription to do this.

"Come on, Bellm, let's go find some gold!" Grover Pool, my somewhat eccentric friend, said, "Union Carbide is paying you forty two dollars and fifty cents a week for lying around with your nose in a bag and I'll furnish the traveling expenses." "Hot Dog! O.K. sure, let's go!" I answered. Early the next morning in his three quarter ton Ford with a camper on the back, we started down the San Miguel River. We discussed the many gold carrying gravel bars that had been worked on both sides of the river; clear on through to the Delores and right on down to the Colorado River, many miles away down the canyon. Both of us had some experience in working placer and recovering gold and the black sand that it came in, but we sure had a lot to learn, and STILL do, as a matter of fact.

The last time any amount of placering that was done in that area was during the Depression in the 1930's when they dug the gravel out of the high river banks and washed it in the river. There was the California Bar and the Chicago Bar and many others back up the line in the San Miguel Canyon.

One prospector or miner, whatever you want to call him, was smart enough to come up with the "yellow stuff" by cleaning up many of the old drifts and tunnels in the various workings with a brush and a pan and then packing it to the river to pan it out. This same enterprising fellow said that while he was working for the cement plant, he used to raise and sell chickens and he found more gold panning out the contents of their craws than he ever did sweeping up in the mines.

Our prospecting trip took us along the high winding cliff road along the east bank of the Delores River where the remains of an old flume can still be seen. It was to have carried water to a big high sand bar at the mouth of the canyon. The story about this flume was that someone slipped up, made a miscalculation, and the water only went about half way and stopped. That early flume was said to have cost about forty thousand dollars back then when the price of gold was very small for the amount of labor and effort involved. Men had to hang on ropes and hand steel pin holes in the cliffs to fasten the flume on the sheer walls. This operation was shut down back then, but there is an indication that at some time water was pumped from the river and the bars on both sides of the river had been worked. The last time there was any work done in this area, the price of gold was near four hundred dollars an ounce and big pumps were available.

Half way through this canyon Grover pointed out high gold bearing bars across the deep canyon, one of which I checked out years later. I found that there was a quantity of fine gold still there. Vanadium and uranium were mined on the high mesas and gold was worked down below. At the mouth of the canyon just mentioned is Mesa Creek. Along the highway on the left side, rusty black sand can still be seen in the seams in the banks above the road. On down the river road is Rock Creek. I worked there in the old original Rajah Uranium Mine, where the ore that Madam Currie used for her work with radium, was originally mined. The remains of gold digging can be seen there all along the Delores. It was on the east bank of the stream here that Grover and a doctor friend had tried to get gold from the large quantities of black sands deposited under the immense vertical cliffs.

On down the river, beyond Blue Creek and to Gateway, then up over the pass to White Water, just across the Gunnison River and on to Grand Junction we went. Then up the Colorado River, bound for Aspen and Independence Pass and Where Else? After lunch, just east of Aspen along side the Roaring Fork River, near the area where my wife and I lived for a few months in 1951, we started up the pass, where a little fine gold was found years before. On beyond the snow covered top of the pass, down into the small valley of Lake Creek on the south side of the stream was our destination. We forded the stream and tried to drive up the ancient wagon road in the mud and didn't get very far as the truck was just too big and too heavy. Grover said that the last time he was up there was in a very old touring car that had wooden spoke wheels--1930's? Maybe? Well, Okay! So much for that!

We went on the Twin Lakes road to the upper lake and looked across at the spring run-off at Lake Fork. We decided it was entirely too deep and the road was too steep and narrow that lead up to the abandoned Manhattan Mine at the end of the valley, so we had to pass that one up too. In the 1960's I was able to fly over this area with a friend in a 1946 Piper Super Cruiser, and we located the mine, which later, my sons and I walked into. We were looking for a vein of quartz that Grover had mentioned and we did locate it, but it was beyond our means to work it at that time.

Grover and I were not really too disappointed as there was still more to see, and we had already seen a lot of interesting High Country. We saw the remains of old stagecoach stations, Lincoln, American and Lost Man Gulches with old mine dumps and prospect holes everywhere. When we topped the pass the tramway across the valley on Mount Champion could be seen with many mines and dumps all around the surrounding hills. It was ten years later when my boys and I forded the stream in our well used 1950 Chevy Suburban with a friend of ours and almost lost the truck in the spring run off when looking for the Manhattan Mine. We found Jewish newspapers dated in the 1914's in one old cabin. They were stuffed in the cracks between the logs to keep out the cold. We found lots of old interesting things way up there in the mountains.

Grover stopped at the mouth of Lake Fork below Twin Lakes and we panned out some fine gold in the creek right along side the highway. Some of these concentrates had mercury in them, either from the gold ore itself or some that had been lost from the tables years ago. Next we went down the Arkansas River where there was still an old dredge bottom rusting in the stream at Granite. There was fine gold there in all the washes and around the rocks in the river. The culverts had been cleaned out every season since they were first put in for the gold that concentrates in them. The dredge from years past was stopped just before the rapids. The story goes that the Chinese diggers avoided this section of the river as some were killed there. At the bottom of these rapids, the black sands lay everywhere and from there and on down the river, small amounts of very fine gold could be found around all the larger rocks in the stream. The source of this gold was from the thirteen to fourteen thousand feet mountains that are at the head waters of the

Arkansas River. Much of it came from Oro Gulch, south of Leadville and at least part of it came from Cache Creek that bottomed out right at Granite. Gold everywhere, but none we could locate at the time that was worth the effort of recovery.

As we were eating our lunch there in the Arkansas Valley, Grover told me of a cabin in the hills across the river from the highway. The story was that, two men robbed the stage years ago at Snowden, south of Leadville, and they escaped with a sizeable amount of cash. One robber was wounded and the two of them took shelter in a cabin that was said to have a view of two lakes in the distance to the west (Twin Lakes?). The wounded man died and was buried by his partner along with the money and some of their guns, and then the other man headed down country and found a job on a ranch somewhere. Fearful of being caught, he never went back for the loot, but he did tell someone, much later, about the incident and so the story was repeated and that's how Grover heard of it. My sons and I looked for this cabin in the later 1960's, and we found many cabins looking out toward Twin Lakes, but we never found the right one.

It was after telling that story that Grover told me of finding three dead bodies in his life. One of them was in a shack at the junction of Lake Fork and the Arkansas River; he was just a kid at the time. He and whoever he was with, notified the sheriff of Lake County. The sheriff and the coroner came down and picked up the partially decomposed body in a very old wooden-spoke panel truck with a screen mesh on both sides. Grover said that it looked like a dog-catcher's wagon. The body was carefully placed in the bed of the truck, but Grover said that it was bounced to pieces on the rough dirt road going back to Leadville.

Back to our trip, we proceeded on down the river to a point below the rapids where we could see several large boulders in the river. Grover pointed out that one had a pin hole in the top of it. The story is that a man lived in a dug-out above the river and had run a cable out to the top of one of the rocks. He worked his way out to that rock and with a pan or a cup of sorts scooped up the gold bearing sand. It was about fifty feet out across the fast running, cold Arkansas River to the rock and it took a great amount of effort to scoop the gold bearing gravel up in a cup at the end of a long pole and dump it in a container and then carry it back to be checked for gold. Of course, the loose gravel continued to refill his shallow hole under the water and most of his effort to get to the bedrock was a lesson in futility, but the point here is that he was able to recover enough values to keep in bacon and beans and a sack of tobacco now and then. As luck would have it, the river went down one year, perhaps it was a dry season or maybe it was when Turquoise Lake reservoir was being constructed, or possibly when Twin Lakes or Clear Creek Reservoir were being filled--Who knows? But the fact was that instead of scooping gravel up in a cup, he was able to dig the rich gold ore up with a shovel, put it in buckets and transport it to a stock pile on the banks of the river. The result of perhaps years of almost wasted effort and then in a few long days of frantic digging, he made enough to set himself up for life. Grover said he knew the man and that he owned one of the big mansions in Colorado Springs and was quite wealthy.

Oh, the river there still contains gold, that's a fact. In 1955 a friend of ours showed up at our home in Paonia with an assay slip showing one hundred thirty ounces of gold to the ton of placer that came from that river just down a few miles at a bridge below Buena Vista. The sample that he let me pan out didn't indicate that much gold, but maybe all he had was a pie tin to pan with and it may not have been very clean. This guy really didn't have much experience recovering gold, but it was worth it to go take a look at what he had found.

We went up the Gunnison and the Muddy, over McClure Pass and down the Crystal River and then up the Roaring Fork to Aspen. We continued over Independence Pass, down past

Twin Lakes, through Granite and on down the river to where the county had just replaced a bridge across the river. "Right here, he said, just about where that concrete foundation is," and that was where he scooped up a coffee can of muck that the county had stirred up while setting the footers of the bridge. Time and circumstances and lack of experience, but the small amount of gravel he just happened to pick up evidently did contain about three or four thousand dollars worth of gold in one very small concentrated area that was now buried by the concrete of the new bridge. What a let down! So it goes trying to get rich recovering gold. GOLD, that's what dreams are made of.

Grover and I continued on our scenic trip to Tin Cup to look at an old mill that had been burnt down. So the story goes, someone was contracted to remove it and clean up the mill site. Legally, he did just that, but not just exactly like the mill owners expected. The guy set fire to the mill. He tore up the flume boards and stacked them and burned them, too. He didn't admit to setting the fire, but he did clean up the site, selling the scrap metal as was agreed on and then he sifted the ashes and recovered the gold that was left, which is said to have amounted to a lot of money, plus the money from the scrap metal. There is always something to learn from others about the recovery of gold, but I personally, don't think any amount of gold is worth going to jail over.

It was at another mine in the Tin Cup area that a man kept trying to hire out, back in the later 1920's. He always made sure he didn't get hired. Why was that? Well, he wore bib overalls and a heavy bulky coat with big strong pockets. Big strong pockets--that's the clue, and after being turned down, as he was leaving, he would always go out under the ore bin out of sight of course to relieve himself, each and every time. After staggering out, this helped give him an unfavorable image, he went back to his camp with his pockets filled with high-grade fines from the ore bin and probably made as much money as he would have working a job, with less work and less hours too. I never heard the end of this incident but it must have paid off for a while. So you see, money can be made producing gold, but it is also true that a person, back then, could get lead poison (from a bullet) or acquire free board and room for a time (in jail) as an added benefit, of course.

We went back home, with not a speck of gold to show off or brag about. That was really not so important, not really, because we saw where and how gold was recovered, saw the mines and the streams and the quartz veins and acquired a wealth of information that has been lost to most people. There are just a few of the "Real People" that have the desire and the ambition and are willing to put out the great effort to locate and recover the gold that is still there. Maybe you are one of them.

WAH MOUNTAIN GOLD

Wah Mountain? Just another gold mine story? Sure, but it's a good one and it's true, without a doubt. Now I can't remember for sure if the name of the mountain is spelled right, but the story is right and the mountain is located on the maps. It is a number of miles north of Canyon City and south of Silver Cliff, not too far from the Royal Gorge. It was the richest gold ever seen in Canyon City up till that time and perhaps up to the present date.

An old prospector packed several loads of high-grade gold ore into town and bought supplies, loaded them on the backs of his burros and disappeared to the north. This custom was noted by several people in several consecutive seasons. The snow and the cold were too extreme to be able to do much mining through the winter months. It appeared that he was operating a shaft by himself that is as much as anyone really knew.

One spring he and his burros just seemed to vanish, just like Van Dyke did in the Frying Pan River country up in the Holy Cross area, but unlike Van Dyke, who left his animals down at Thomasville and went back to the old country each year, the prospector did not return. He left no trace of his activity, he just vanished. What happened? Did he just up and leave? He seemed to be producing good gold. Perhaps there was an accident or even something more violent? Gold brings out the worst in many people. You might just ponder on that a bit.

Yah, sure, I got involved back in the early to middle fifty's clear over on the western slope of Colorado in the Paonia Valley. I had moved my family from the old ghost town of Marble, where I had been working in the long abandoned Yule Marble Quarry mill yard, salvaging existing blocks and crushing the smaller pieces for a company in Glenwood Springs. There were just no decent wages to be made back then.

We then moved to Paonia where I worked for a cattle rancher to pay the rent on a cabin of his that we were living in. He hired me to help him open up one of the old Lost Bennet Silver Mines on Emerald Mountain west of Crested Butte, up near the head of Rustler's Gulch. The mine was way up the side of the mountain on a road that had fifty seven switch backs up to the Galena mine, putting it close to thirteen thousand feet. Emerald Mountain is fourteen thousand feet high. Now that's another story, but because of this job, and maybe a few other reasons, the Wah Mountain experience began.

One of our many "Real Friends" in the Paonia area was the Wright family. They were a mighty fine and very hard working couple with a family of four, if I remember correctly. Dick had been a coal miner and a hard rock miner and had mined in the Silver Cliff area during the depression. That was where he became involved with Wah Mountain. He and his wife, Marge, had found the mine, a caved in shaft, long abandoned. "You are always chasing gold mines, Harvey, so we're just going to give you one. You can have it free and clear. We don't want any part of it, and you have to leave us completely out of it," Dick said. So there I stood with my mouth hanging open, dumb as a rock. You really need to know more about this fine old couple to be able to appreciate them as my wife and I do. Dick had to quit the mines and became a mechanic and Marge, well, she worked like a man all of her life and always outside, summer and winter, working teams of horses and mules in the fields. She operated the first diesel farm tractor on Roger's Mesa where they lived. She was one of the best mule handlers, much better than most men. She had a rough voice like Tug Boat Annie or Ma Kettle and she dressed in Levis and work boots. She was as mild and kind hearted as all outdoors, and she would never allow anyone to abuse her teams or misuse them in any way. Yes, that's where the real gold is and the beauty of it, too. She was solid gold and a yard wide. You would have loved her, too. She worked so hard, raised four young ones and drove a 1932 Model A Ford Coup. That was Marge.

So the story they told me goes like this; In 1931 or 1932 Dick and Marge packed their two burros with their camp goods and tools and hunted Wah Mountain until they located the old miner's camp. How did they come to the conclusion it was the right one? The tent and the complete camp was still there, the remains of groceries and supplies and personal things, all rotted into the ground. They also found the remains of one of his pack animals that had been tied to a tree with the halter still on his head.

What would you think? Most likely the same as they did. They were sure it was the right place, but the mine was not there. They had not found it in their searching for the camp. I'll bet that they found lots of quartz waste there at the camp where the old miner broke the ore to get the best of the gold. Eager with expectation, they set up their camp and began searching the area. They started their search by tying a rag to a tree and going in a straight line along the hill, then moving at a right angle and tying another rag and making a search in a straight line, doing this again and again. They finally found a caved in vertical shaft with it's rotted timbers, broken windless and a scattering of mine tools left abandoned in the dirt. They found the camp and now the shaft and so what about the old miner? Where else, but at the bottom of the hole. He was just a pile of bones by then, no doubt about it.

They moved their camp to the hole and rebuilt and set up the windless. Dick set up the re-timbering operation and Marge went to work cutting and dragging timbers with her burros. It's a mighty tough deal to hang down a shaft of rotted timbers for just a man and his wife. The rotten timbers had to be pulled out and the new ones lowered down, put in place and made secure. They worked daylight to dark, day after day, and the deeper they went, the more difficult and dangerous it got.

Tired and worn out they never gave up, expecting anytime to find the gold at the bottom along with the old man's bones. Then out of the blue, Dick's worthless deadbeat brother, Paul, showed up at the camp and told them that their dad said that "He could have half of the mine." After all the hard work, the sweat and blood, the usual scrapes and abrasions, the sore muscles and always the frustrations and heartaches, along comes Paul, who wouldn't work, didn't bring along any supplies or groceries and to top it all off wouldn't lift a finger around camp. He even expected to be waited on. Just what would YOU do? Probably just what Dick and Marge did, they kicked the new timbers down the hole, packed up their camp gear and headed down the mountain. If Paul wanted it he could have it. Me, I guess that I might not have been as nice as Dick and Marge because after all that work and effort, I would have seriously considered giving Paul a shove right along with the new timbers. END OF STORY? NOT HARDLY!!!

It was the first or the second hitch at the Climax Molybdenum Mine that I and my family hunted for that shaft on Wah Mountain. We made several trips and looked and studied and searched and after a great deal of effort and time came to the educated conclusion that the county had constructed a new road up Wah Mountain and had evidently covered the shaft. So what? It's still there, the covered shaft, the gold and the old man's bones, and the expectation and thrill of getting involved.

END OF STORY? Well, of course not! Just because I can't take the altitude and the cold and what ever else it takes to get the gold that doesn't mean that YOU can't! It just might be your turn now.

SO GET WITH IT!
THE BEST IS YET TO COME!!
I KNOW FOR A FACT!!!

Ouray Gold
The Pay Back

There was an ounce and a half of bright yellow fresh gold there in that pan, maybe more. "Where'd you get that?" said the owner of the mine. Ben looked up at the fellow with a look of contempt and said something quite unprintable, but very appropriate, dumped the pan in the ditch, gold and all, turned his back and walked over to his car and drove down the hill with his wife and two young boys. It all started when Ben and his wife were operating a small restaurant in town and met some of the old timers that worked gold in the mines there, just above the town. There were many stories told of the mines such as the Camp Bird, the American Netti and the Winaucca Mine. Smuggler's Trail starts right there at the edge of town and leads up to the old boarding house at the portal of the American Netti Mine. A few of these same story tellers were still high-grading gold from the upper levels and using the old trail. A lot of coffee drinking and story telling went on and Ben and his wife were nice to the old miners.

The little restaurant went under so these old miners suggested to Ben that he should try to get a lease on the Winaucca Mine and work it. Ben was not a miner, but he listened to what all these old miners told him and it sounded good to Ben and his wife. The owner, who was a real estate man and no miner, just a get rich quick any way you can and don't get your hands dirty kind of man, provided a cabin for them right at the portal of the mine and furnished the equipment and operating expenses for the six month lease period. The agreement was for Ben to work the mine for the six months and the ore would be sent to the mill just below town. The owner would get half and Ben would get half.

It was like a god send to them, a place to live, expenses paid and half the gold. They left town with many bills unpaid and the promises to pay them at the end of the six months. Moving into the cabin they attempted to start mining. It was a real thrill, with carbide lights, hard hats, rubber mining boots and a prospecting pick.

One of the old miners showed them the gold vein there at the face of the drift which was down a slight incline and around the corner quite a long way, really. Being new to the mining game, Ben never thought to ask why someone else wasn't mining here and producing gold. Or just WHY the old miners that were high-grading in the American Netti were so eager to help.

We need to remember that there is a degree of good in most bad men and a degree of bad in all of us, but we have to realize it and keep it under control. People use other people to get ahead, and many of these have little concern for those who do the hard work.

We know for sure someone actually had to help Ben set up the worn out Cleveland Hammer for drilling, hook up the air and water lines, and operate the compressor and maybe give him some pointers on how to drill. Ben fought the machine with the help of his wife and managed to get three shallow holes in each corner of the face and a hole or two in the center. He managed to load the holes with dynamite and shoot them. For one with no mining experience, he really did quite well not to kill himself with the machine or the explosives. He and his wife soon found out the proper sequences of drilling a round and shooting it, hand mucking the ore into a mine car and pulling it up and outside to the ore bin. I'm sure they had a lot of help (probably mostly "advice") from the old miners that drove up every so often. They would help Ben get going and then they would just disappear, leaving their car out at the cabin. Well, it was a big mine and it was connected with the mine above it, the American Netti. That old mine was deep and cold and wet and it had terrible cold updrafts in the old unused raises. It still had ladders and you couldn't see the top of them even with a real good light. Guess those old miners were still doing some mining on their own. They would cut samples of the ore and could pan out colors right there at the mine and show Ben the gold. It was good ore, in fact very good ore, perhaps too good. Those old timers were still driving up to the mine to help Ben and then disappearing for hours at a time during the day.

Ben and his wife worked six months, six months of hard dangerous labor. A truck finally came and hauled the ore to the mill. Ben and his wife and their two boys and the old miners and most of those that Ben owed money to were right there to see the results. The old timers checked the tailings coming out of the mill continually, and no amount of gold was lost in the tailings, the mill recovered it. It was just a short while until Ben saw the check, it was for seven hundred and fifty dollars and only half of that was his. What a terrible disappointment! So where did the gold go? The old miners checked the tailings and it wasn't going out there, so where was it? The Real Estate man shook his head and said that he was sure sorry, but, anyway, the six month lease was up and they had to get off the property.

Ben walked back into the mine one more time, to be the last time, and he thought about the showing of good ore that he had seen high on the right rib of the drift. He picked out about a good sized tea cup full of it and was panning it out as the mine owner came up and looked over his shoulder. The owner was no miner, just another conman using other people's money and labor to get him rich with the least amount of effort possible. That greedy mine owner looked and looked and looked for that gold. He let his business fail so that he could keep looking and looking. His desire and greed must have gotten the worst of him and he ended up putting a forty five automatic to his head and committing suicide.

Later Ben was told by the old miners that the mine owner also owned half of the gold mill. And the GOLD? It was there in the mill, actually hung up in the ball mill; it just got pounded together in globs and hung up in there to be cleaned out later when every one was gone. Someone got away with that gold, it was common knowledge that it went into the mill. So who took it? Who knows? That real estate man probably had his share of the gold hid out somewhere. He had probably worked this stunt more than just once. Then if he was a thief, his milling partner had to be a thief also. It is easy to steal from a thief, it's expected and it's easy to lie to a liar they expect it, but remember, in the end there is nothing that thieves and liars can do to an honest person. In fact, such men are afraid of an honest person.

So what about those 'good old boys' that were helping Ben, parking their cars at the mine and disappearing for hours at a time? Why climb all the way up Smuggler's Trail to the Netti to high-grade gold when they could park at the Winaucca and climb up that windy old raise to the upper levels of the mine above them, never to be seen on the trail? Think on that for a moment. Would you sneak up that very old raise ladder almost three hundred feet and underneath a loose slab that weighed hundreds of tons, then walk in the mud to another old ladder and climb higher up into the old caved-in work areas several times a week to pick out a little pretty yellow gold? Well, they did! Something to do, I guess.

I climbed that three hundred feet both ways, several times a few years later. Yes, I was looking for Ben's gold and the old miner's gold too, but I never found it. WELL--IT WAS SOMETHING TO DO!!!

GREATERVILLE
FRED'S GOLD &
THE MEXICAN'S JEWELRY ROCK

"You're just the man to find it!" Fred blurted out all of a sudden, "That vein of gold over there at Aliso". Aliso? Gold? Gold, I understand, but Aliso? I never heard of Aliso or any vein of gold there. I was looking for placer gold and was just checking out the Greaterville area. I found a fellow working the bottom of a dry wash collecting a little gold. After talking to him for a while, he told me to go on up the road to Fred Harm's camp and talk to him and so there I was, drinking coffee and swapping stories. Fred was an old one-eyed, fat man, no offense intended, just a fact, and that's exactly how Fred described himself to me. Fred said to me, "Yes. I think you are the one to find it!"

Fred's camp was up on the left side of Opher or Hughes Gulch, as there is some question of the correct name of this little dry wash. He and his partner each had a small travel trailer on a lode claim of his, but had given up working the claim. He said that it had gold, good gold, at one time. His son took out one piece of ore that brought him enough money to buy a new car. "It was a foreign car of some kind, Swedish, I think." Fred said. "Was it a Volvo?" I asked. "Yes! That's right, that's what it was alright."

"Well, Fred, why in the hell aren't you up there digging like mad right now?" "Well," he spoke slowly, "We did dig, we dug all over that mountain, bull-dozed off the whole front of the vein area and that one piece of gold was the first and the last of any quantity of gold to be found there." Then with a sick smile on his face, he said, "I went back to prospecting and produced a little gold, mostly placer, off of my other claims. It's a damn sight easier and besides, I have a couple of pension checks coming in each month, enough to keep me going until I die. Prospecting's the best, because it is a great deal

140

easier, safer than and not nearly as expensive as development on a mine."

Fred had made friends with an old Mexican rancher, that lived near him, helping him out doing some mechanic work on his tractor and such, and they became quite good friends. The old Mexican had a habit of stopping in at Fred's camp and having coffee with him early some mornings, and then he would ride on up the road on his horse. After many such trips going by Fred's early in the morning and back late in the evening; the old man showed Fred what he had in his saddle bags. GOLD! Gold in quartz, jewelry rock rich in just the gold alone, but even worth much more as specimen pieces if the gold was left in the quartz. The old Mexican had been working a small vein up over the mountain for years with hand steel, pick and shovel. It was much like going to the bank, because as he needed money, he went up the trail and made a withdrawal. But now, he was getting up in years, and to make it up to his "bank" was just too much for him.

One day while he was visiting Fred, having coffee with him, he said, "Fred, you've been a good friend to me, always helping me out, and now I want you to have the gold that's up there on the mountain." He told Fred his knowledge about the country and the directions of how to find the six inch vein of quartz. He explained to

Fred, "No one is going to find it unless they are told exactly where it is. I want you to have it, not my son, it's yours alone." We came to our own conclusions as to why he did this, he never said, but gold can destroy as much as it can help. It must have been about this same time that the old Mexican told Fred about his lode claims in the Dos Cabasos area. He said, "You can have those claims, too. I can do nothing with them anymore." Fred located these claims and proved up on them for several years, even driving drift and sinking a shaft on one claim.

So, there I was, having coffee and swapping stories and Fred decided that I was the one! So he gave me the directions to the vein, told me just how to get there. He said that from the vein, you could see Greaterville, to the west Tucson was visible, and to the south, Aliso and the old corral could be seen. "It's so easy and when I get to feeling better, I think that I can go over to Aliso and go right to it!" That was Fred's remark.

We had begun to feel like we could trust each other. We were feeling quite comfortable with each other, as our interests and knowledge of mining and minerals were discussed. Agreeing to put forth the effort, I took my leave and drove up beyond the radio tower to the start of the wilderness trail, had supper and made my plans for the next morning. At daylight, I was climbing up the trail it was easy to believe that the old Mexican had fallen off of his horse two times, as he had told Fred, and this was just the easy part of the trail, so I was to find out. The trail was made more difficult for me on foot with a pack because those who traveled before me on mountain bikes and horses, along with the bad storms and flash floods common to these hills, made the trail virtually impassible. Getting to the top of the pass between the valleys, I came to the conclusion that this was the meanest, roughest country to hunt in for only a six inch wide vein of gold. It was steep hillsides of loose broken rocks, mesquite bushes and cacti so thick that a person couldn't walk through it. It began to soak in, and I thought, "BUT IT IS SOO EASY! Sure, maybe, but that old man didn't come this way on a horse, as Fred claimed." I tried to follow a fence line that was put in place there many years before, but it was so choked with sticker bushes of every kind that I had to chop my way through, making many detours, climbing up and down the steep loose hillside.

I checked out every indication of mineral and every place on the mountains where Tucson, Greaterville, Aliso, and the corral could be seen. None of these places could actually be seen, but I could determine exactly where they were from several places on the top of the ridge. I had only checked out about half the ridge. There was quartz in many places and quartz float everywhere. There was also some rose quartz, but there was no mineral. My feet hurt, my hands and face were scratched in many places and my legs were burning from the broken off points of stickers still imbedded in them. I headed back around the mountain slope, down the hills and up the other sides of many small steep washes in the thick brush. Finally, reaching Aliso Trail, I continued up through the pass and down the steep trail and finally back to the Chinook.

That was trip one, lesson one, and my conclusion was that no eighty year old man came up this same trail that I had just been on! So I took a shot of Brandy, put the coffee water on, sat back and rested my poor aching body. Pulling down my britches, I proceed to scrape the many little black stickers out of my legs with my knife. So, it was home again, back to working Ed Smart's claims and always thinking about Greaterville and the next week end trip.

This time, I used the Jeep pickup, after welding standards on the driver's side to fasten a platform for a bed up off the ground. Sleep on the ground? Not me, not around here! This time I went up the Gardner Canyon road and found the road to Aliso. Down around the bend from the spring I found the remains of a corral, the only corral in the area. A person was supposed to be able to look up the side of the fence and see the vein on the far mountain.

That sounded reasonable, except for the fact that the corral had four sides, what was left of it. The one logical side did point in the right direction, but, always there seems to be a BUT, there was a good sized mountain blocking the view to the far ridge where the gold was supposed to be.

I headed up this immediate mountain with my prospecting gear. The first distraction was a promising outcrop of white quartz, so of course it had to be checked out. There was no evidence of mineral all along the mountain side, so I went back to the area where I could see the corral and then up the hill until both the corral and the far hillside could be seen. There on the far mountain was a limestone ridge, and it had to be, just HAD to be the one Fred mentioned. "Find the limestone ridge, where it meets the trees and start looking." he had told me. Now before that could be done, I had to work my way down this mountain and then find my way up the valley to where I could get up over the limestone ridge, which was cliff in most places. There sure was a lot of hillside to check out.

I was working myself down the immediate mountain side and just ahead of me was an animal like nothing I had ever seen. It just ambled off down through the brush, seeming to ignore me. I had been told that many strange and unusual snakes and animals came up out of Mexico and had been seen in the area. This one was brown, smaller than a bear, larger than a ground hog, and looked like and adult. It walked with a rolling motion and looked like it was all muscle. This critter, I found out later, was called a "Desert Monkey" or Coati Mundi. Stories are told about this animal killing all the chickens in a hen house and when a dog took after it, it killed the dog, no contest. I pack a 38 Service Revolver, but I was looking for gold, not trouble. There was enough excitement and thrills for me without asking for that kind of trouble.

I went on down the hill to the bottom and up the wash a distance to climb the loose steep side of the mountain to the limestone ridge. Working along the ridge, towards the end, I found access to the top. This was quite a beautiful little flat, above the valley, with trees, a view of the Mule Mountains and all the mountains to the south and the west. This HAD to be the place where the vein was, or close, anyway. Looking carefully, I could see quartz float all over the area. I climbed to the top of the ridge and none of the indicated landmarks could actually be seen, but I did see the tree tops of Aliso, where there were indications of a corral. Looking behind me, was where Greaterville used to be and looking west I could see where Tucson was and all the surrounding country. All that I found this time was cow manure, which proves that animals found a way up there. So could a horse and rider if he was very careful.

It was time to get out of there, the air was getting cool. Taking a different route back, there was much to be seen, but traveling was going to be difficult and I was beat. It was late, when I made it back to the Jeep and I had no choice but to spend the night. Fixing something to eat and a cup of coffee, along with a shot of Brandy to warm things up, I sat on my bed roll on the bench on the Jeep, relaxing by a small fire. It was getting very cold, and so with my chainsaw, I cut up a pile of fire wood to last me the night. The fire helped, but I just couldn't stay warm, even with my back against the Jeep. I put on more wood and built a bigger fire so it would burn all night long. I just couldn't stay warm, I figured out that there was a down draft from the surrounding mountains and it felt like it was down below zero. I've slept out in the snow banks in Colorado High Country, and my clothes and bedroll back then were not nearly as adequate as what I had now. Most of the night was spent sawing up the remainder of the posts and poles of the corral to keep the fire going, while cat-napping sitting up with the bedroll wrapped around my shoulders.

When daylight came, I threw my bedroll and the rest of my stuff in the back of the truck and took off up the steep road to escape the cold air and get into the sun when it came up.

Nearing the top of the road, I looked back and saw my bedroll on the piece of plywood lying in the middle of the road so I carefully backed down to pick it up. I finally climbed back to the top just as the sun was coming up in the east over the Mule Mountains. It felt good to be warm again and heading home. That was trip number two, and I was already thinking and planning for the next one, determined to find that gold! It isn't that I don't have some gold of my own, I do, from working the washes in the Bisbee area, but this is a challenge and this gold is still in the quartz and perhaps I'm hoping that the gold could be in rose quartz as there was some rose quartz in the veins there. So I tried again.

Early in the quiet cool morning air, I saw an extremely steep, washed out, rocky old road that was pointing in just the right direction. That little 1950 Jeep pickup with new tires and a 318 Dodge V8 engine was just barely able to reach the top. Starting down the other side, my mountain with the vein of gold was still a long way off. Not in miles, mind you, if you were a bird. Parking on a small flat, I started out on foot, down the steep washed out road, with my gear. This time, I took my Gold Spear, and the Gold Bug, (both metal detectors) plus the Ruger Automatic and the 38, just in case I ran into some of those strange animals from Mexico, besides I'd heard a story that a man was attacked by a bear in this area not too long ago. I know that that's not too common, unless the bear is wounded or protecting young, but I am way out here all by myself singing "Mariah" (Now, I'm so lost, so goldurn lost, not even God can find me--so the song goes). I may be a little insane, but not so stupid. Anyhow, the road that I was now following cut right through several veins of quartz, but checked out to have no value.

At the bottom of the road, there was a stock pond long abandoned, but filled with muddy water and there were animal tracks all about, just what kind I couldn't say, but I am after gold, not anything else. I felt better about the extra weight of the guns. I headed around the pond and up a smooth limestone wash filled with many rounded well-washed rock. There was no trail and no place to walk, so I climbed over rocks and ledges and worked my way through Mesquite and cacti of various kinds and sizes and because I was packing the Spear, which was about four feet long and the Gold Bug, it was difficult traveling because I kept getting hung up on the bushes. I began working myself up along the side of the mountain, up under the limestone ridge and looking ahead of me I saw seven of those mean little monkey critters (Coati Mundi). I froze, just stood there and watched, they surely heard me, they could see me, but it was quite plain that they owned this part of the mountain and I wasn't even worth their concern. Yes, I was packing two loaded hand guns and had a brush knife in one hand, but as far as I was concerned, that was their part of the mountain. I'm no coward, but I'm no fool either, I left them alone and they did the same for me.

Getting past them, I went up around the ridge to a little park like flat, and the prospecting began. I figured that the old man had to tie his horse somewhere close to the vein and this spot looked likely. The Gold Spear turned out to be of no value here, but the Gold Bug picked up lead from spent bullets and many, many small pieces of rusty tin from old cans. Working the hill side for several hours with the Gold Bug, I still couldn't find the drill steel that was supposed to be stuck in the vein, nor could the Gold Bug find any of his hand tools.

I prospected all over the side of the hill from the top to the bottom and did not find any sign of mineral, same as before. I went along the top of the ridge in both directions, there was quartz everywhere and all kinds of possibilities, but my vein wasn't to be found. In spite of my sore back and feet and the scratches and stickers buried in my hands and arms and legs, the air was pure and clean and the view of the mountains and valleys made it worth while, anyway.

Finding a trail to follow above the ridge somewhat in the direction I needed to go, coming down the end of the big ridge, there was what looked like, a satellite dish in a cargo net. It had to have been placed there by helicopter, as it must have been twenty feet across. From there, I could see where I had parked the Jeep way down, across and up the other side. There were several weathered incline holes in the limestone, some big enough to climb down into, but with the snakes and scorpions and spiders and such, I wasn't eager to go into any of them, but if there was a chance of there being gold or other precious mineral down there, then most likely, somehow I would try anyway.

Back at the Jeep, I met two boys and a girl in Army Fatigues who were hunting hogs with hand guns. I drove back around the mountain range to Greaterville, to talk to Fred. It was a long drive on rough roads back around Granite Mountain to Fred's camp. After discussing the situation with him, Fred said, "Let's go to Dos Cabasos and look at some claims over there."

Early the next morning, in Fred's truck with him driving like the Devil was on his tail, we were on our way to Wilcox. A quick stop at the Dairy Queen for ice cream (last chance for ice cream because there was no refrigeration at his camp) and then on to the claims near Government Mountain. Much of the dirt road was washed out and we had to go through some private ground and through several fences. I opened the wire gates after checking closely for rattle snakes which seem to like to travel down the road and sometimes rest in the shade of the gate posts. No snakes that time!

The gulch to the mines was pretty much washed out. By rolling the bigger rocks out of the track, we worked our way up to the property. There on the left, was a corrugated tin building on a concrete pad and there was a portal of a mine just ahead of it. Above the shack, was the dump of another hole and across the dry stream bed was yet another mine portal.

After having a lunch of sardines and crackers, I fastened my headlamp on my mine hat and we checked out the hole next to the shack. Inside there was a crosscut drift to the left and at the face in the lower left corner was a small vein. After examining it closely, silver metal could be seen with my glass. Fred said, "It was silver, alright, and there was a lot produced here but the story is that none of it was hauled out, and bars were buried somewhere near the blacksmith shop outside."

We went on to the face of the main drift. There in the bottom left hand corner was another vein and after examining samples closely, this tiny vein had yellow gold in it. I looked closely at the remains of the shop outside, thinking about maybe using the Gold

Bug to try to find those silver bars. We went on across the dry wash to another mine in the bottom of the wash. Fred had driven most of that existing drift with an electric drill, the formation was that soft. At the face and in the bottom left corner was another small vein and yellow gold could be seen in the samples. So what about these veins in the left hand corner of all three faces? I don't know, but there was not enough mineral showing to get much excited about.

Above the tin building was a white dump of soapy white scheelite (tungsten) ore and it contained metal which, after looking closely, was gold. "Fred, you have gold showing in the tungsten pile." I said. Fred was inside the portal at a station where a shaft was sunk, checking for rattlers. It was still really too cold for them, Fred knew that and I knew that, but perhaps the snakes didn't know it, so we needed to be sure. Fred said that he drilled and blasted in the shaft, and had hired two Mexican boys to muck it out. "I guess that I should have checked it out a little closer." he said, and then went on to explain, "I think this is where the Old Lost Adams Mine is, next time you're up here, go up the wash and dig under the dry water fall."

I made another trip later and almost turned the Jeep over with a camper on it, and I dug where he said. I dug a hole three feet deep and five feet wide and there were riffles in the bottom that were naturals to catch gold, but all I found was three small flakes that I wasted two whole days on. So it goes, chasing the yellow stuff.

Trip number four to Greaterville took me to the radio tower and up the wilderness trail to check out the west end of the ridge in question. Working up along the western most mountain that looked out toward Green Valley, the view was fantastic and near the top on the Mt. Baldy side, were a number of old diggings and all of them were very promising. There was a lot of pretty rose quartz with indications of mineral, but as the original directions came to mind, no man on a horse ever traveled on this side of the mountain, not up here, where these diggings were.

So I forced my way along the steep hillside, chopping through the mesquite and the cactus to the Aliso Trail and staggered back down the trail to the Chinook which is what I was driving this time. I had my shot of brandy and several cups of very strong coffee. I did a quick wash job and put on clean socks, and then I moved the Chinook where I could see out over the valley, and even got to watch a little black and white T.V. from Tucson, before I passed out for the night.

The next morning, after driving down the road to the Morning Star Mine and looking over the dump there, I climbed down the incline to the water level of the flooded mine. There were cross cuts going both ways that contained a little white gold and or silver at both faces of these small crawl holes. I was told that there were still some Mexicans ambitious enough to dig in there at times. There are indications that there was gold there right at the grass roots. The mine was closed during World War II and allowed to be flooded again, to cover a theft. That's not too hard to believe. This was the original Saint Louis Mine, according to old records. Up the gulch was a small operation trying to recover some very fine gold, but it appeared that it was not a paying operation. They soon gave it up. They could only write it off to experience. There was a lot of activity in this gulch at the Turn of the Century. Records show that a lot of gold was taken from this area. Sad to say, I haven't yet found my gold mine, but I still dream about it and plan to try to find it again.

PART 3
URANIUM MINING

THE AMERICAN EAGLE MINE
BIG GYPSUM VALLEY
ON THE COLORADO PLATEAU

One of the biggest rolls of uranium ore known was found in this mine. It was three thousand feet in length and just two hundred feet beneath the surface of the ground. There was a four hundred foot inclined shaft to the upper level of seven step faults all trending to the west. I re-opened the mine and broke and shipped ore at that mine at later date, but it was only low grade.

We pulled a Sullivan compressor from a mine on Wild Steer Mesa down the back side of a mountain and through Gypsum Valley to Big Gypsum and then across the Dolores River that cut crossways through the big dry valley. The snow capped LaSalle Mountains could be seen from there to the north. It was desolate and dry and as lonely as it comes. There were just three of us working the mine and I was the only "Real Miner." Lots of miners were out of work as the 1950's uranium boom was about over.

We made the old worn out hoist run and strung a signal wire from the top to the bottom of the mine. There were no mine cars in the mine so we procured a couple from another abandoned mine several miles up the valley. To get them to the mine we tied them together and chained them to my 1950 Chevy Suburban and pulled them right down the dirt road, across the river and somehow got them on the track on the incline.

The air line was set up and a water line patched up enough to be able to use. We had to haul our drill water in fifty five gallon drums from the river a half mile away using my suburban. We baled it out of the freezing river and poured it into the drums and at times doing it after dark. We used carbide cap lamps underground and we drug the Cleveland air hammer and jack leg and the drill steel, blow pipe, shovels, picks and bars down the seven slip faults to a face of low grade ore. We drilled, blasted and mucked out the best that we could and got it to the surface. We had a small ten horse slusher and a ramp to load the cars but there was still plenty of hand mucking. There were three different air tuggers we used to pull the loaded one ton mine cars to the incline and then they were pulled up the incline to the ore bin.

We decided to work four ten hour days and take three off. We were forty miles one way from Naturita, all but five miles of that was dirt road and we traveled on our own time. So I began drilling more holes, forty to fifty and even as many as one hundred, all five foot deep. All our fuses were seven feet in length and our fuse burned at forty five seconds per foot. I used an extra carbide lamp to spit (light) the fuses. I cut one four foot fuse extra for a timer. When it burned out I had forty five seconds or less to find cover from flying rock and the continuous concussions. My young helper and friend would help me collar the holes and set up my jack leg. He made up primers and hauled fifty pound boxes of dynamite to the face. The only time we rested was when we recharged our carbide cap lamps and that was a five to ten minute job. No smoke breaks, no fifteen minutes off every two hours. We were men doing a man's job. We had several humorous (and almost deadly) incidents because of just too many holes to shoot and we were tired, always tired. My partner's job was to keep me in lit carbide lamps to use to light the many fuses scattered over a large distance. He watched the timer fuse and pointed out each fuse to light as the smoke from the fuses just lit kept getting thicker and thicker. Always a worry about how much time was left and if we would miss lighting some of the fuses and then the round wouldn't pull right. When that happened, we would have to wait for the air to clear out and that could take up to several hours, then we'd have to go back down and light the damaged fuses. Not that I am complaining or anything, but the life of a miner was never easy and we were making all of two dollars and fifty cents and hour and it was "put out the ore" or "get out of the mine".

Once my partner screamed that the timer fuse had run out, but I had three or four more fuses to light. He ran but I stayed and lit the last of them. He was running up the ore body and climbing over the slusher ramp yelling at me all the way to get out! I finally started running with one carbide lamp on my hard hat and one in my hand, both of them were getting low on water and carbide. He was ahead of me when the shots started going off and the rocks started flying and the concussions of the blasts going off blew out our carbide lights. We kept right on running up the center of the track in the dark and we finally stopped when the noise quit and I was ahead of him. We were both running up between the rails that were just eighteen inches apart. We never figured that out, but we laughed and cried a bit and laid there and waited for the smoke and dust to clear. I will say that it didn't happen twice, that's for sure!

One Monday morning, the top man (the hoist man) didn't show up for work and we found out later that he had some kind of seizures and hadn't told us about it. He got to worrying about it and finally quite because he didn't want to be responsible for injuring or killing anyone. Besides that, my partner was having problems at home and trouble with his transportation and several big truckloads of ore only ran about 0.10 because we never were furnished a Geiger counter even though we tried to pick the best colored ore we could it wasn't good enough so that was the end of that job. Well, too soon old and too late smart and I went to work for another mine operator who hired me to break ore for him and set up mines and build ore chutes and develop water for his operations. That's another story in the life of a hard rock miner.

138. ENCO OVERSHOT GOTMAN ELECT BUGGY
PARADOX 5+6 DECLINE TO K-LEX Hole

PARADOX 5&6 INCLINE
AND THE SUGAR SAND

Down the hole we went again in the cold moist air, into the cool moist air filled with powder smoke and diesel fumes, only this time we were on a man-trip that was being lowered into the depths of Monogram Mesa, down a thirty percent incline. This inclined shaft was spacious enough for hoisting muck or lowering timbers and all else needed underground. Union Carbides's problem at this mine was the limited amount of ore that could be brought to the surface, because the haulage incline was the man-way as well as the supply route for every body and everything.

A circular vertical shaft was being pounded down. It was to be a hole large enough to hoist ore as well as miners in an emergency. A cable-tool rig was used instead of rotary, because a cable-tool always makes a straight, vertical hole.

Red, my mining partner, and I had been transferred from the Paradox D for this great privilege, more for our "sins" I believe. This seven by eight foot full timbered underground decline, commonly called an incline, was a beauty. Sand was sifting down out of the "back" every time that cable tool bit hit the bottom of the drill hole. About every few seconds, THUMP, and yellow grainy sand leaked everywhere. THUMP and loose sand was falling twenty times each minute, one hundred twenty times each hour, nine hundred sixty times each shift. The THUMP never stopped, and it continued to grow louder and more violent as we mined closer and closer to come together and join in our combined efforts to develop a means to hoist ore and men and increase the air flow, that would reduce the ever increasing danger of radiation poisoning that almost every Uranium miner became sick of and finally died of, sooner or hopefully later.

My partner and I checked out the big electric hoist secured in a cut-out at the top of our incline, and then half walked and half slid down the sand covered planks to the 12B mucking machine near the face. It was a strange contraption with spools mounted on each rear wheel. A cable was attached to the right spool, and then extended up the incline, where it was threaded through a chiv-block that was fastened to a tie, or a sleeper, as some call it, in the center of the track. The cable continued back to the left spool, where it made several loops around it and was then secured to the spool itself. The mucker would run down to the broken ground at the face and the bucket filled, then with the help of the spools mounted on the rear wheels. It could pull itself back up the grade to the rubber tired, battery powered, underground mine truck. This mine truck was then winched up the incline where it moved on its own power to the dump pocket.

Now, surely anyone with a few years of college would see the ingenuity, the feasibility, the practicality of this simple arrangement. Red and I certainly did, and neither of us went beyond High School, but, and there is a big BUT, right there, things are not as they seemed; if there was not the exact amount of cable on each spool on the mucker, a loop would crawl off and the mucker would race ahead and then jerk to a stop, which was not too terrifying, providing the bucket was not above you, and about to dump its load of muck into the mine truck. When this happened, and it did on a regular basis, the mucker, being top heavy, was likely to fall over on the operator and crush him against the timber. We always managed to push the dump lever forward fast enough to avert a disaster.

When the mine truck was sufficiently loaded, Red fired up the tugger and tightened the cable as I shifted into forward and the truck began growling up the grade. The electric motor began heating up and Red had the bands on the tugger smoking by the time I topped out, and we decided that we would cut the load down in the future. After the load was placed in the dump pocket and Red had hooked the cable back on the truck, I took off down the incline. With the brakes locked and the wheel sliding on the loose sand for about fifteen feet, Red caught up the slack in the cable and got me slowed down before I ran over the 12B mucker.

Now, we were using crown bars, which might well be explained at this time. These were two eighteen feet long eight inch "I" beams hanging on the caps of two and sometimes three square sets. They are used to help keep the big rocks off our heads while we muck up the waste and drill and set up new square sets at the face. Lagging was placed across the beams ahead of the lead set of timber insuring some measure of safety. Again, this sounds logical, and seems like it would work quite well so here we go again. These two crown-bars are extremely heavy. They are suspended overhead by six hangers made from one inch solid cold-rolled steel. They were held in place by wood wedges so they wouldn't slide ahead and come out of the hangers. We were able to allow then to slide ahead slowly by using our buzz-wrenches (ten inch pipe wrenches) as a clamping device. There was no place for error or carelessness. All this time the drill rig on the surface was pounding away, shaking the ground with every thump. Well, that's what under ground miners are paid for and our situation was no worse than what other miners were doing.

The electric mine truck we were using was manufactured with a particular purpose in mind, to be used underground. It was much like a three wheeled tricycle, except for the fact that the driver sat above the single wheel and faced the opposite direction. This truck had the rear axle in front and was steered by the single wheel in the rear. The drive axle had hydraulic brakes and there was a hand brake that locked the drive line. It was a dump bed on wheels that was driven backwards and had the ability to negotiate a ninety degree turn fast enough to overturn and could crush the operator against the timber or the rib. It was rubber tired and self propelled and was not confined to the mine rail, which made it what we called "Trackless Mining". These mine trucks came in many shapes and sizes, battery powered and later diesel powered, and even with exhaust scrubbers which caused many problems.

By being knowledgeable of what can happen and has happened before to us and others, is what kept us alive. So, if the mine truck came down the incline out of control and smashed into the 12B mucker, it could cause bodily injury, death, or a cave in, with disastrous results, as did happen in another incline when a runaway mine car hit a miner standing behind a 12B mucker. The mine car hit the miner, crushing his body into the back of the machine and smashing off his arms, legs, and even his head. Accidents such as this make us very safety conscious and we tried to make sure it did not happen to us. There were everyday occurrences above ground just as serious, but every aspect of mining is serious and underground miners are some of the most safety conscious people alive. It is a fact that men working under the most dangerous conditions have much less serious accidents.

When sufficient waste is removed from the face, the jack-leg is set up, attached to the air hose and the water hose and then drilling commences. The burn holes, the relievers, the rib and the back holes are punched in quite easily, but the lower holes, drilled to pull to the configuration of the incline are at a steeper angle. This makes the drilling almost too easy, but also cuts the soft sandstone faster than the water can remove the cuttings, and so then the steel hangs up unless the operator holds back on the machine just enough to keep the steel rotating. The steeper the holes, the more effort it takes to avoid hanging up and when that happens, a great amount of strength is required to free the steel and pull it back up and out of the hole. As a last resort, the machine leg is swung around to the face with the machine running wide open and the leg exerting its four hundred foot pounds of pressure. While the operator is holding up the entire works in his arm, the wild running machine frees the steel. If the miner is fast enough to close the throttle and shut the leg down before the whole mess is on top of him, he is very lucky. But, on an incline, most likely he will have to stand the machine, leg, and drill steel, right back up in position to drill a few more of the same kind of down holes. So now, when all the holes are completed and the water and loose sand are blown out with the blow pipe, the machine, leg, steel and the water hose are man-handled up the grade and placed in a protected place. The air hose is attached to the mucker and the bucket is swung to the side to protect its controls and then the explosives are slid down to the face along with the prell-gun. The round is loaded and the immediate area is cleared of tools and all else then the face is ready to blast.

It is still well to remember that the big cable-tool rig was still pounding away and shaking the ground above our timber and sifting the loose sand down on the equipment and the men. After the blasting we mucked out the round and eased the crown bars ahead to slow down the falling rock and forced the slide rail ahead for the mucker. We laid sleepers for the rail, piped air and water ahead along with the ventilation bag. We lowered posts and caps and lagging and plank for the mine truck to run on. We kept the incline full timbered right to the face and the crown bars right against the face and we drove that incline deeper and closer to the proposed new ore shaft.

This was a contract mine and was supposed to be set up so that good miner could make more than just day's pay. The shifter was trying to make a name for himself with the company, but he didn't realize that by not working with the development crews, he was destroying their initiative, slowing down production and causing the whole crew to want to transfer to another company mine. The company treated men, willing to work, quite well, even providing jobs for some men that would always be just day's pay miners. Shifters did not always work for the best interests of the company or that of the miners and it became just a matter of time until they were replaced. Union Carbide was quick to make needed adjustments when a bad situation came to light.

Good miners did what they had to do in order to keep producing ore and advancing development of a mine regardless of difficulties. At the 5&6 Incline we had to force our way into the tool room many times to get needed pipe fittings and hardware and other such supplies that would have been made available to us any time in the other contract mines. We all worked and shared what we had.

Every miner on Monogram Mesa knew about the 5&6 Incline, even the crews at Mineral Joe 2, which belonged to Climax Uranium Company. No one wanted anything to do with it either, but Red and I kept at it because it was "our" incline and we gained much respect from the other miners because we kept at it. We fully intended to see it to completion, which was only about twenty feet.

The incline came to a sudden stop because of several incidents. We were getting too close to that big drill hole coming to meet us. The sandstone face and the rock above the extended crown bars was breaking loose and falling around us. The 12B mucker began slipping its drive gears when we backed up to the mine truck to dump the bucket. It would free-wheel out of control to the bottom of the hole with bucket overhead and run off the slide rail into the muck at the face. We explained the situation to the shifter and because he wouldn't believe us he filled the bucket and backed up the grade to dump the load and back down the incline he came, out of control, with the bucket of muck overhead and rammed into the muck pile. He came off the track and the 12B almost fell over on him and then the fool got mad at us. The old mucker was hoisted out and sent to the shop. We stood the last set of timber at the face and it took weight and the cap split and came off the post. The shifter laid the blame for this on us and we were to replace the cap and repair the timber on day's pay. I said, "NO!" and we got the Mine Super down there. He brought an engineer and measured our advance, and had him re-measure until he came up with another ten feet. The Super then smiled and said, "She is deep enough boys, report to the Nil Mine Monday, there is a good contract for you." And that is another story for another time.

Rafting Down The Drift In Union's Nil Mine

More than forty five years ago in the fall of 1963, just after hunting season, going back to work on Monday morning, we left our pie cans in the lunch room and took off to our respective working areas. Much to my surprise, I couldn't get to my diggings. I reached the powder magazine and it was getting wet. My working place was about a thousand feet farther down a slight decline, around the now flooded sump, and then back up a few feet above the flooded area to a new stope that I had just opened up. I went back to the lunch room that doubled for the shifter's office to inform Don Rapp, the shifter. After he took a look at the situation, he told me to do something about it. We both knew that the pump had quit and most likely it quit right after we shut down for the hunting season. So we were looking at nine days of flooding.

It was three hundred feet to the sump and another three hundred feet to dry ground. He told me, "Get that damn water out of my haulage drift!" and he walked back up the drift because he had the rest of the mine to check out. "Do Something! he said, That's why Union Carbide is paying you two dollars and twenty seven cents an hour." "Hey, Don, do I look like a Duck?" I said. "NOOO, you look more like a cross between an ape and an old bear," he said as he disappeared around the corner. Then I thought, "Boat, float, raft, RAFT. Raft, that rhymes with Rapp and that's the shifter's name, and so that's what it was going to be, a raft.

There was plenty of round timber close by and all cut to eight feet but that was no good. The only lagging was clear outside. My eyes happened to focus on the powder magazine door--there was my raft! Just right! I went to the tool room for a short scaling bar, a cold cut and a bag of drift pins. With a little determination and a five foot bar, off came the door. I spiked it to several timbers and there she was, ready to go. It was the only raft I had ever seen with two big signs on it, one of them was, "DANGER POWDER MAGAZINE," and the other, "NO OPEN FLAMES."

Away I went, first on my knees and finally flat on my back, pulling myself along down to the sump. The motor was about to take in water, but hadn't yet. I pulled myself back to the door less magazine and saw Don and an electrician, who was called in from Uravan. Don looked at my raft and at the powder magazine, but said nothing. I loaded the electrician on the raft and we went back to the sump. On the way down, I explained that there was no way to get to the breaker box without getting wet. This reminded me of the story about an electrician at Climax Molybdenum that had fallen into the same sump twice with a belt load of tools and was called "Steamboat" after that. So I said, "If you don't get drowned or get electrocuted, you might pick up a new name, too." We were able to float right up to the pump, and very carefully, so as not to ground it out with the rising water. And it was then he showed himself to be a "Real Mine Electrician." He pulled out his ten inch pliers and rapped twice on the motor housing and the pump took off running. "Why, I could have done that myself!" I said. His answer was, "No, that is my job and your job is building rafts out of powder magazine doors!" I believe that Don Rapp had something to do with that comment.

We were talking and this electrician told me that he had heard of me. He went on to say that he had worked at Cripple Creek and knew the Hansen Brothers when they had the lease on the Ruptured Duck Mine and hit high grade gold ore. He told me about the eight inch section of their ore bin in which they saved the richest ore samples, and when they went to empty it there was nothing there. He had a smug smile and said, "Ask them about it. I got there first."

There was air and water and ample ventilation in my stope. I used the raft for a week or so, hauling explosives and whatever

176

was needed. Don gave me a pair of waders that must have been made for the Jolly Green Giant. They were, "One size fits all." But waders are just not like panty hose. It was a sad day for me when I tried to use those waders. At the beginning of the shift, I took off my mine boots and wet gear and even with my mine light battery inside the waders, I could see that they were not going to work. Most waders come up to a man's arm pits where these could be pulled over my head and I could put both my arms inside too. The crew and Don Rapp got a good laugh watching me load explosives and my lunch bucket and whatever else on the raft. While walking alongside, the water got a little too deep in places and the mud on the bottom was slick and down I went. The waders filled with water and I went under. The two enormous feet of the waders came right to the surface while I was on my back in the mud under four feet of water. Let me tell you, mine water is a mixture of grease and oil and urine, ammonium nitrate, sulfuric acid and more. I finally got right side up and my head above water. I washed out my socks in muddy water and managed to get my mine boots back on. Dragging the raft and the foot floating waders, I pushed and pulled the raft back to the magazine and then on to my working area. The water was going down, but the mud was getting deeper and we had to put up with the mud for months.

One of the crew, Walt Campbell by name, lost his wrist watch in that mud and was most unhappy about it. By chance I happened to be looking down and found it at the bottom of a foot track. Walt wanted to give me five dollars for finding it, but I refused, so he said that maybe he could at least give me a dollar for each of my kids. I laughed and said, "Alright, but it's going to cost you six dollars, I have six kids!" He dug it right out and handed it to me. That watch was very special to him, as it was dropped out of a plane onto an airstrip at Pearl Harbor in the early 1940's. He still had it and it was still working.

Don finally brought me another pair of waders half the size and still way too large. He let me know that the magazine door ought to be put back on before the Mine Inspector or the Superintendent made an issue out of it. It was the only time I ever rode a raft underground. I worked in that area by myself for at least a month, breaking ore and heaping it up until it was possible to get the Plymouth diesel trammer in to move the ore and ship it. Union Carbide was a good company to work for and if the price of uranium hadn't fallen so low, I might have stayed there

Union Carbide's Nil Mine

A hunting rifle with a scope was used to direct the first eighteen hundred feet of the portal and from that point the mine was developed. One area where I slabbed up ore in the floor was quite close to the first uranium mine that I worked in. It was the Mineral Joe 11. When blasting one of my rounds, I caused a cave-in in the Mineral Joe. I buried a 12B mucking machine and three mine cars. That got me a visit from my old shifter and he remembered me for sure! Then it was a year or so later in another section of the Nil Mine I blasted right into the Mineral Joe. It was like a family reunion with old friends. This was also the only mine that I ever floated up and down the drift on a raft. This is the first mine where the little Mel Roe Bobcat loader was put to use under ground. It was three phase 440 Volts with a big long electric cable always dragging behind it. We watched the shifter crawl up into the seat and fasten the safety belt and head for the ore pile but he couldn't fill the bucket even after several tries. I laughed at him and he said, "Alright wise guy—you show us how it's done!" So I answered, "Fine, no problem for me." And I climb on and fasten the much needed safety belt. Feeling out the controls, I charged up to the muck pile with the bucket adjusted to the proper angle and scooped up a full dipper the very first time! No problem at all! Then wheeling like a real "Pro," I ran up to the electric mine truck, lifted the bucket and dump the load, but with a slight miscalculation on the controls. The bob cat was upended with all four wheels off the ground and the loader bucket was wedged against the roof and stuck in the bed of the mine truck. Then the laugh was on me! And I was hung face down, hung with the safety belt. Using the unfamiliar hydraulics to their limit, the loader bounced back on all fours. We did end up with two of the little critters at that time and we loaded hundreds of tons of ore with them.

Union Carbide wanted more ore so they gave me a broken up Alice Chalmers #3 crawler loader tractor. It had leaky worn out hydraulics, broken main frame and worn out tracks. A block of wood had to be kept close at hand to back up on to put the tracks back on. The mechanic and I did too good a job repairing it and keeping the ore mucked out at the same time. Carbide liked our work so much they took the #3 and gave me a #5 crawler loader. It was too big. The mine roof was too low and it was too wide so there was always the danger of breaking a compressed air line and that could get a man killed. When the loader would wedge itself against the roof, my head was forced down between the steering clutches and all I could do was spin the tracks back and forth to break loose. A lot of muck was moved with that old #5. Then I had to build a bridge across the drift that was below our haulage area. It was constructed with the largest mine timbers available at that time. Then while mining out a body of ore on far side, a hydraulic hose ruptured and covered me and my safety glasses with hot hydraulic oil. I set my dirty glasses aside and a safety man came in and proceeded to chew me out and what I told him prompted him to leave quite hurriedly. He had a dislike for me ever since I saw him try to bend a nail down on and old timber by kicking it with his rubber mine boot and that was over at the 5&6 Incline. I told him that he knew better than that being the safety man and several of us laughed at him as he limped down the drift. He would have given any of us a correction slip for the same stunt. At this same time another old miner, Joe by name, was mining out a face of ore on the same level about eighty feet from me. Just as the repair work was finished, I looked up and saw Joe coming down the drift toward me, when he saw me his eyes got big and his mouth fell open and we very briefly stared at each other. I quickly fired up the loader, charged across the bridge and chased down the drift right behind Joe. Both of us were in the clear when the blast went off, but it was close!

Old Joe felt so bad and was so embarrassed that he turned around and hung his head and he just stood there. Then Joe looked up at me sad-like, he looked straight at me and waited. All I could do is look at him straight in the eyes and nod my head at him and smile. After all we all made many mistakes, some life threatening.

To somewhat illustrate Joe's frame of mind, a new young motorman was hired. He hauled the ore to the portal. First thing every Monday morning he had to haul out the "honey pot" and dump it and he just didn't have the stomach for it. It was part of his job and an issue was made of it. Some of the men in the lunchroom were giving him a bad time about it and he got embarrassed about it. He got flustered and his finger got stuck in the handle of his thermos cup, he got mad and pulled out his rap-wrench and beat the cup to pieces and his finger was still stuck in the handle of the thermos cup. All of us couldn't help but laugh and I turned and looked at Joe and said, "You're not laughing, Joe." He looked back at me with a poker face and said, "Tain't funny!" All of us roared out laughing again. Old Joe was right and that poor motorman was forced to quit and all of us were sorry because we liked him.

There came a time when no more waste could be dumped over the hill. "Get Bellm to push it over with the Cat. When the motorman doesn't show up—Get Bellm to do it!" And so it went. One day the shifter told me to take down and haul out some four hundred feet of metal vent line and gave me a helper and said it had to be done in three weeks time. My partner ran a small battery powered trammer and I stood on top of it and chopped down all four hundred feet of it in one afternoon with a timber axe. When the shifter saw it laying in the center of the drift, boy, was he shook up, to say the least. We figured that he ran outside and made a telephone call to the Superintendent in Uravan to cry on his shoulder. We had tried to explain to him that it didn't matter anyway, the drift wasn't in use. So we tied long lengths of vent line behind the motor and drug it out following the muck train so as to not interfere with production. It was all out and stacked in three days. The next item was a fifty horse slusher that I had to set up outside to move waste. It was the worst of circumstances and there was nothing to work with but we got it set up and I ended up running it, too.

BEAVER MESA MINING COMPANY

To get there you have to go west of Grand Junction up the Gunnison River to White Water then across the river up Nine Mile Hill, then across Unaweep, then down to the little town of Gateway and then across the Dolores River and, then up the steep John Brown Hill to the Beaver Mesa mining camp. My job was at the Pack Rat Mine, drifting and breaking ore. The ore and the waste were trammed outside and dumped in their respective piles down below the haulage area. The ore was loaded in ten wheeled trucks and eased down John Brown Hill. When the steep hill was icy, the truck drivers had to go to great extremes to manipulate the tight steep curves.

Late one night, Freda and I came up behind a dozen or so vehicles stalled beside the road. They couldn't get across the wash below the damaged bridge. It was then and there that I stole the biggest and most expensive thing I'd ever stolen in my life. It was a new bright shiny D-7 Cat sitting there blocking the damaged bridge. "Hey, there's Bellm, he can get us across the wash!" And reluctantly, I did. Every vehicle had to back out of the way. I fired up the cat and took it down the wash behind a big load of hay on a truck and shoved him up the other bank to the road. Then I built a passable road for the rest of the vehicles. It was late at night and when the cat was put back in place, I even tried to wipe off my fingerprints. In a case like this we did what we had to do. Later, I thought for sure that I was caught when our neighbor asked the superintendent if he could put a cellar in the dirt bank behind his trailer. The answer was, "Yes, if you can get someone to operate that D-6 loader." His answer was, "Well, I know Bellm can do it." And I did.

The neighbor across the road one cold night called me over to get his oil stove working. I had to lie on my back on the cold floor and it was very painful. "Here, Bellm, drink this," he said. I knew that it was only some of his green home-brewed beer. It never had a chance to age. I surely needed something much stronger, but that goblet of beer was definitely wicked. He had poured the liquid off of the frozen beer that was on his porch and it had to be straight alcohol. After two glasses and getting the furnace burning, I couldn't get up off the floor.

At this time most of us killed deer for meat and we were careful. There was a game warden scare and somehow it was left up to me to go hide the camp meat and all the extra fish that the families had. It was getting dark. I went too far out and did too good a job of hiding it and it took several hours the next day for us to find it.

Two families of us went fishing down into Beaver Creek. We had an old secondhand telephone truck with a utility rack on it. Late that day we were coming back from our fishing trip and the gas line plugged. We broke the fitting off of the bottom of the gas tank and had to plug the hole with a pencil. Salvaging the windshield wiper vacuum lines, we siphoned gas into cool aid jugs and other containers and I rode on the driver's side with a small bucket between my legs and the women would pour gas into the bucket, that is, what didn't go down the front of my pants and down my legs. Feeding gas to the engine this way we almost got home, with me blowing on the gas line.

Then there came the day that a full third of us miners were laid off. I can remember easing down John Brown Hill with a twenty eight foot Pan American trailer pushing our 1950 Chevy Suburban. We had to keep the hub caps packed with snow to keep the brakes from burning up. Then two of us found a job with a VCA (Vanadium Corporation of America) leaser producing ore from the old original Rajah of Madam Currie fame. And that's another story in itself.

EMPIRE ZINC
EAGLE MINE
GILMAN, COLORADO

This mine was located half way between Minturn and Redcliff on Battle Mountain. A most unusual thing about this mine is that there is no waste dump and never was. All the mining and milling was done under ground. The waste was piped from the bottom of the mine half mile down stream. There were very few buildings on the surface for an operation of such great size. There was of course a hoist house. An uncle of mine was a hoist man there in the 50's.

After we changed into our work clothes, we were marched to the open cage that held ten men and an eleventh man was pushed in and the cage door slammed shut. We were pinned in with our arms pinned down to our sides, the gate was closed and the hoist was belled to drop us down and "drop" is the only way to describe it. We fell six hundred feet in a minute or less then our stomach rose up into our throat and then dropped to our ankles as the cage came to a halt without even a jerk. The cage door was opened from the outside and we stepped out into a large underground area that housed the ore bin that was filled by trains that were hauling from the Pando ore body from the south five miles or more away. Pando on the surface was where Camp Hale was located, that was where the 10th Division Army Ski Troops were trained. There was another set of rail from the ore bin that led to a body of galena ore that was underneath the Vail Ski resort.

I was nineteen years old at that time and my job was beating chunks of ore down through the grizzly rails with a double jack and an air hammer. Below the ore bin were jaw crushers, ball mills, rod mills, and Humphrey Spiral Separators that were used to separate the ore from the rock. The crushed ore was then floated to the surface in large vats with the use of pine oil to be skimmed off and piped to the cyanide plant farther down below.

There were two decline shafts extending down to a spur of the D&RG Railroad tracks. I worked on the bull gang and I was young and strong and had a lot to learn. Several of us unloaded thousands of iron balls for the ball mills from open railroad cars with scoop shovels. Another job was smashing up empty cyanide tins and loading them into an empty railroad car. Working on the railroad tracks was a dangerous place to work because things rolled off of the mountain. Once a wheel with a tire mounted on it and it lit on the railroad track and bounced and disappeared into the air.

When it hit we were all running for our lives and didn't wait to see where it lit the second time. I was told that another time a wheel came down and bounced across the track and the creek and tore into the side of a building.

About the only thing that the D&RG Railroad didn't deliver to the mine was timbers. The mine timbers were cut to size at a sawmill at Vail at that time and they were lowered down from the surface.

That winter was a bad one and they didn't make tire chains for the tires on the little Crosley that we were driving at the time. I can remember walking out to the highway to catch ride to the mine when it was thirty below. I finally gave the job up because it was so impossible to get to work.

My next mining job was at the top of Fremont pass for Climax Molybdenum Company that was above eleven thousand feet.

CLIMAX URANIUM MINERAL JOE 11 MINE

This mine is at the south end of a valley on Monogram Mesa. My job was slabbing out a face of low-grade ore that had no real value but enough to be profitable. With too much time on my hands I drilled a hole in a "likely" mound on the floor and the cuttings were blue-black and I mined out about three hundred tons of very high grade uranium ore. My partner heaped it up with a slusher and then we were told to only ship ten tons a day to the outside bin.

This mine like all the others had a few genuine characters and tall slight built Jim was one. All of us carried dollar watches wrapped in toilet paper in a chewing tobacco can and Jim would ask me what time it was and I couldn't find my watch so he would open up the tobacco can in his hand and tell me what time it was and hand it to me and it was my watch. He did this several times and I never knew when he took it. Jim went to Meeker, Colorado, on vacation and married a young girl and they had their honeymoon in her parent's home. When his vacation was up and he got ready to go back to the mine, his new wife told him she wasn't going anywhere with him, she was staying with her parents and that was the end of that marriage.

One new hire was an ex-con, actually a nice well educated fellow and we became friends. He told me that he got bored while in the Army and he and a buddy robbed a filling station just for something to do. They then drove down the street in a pink Cadillac throwing the stolen goods that they didn't want out of the window and that's why the law stopped them. At the time he was working at the mine, he lived in a room under the Yellow Rock Café in Naturita, Colorado. He had a raised bed in the center of the room that looked like a scene from an oriental picture. The few times I visited him there he poured me ice tea and whiskey from a thermos. He was clean and neat and polite and good looking and all the girls loved him, from the young ones to the old ones.

I already have a story written about Beardsley and Hard rock and the Vicks and the mentholatum jars.

Another character was elderly Harold and every Monday morning he would show up pretty well hung-over, but after he was lowered down in the shaft where he was working he would hand tram one ton mine cars to the hoist all day long. He was always reliable, underground that is.

The shifter's father was a top-lander and he liked his beer. I told him about Heinekens Beer and after missing a few days work he came back to the mine. He said, "Damn you Harvey I couldn't find any of that brand of beer, but I bought another case of beer just as good and coming back from Grand Junction I wiped out two guard rail posts and it cost me seventy five dollars a piece, and I could have bought a dozen for that price, if they would have let me."

URANIUM AND THE OLD RAJAH

There was lots of uranium on the Colorado Plateau and the only use for it for years, was in making yellow paint. Then Madam Currie stirred up an interest in it for use in medicine. It was hoped to be the cure for cancer. Somehow, she had worked out a way of isolating radium from uranium, which was relatively common and almost useless. It was found in the sandstone mountains of Southwest

Colorado. There was money to be made if it could be mined and shipped to France. This was at the Turn of the Century.

There were gold and silver mines in the La Salle Mountains. There was copper in the old Cashin Mine, although it was too pure to mine, unless it was chopped out by hand with timber axes because if you drilled the copper vein and shot it, the copper would just hang there in a mass. There was also silver there as we knew of several wagon loads of rich galena that was picked off the surface ridges close to the Cashin Mine and abandoned there because it was too far to take to a mill. With no railroads closer than a hundred miles and not many roads, pack animals couldn't carry enough volume to make any profit. Placer gold was found in the Delores River bars and then later they mined uranium and eventually cattle and sheep moved in.

The Rajah was just one of the mines that furnished the ore for Madam Currie. It was located several miles up Rock Creek on the Delores River. The ore there was multiple bands of yellow and black material in sandstone. The ore looked like the stripes on a tiger from India, so they settled on "Rajah" for the name of the mine. The uranium ore was black carbonite and yellow carnitite, and was also later found on the surface of the ground in the area north of Paradox Valley above the west side of the Delores River on Beaver Mesa, Wild Steer Mesa, and Bull Canyon south of the LaSalle Mountains.

Now, to get back to Madam Currie and her radium. It took about seven tons of carnitite ore that ran over two percent to make just one gram of radium and there are thirty one grams to an ounce. So it would take two hundred and seventeen tons of high-grade ore to make just one ounce of radium. The radium was hand sorted out of the ore by women using extremely powerful microscopes and needles stuck in the end of pencil sized pieces of wood. Radiation poisoning must have killed them just as it did the women that died from wetting their paint brushes on their tongues when they were painting luminous dials on watches. In those days the ore was hand steeled and blasted out with black powder, up-graded and loaded on pack animals and then hauled by pack string up over the mesas north to Beaver Mesa then down John Brown Hill through what is now Gateway, up over the Uncompagre Mountain Range and then to the railhead at Grand Junction, Colorado.

Where the Rajah Mine was located was an unusual piece of mountain that stuck out all by itself and looked as if it had been placed there all by itself by some huge hand. To the east of the mine there was more uranium and lo-grade copper ore. Just across the side valley, on the mountain at about the same height, was high grade copper with some small pockets of high grade yellow carnitite ore.

I re-opened the Old Rajah Mine, and others in the same area, we produced many tons of ore. I and my partner, Gene Hinkle, along with about eighty percent of the miners working in the Beaver Mesa Mines were laid off in 1961. We were contacted by a VCA (Vanadium Corporation of America) leaser by the name of Woody Gripe, who needed miners to work in the Old Rajah Mine. I went to work there, but for some reason Gene decided to take his family back to the eastern slope. As it turned out, he was the smart one. I moved my family and our old Pan American trailer to the site, and began getting set up to mine. We dug out the spring, built an outhouse and did our best to move out the tarantulas, scorpions, and snakes as we cleaned up the area. We were young and strong, with five small children. We had a place to live, a job and felt lucky because there were many out of work at the time.

No one seemed to know the complete history of the mine, but we found many old Tuxedo tobacco cans that date way back, and Eagle sardine cans, and I.W.W. written with a carbide lamp in many places. That stood for International Workers of the World, but the mine owners said it stood for I Won't Work. The portal of the Rajah was on an almost vertical cliff about five hundred feet above the creek bottom. There were several switch backs that were so sharp that you had to drive up one and then put the vehicle in reverse and back up the other. There was an old Sullivan gas powered compressor in the road beyond the ore bin, and that was the end of the road. Getting there with the old English Ford dump truck took a lot of tricky manipulating to get it back under the ore bin. We had to stoop to push a wheelbarrow through the tunnel to the old ore passes. The face straight ahead was caved in, and filled with rubble, but the cross cut to the right had three ore passes on the west side of the drift. The upright timbers were so close a person couldn't get their hand between them. In places it was almost a solid wall of upright timbers on each side, and our hands were continually scraped on the rough wood. The wheelbarrows had to have the sides mashed in so they would fit. The back lagging was filled with all sorts of wood to cushion the falling rock, with handkerchiefs and rags stuffed in to hold back the sugar sand. We made a few mistakes in trying to remove some of the rags, because then the sand would run out, the rocks would begin moving and then the big rocks would cave down into the drift. The dust was always unbearable. We could bleed forty hundredths ore from the back lagging in the old drifts. When we poked it, it would run and the rocks would fall, then we had to shovel it up, sort out the waste and haul the good ore outside to the ore bin and pile the waste aside underground that was later used for back fill. Some of it was hauled out and dumped over the cliff into the valley below. We had to do all that and the Boss wanted eight ton per man, per day.

There was one Navajo by the name Tony Justin, and one "bellagana" (Navajo for white man) miner and the leaser and his wife for the crew. She came up and hand mucked at times. We (me, mostly) carried five gallon water cans, five gallon gas cans, some drinking water, a carbide lamp and whatever else was needed one quarter of a mile up the northeast road to the Big Chief #1 and #2 which were two other mines in the lease. Tony used one wheelbarrow and I used another. He was afraid of falling rock, but not afraid of hard work. I poked out the ore and we shoveled and sorted and pushed about forty wheelbarrow loads to the surface with our carbide lights banging on the low back of the mine. Eight tons a day? You Bet! And we didn't think a lot about it.

Tony moved his family up to the mine. A wife and three kids and she was a traditional Navajo, wearing squaw dresses and the little boy ran around with the crotch of his britches cut open for easy access to go to the toilet, but they didn't build an outhouse like we did, they used the bushes. The boss supplied them a trailer to live in. Tony got his brother-in-law to come to work and then next it was Tony's father-in-law, David, with his velvet dressed squaw. They lived in a walled tent with a wooden floor, just below where we were parked. They cooked in front of the tent on the top of a half of an oil drum. They made fry bread which was similar to a tortilla, cooked mutton, coffee and beans. The Navajo kids showed my kids how to find cedar berries, dye them in pop bottles, and string them for necklaces. I stress the word "showed" because the kids didn't speak a word of English. The women made my wife a Navajo squaw doll all dressed in traditional Navajo clothes and it was tied in a miniature pack board like the ones they carried their babies in. It was interesting living near them and learning some of their traditional ways. Many were the times that old David stood in the snow, bare to the waist, washing off the sweat and dust outside in front of his tent. We found that the women weren't that clean, because the smell lingered on in our trailer long after they had left after visiting. We also noticed that as it got colder they would just add another skirt.

Then the ore almost quit running out of the ore passes, and I found out why. The ore was coming from an old caved-in face. I set up the old Cleveland jack leg, filled the jack tank and fired up the old Sullivan compressor. The old compressor ran well enough but after the first small round was blasted, I had to cut washers from an old suitcase to use on the piston that was inside the leg on the air hammer. I had to hold the leg good and straight to get it to push. After a half a dozen short rounds, we dug into an open cave area filled with the yellow ore, carnitite. That bonanza yielded about a half ton, but that gave us enough "sweetener" to ship some low grade we were getting from the ore passes. I lay on my side and worked back up the crevice to the left around the old cave-in at the face and located the source of the ore in the caved in stope. It could be seen, lots of yellow and black and gray ore, still in place. The rocks were falling and the ground moving continually. It was no good and too dangerous. So we went outside and we measured and guessed and I started sinking a shaft just ahead of the caved-in stope. I drilled down holes with the jack leg, with the leg removed. I drilled dry and blew the holes with the machine. Then I drilled with water slowly enough so as to not chip out any big pieces. I would then place a foot across the muddy drill hole, throw the machine handle to blow and close my eyes. I also tied my pants legs with a piece of fuse to help keep most of the mud out. I made up the primers, crimping the caps with my teeth, which is not as bad as it sounds. With my tongue against the closed end of the cap, the fuse cut clean with a good sharp pocket knife, no rocks or dirt on the end of the clean cut fuse, and the caps about the same temperature as my mouth and having a couple of back teeth out on the far side, it was pretty safe. Anyway, I am still here. Besides, even with a hand crimper, if it were worn badly and the fresh cut fuse got a rock stuck in it, you could push it in the cap and crimp it a little sloppy, and "Look, Ma, no hands!" That is if you lived through it at all. As real experienced miners became scarce, safety methods improved, and it was a good thing. I've know many men and children who have lost eyes, fingers and maimed hands because of carelessness and ignorance, or both.

It was possible to go above the Big Chief and the Ocean Spray and ease into the back of the Rajah to the good ore producing part of the mine, that is, if you walked softly and didn't touch or bump anything. Even gusts of air would make the sugar sand leak out of the back lagging. There were piles of waste shoveled up into the back with stones carefully made into cribs for support. Most of the men that followed me through the back side made excuses to walk around the mountain rather than go back through the mine a second time. In my spare time, nights and weekends, I found seven different levels of the old mine that were evident, but only three were shown on the few existing maps that were available. There was an underground ore pass from the upper level to the bottom haulage drift that had a mine car to move the ore to the bin. To crawl through the upper levels and then look back and see the loose timber and falling ground caused me to see more of the bad area while looking for a safer way out. I never found one either.

The face on the upper haulage drift was dead, barren and void of uranium. It was just flat cut off. The back lagging in the drift could be bled of forty hundredths ore with a stick or a wire. This was done just a little at a time so when the sand left the hole, the big stuff just came down slowly wedging itself together and hopefully not breaking out the timber. Going very slow and easy, we got about two hundred pounds of high grade ore into the buggy. We would have to move the wheelbarrow ahead or back and then bleed the lagging some more just a little at a time. The ventilation was sometimes almost too good because it kept the dust in the air. We had to keep neckerchiefs or rags across our mouths and noses to keep out the dust, and then sometimes we would have to tear them off and force them into the crevasses to stop the sand from running. There was a hole in the floor on the west side of the drift that we could dump the ore down into an inside ore bin, but it had to be slid carefully out the front of the wheelbarrow so as not to stir up excess dust because there was a strong updraft there.

Back at the Rajah, I fastened the Butterfly Ingersol dry machine to the old worn out leg after making sure it still ran. I fired up the compressor and found the Butterfly Ingersol only drilled or blew out the exhaust hole. If I drilled dry, the leg worked, but when I changed holes with the machine not rotating, the air would escape out the exhaust vent and the air tank would go too low to drill so I couldn't raise the leg or collar the next hole. Somehow I fought out about twenty feet of drift big enough to work in and broke into the high grade ore. I supported the bad ground with cottonwood and poplar poles, and anything and everything for lagging. The boss's wife had helped hand muck most of the broken waste into a wheelbarrow and dumped it over the dump. There was a ton and a half of good ore that went about one and a half percent that we put in the bin. We fought the old Ford truck up that hill and got it off the mountain.

Tony and David had mucked out the shaft to almost fourteen feet. The shovels of dirt came out slowly and as regular as clockwork, never stopping till the bottom was clean enough to drill and shoot again. The boys helped me set up the jackleg, and when I pounded the drill steel into the knock-off bit on the bottom of the shaft, I could hear rock falling below me. We had made a mistake and were sinking a shaft right into the caved stope. We quit the hole needless to say.

Money from ore was getting smaller and smaller. The Indians, when pay was late, would say, "No ore, no trucks, no money, we quit!" Then I would say, "No ore, no trucks, no money, that's right! So make some ore, sweeten it from the Rajah and we get some money!" VCA (Vanadium Corporation of America) was starving us out with all the old excuses, "The ore isn't good enough to ship," or "the road was too bad and they couldn't get it repaired," or "the ore at the Big Chief has too much slime in it," (which really meant the copper content). That ore is still sitting there in the bin. Tony's brother in law finally quit. He said he couldn't take the bending over pushing the wheelbarrows. We kidded him about having "T.B." two bellies, because he had a pretty good sized gut to bend over when ducking the low back to push out the wheelbarrows. It wasn't too long after that that the other Indians quit, too.

All that time we were thinking that we could ship the big ore pile up at the Big Chief. My wife even searched the old mines with me, hoping to find some good ore to ship. Up the old bald headed raises, and down the dog-hole shafts, sprag, wedge and chipped out hand holds and foot holes. The only good ore left was just below the upper haulage drift next to the surface. A short drift had to be mined, and there had to be more of the one and a half percent uranium below the rubble-filled incline. The leg was working fair on the Cleveland machine, but the old hammer was just worn out. Looking for camp meat one day, I had found an old Butterfly Ingersol hammer in the portal of an abandoned mine. It had no leg and no water attachment, but could use the drill steel we had. The handle on the valve end had a two foot rod across it with air hose sleeves on each end so two men could man-handle it into the face. My oldest boy was in the fourth grade and I hauled that old machine to the Rajah and set it up. On that same trip, we found another inclined shaft with a ladder going down the man-way side. With my carbide light I went down the shaft. There was good air, and the ladder seemed in good shape, but about one hundred and eighty feet down, the section of the ladder I just crawled down on swung loose and turned halfway around. There was one piece of rusty number nine wire holding one side of my ladder. Looking up, I couldn't reach the next ladder section. The bottom of the shaft could have been another one hundred feet down with no landings. Carefully, I swung the loose section back around and tied the loose end back to the top ladder with the rusty wire. Breathing a little easier, I continued to climb down. I was on the bottom sixteen foot section. It didn't matter much if it was sixteen feet or one hundred and sixteen feet, because a fall could have broken an arm or a leg easily.

Finally the time came when it was my turn to say, "No ore, no trucks, no money, so I quit!" I sold my 38 service revolver for a twenty dollar bill, came into a hundred dollar windfall and went to work for Union Carbide on Monogram Mesa. Finally I was back to a steady job with a regular paycheck. I was still mining uranium and top miners were making more than two dollars and fifty cents an hour then. We had it made. Well, rather, we made out.

There is really much more to the story, such as that old English Ford dump truck I talked about. It had swallowed a valve and someone had put a piece of tin across the valve opening. Later I put in a short Chevy valve so the cylinder wouldn't fire into the oil pan. We would take the truck up that mean road, shovel in close to a ton of ore, put the truck in its lowest gear and still have to drag the brakes all the way to the shipping bin at the bottom. After two trips, we pulled the head and replaced the tin blocking off the valve hole. It was time consuming but necessary if we were to get a payday.

There was a Jeep pickup that had a Studebaker engine half-way mounted in it. Now that Jeep, when I got it running, had one half inch nuts for spacers all around the bell housing between the engine and transmission. The clutch linkage was on the wrong side so I had vice grips fastened directly to the clutch throw-out shaft on the left side of the clutch. The clutch had to be used with the right foot, which should have been used for the brakes and foot feed. There was just a piece of bailing wire from the carburetor through the firewall that was controlled by your right hand. I didn't need my right hand to shift gears anyway, because all that was used was low range in the transfer case and forward and reverse. I forgot to mention, there was only one motor mount. I had made it from a piece of truck frame cut out with a hacksaw and hand forged into a usable hanger. The forge used was made from a Chevy wheel drum with a six volt heater fan for air, using jack oak and sage brush for fuel. The anvil was an old bell-housing set on a plank. Even the bolt holes were punched through with the anvil and forge. The one motor mount took too long to build, so I hung a tire chain wrapped with inner tube from it to the opposite side of the frame. There was also no room for a fan on the radiator so I used bailing wire to attach two six volt fans in front of the radiator and the grill to cool the radiator.

I took my boss, Roy Gripe, up to the Rajah in that Jeep. It went like this: "Load all the full gas and water cans and make sure the radiator is full. Start the engine, then twist two wires together so the front fans could attempt to cool the radiator, put the right foot on the clutch, place the transmission in gear with the right hand, then pull out the bailing wire throttle, let out the vice grip foot pedal clutch, and we were off! Drive up a steep grade in four-wheel drive low range, stop on the curve, push in the clutch with the right foot, and hold the foot brake with the left foot. Shift into reverse, let out the clutch and then back to the next curve. Go through the procedure again, and drive to the next turn, then back again to turn four, and then drive to the ore bin." Coming down was somewhat hairy as the Jeep wanted to free-wheel all over the place in reverse. After the "only" trip he ever took with me, Roy decided I was saved, sanctified and just waiting for the rapture because I didn't kill us both. (He claimed to be a Pentecost Preacher, so I guessed that he would know about those things)

Another source of annoyance was the rear tires, they were eighteen ply re-capped Dunlap airplane tires, and when one of the old tubes got low, the tires spun on the wheels, cutting off the inner tube stems, but they never went flat. At least the old Ford dump truck had a clutch, brake and throttle in all the proper places.

Besides all that, my wife had to drive our school-age kids several miles in to Mesa Creek where the wife of another miner then took all the kids to the Uravan School. She had to make the trip mornings and evenings and ford the creek. With the Spring runoffs, the Chevy Suburban we drove sometimes fought to get across the creek, especially in the afternoons when the water was up. Then we would have to get the Ford dump truck to help get through the high water. The county gave us a little money for making that trip twice a day, five days a week.

That is just one episode in our lives, it ended up costing us about two thousand dollars in lost wages, but we didn't cry over the spilt milk. We did gain much experience, and lost some of the extra weight we had while working the more prosperous mines and all of us were healthy and happy, and we survived. That was more than fifty years ago, when the men were "Real Men" and the women were "Real Women", and we liked it that way, and still do.

URANIUM MINING IN THE COLORADO PLATEAU PARADOX D MINE

Monogram Mesa, Bull Canyon, Wild Steer Mesa, Big Gypsum, and Dry Creek Basin are just a few of the uranium camps in one area where fortunes were made and lost. It is all a dry, windblown sandstone country of Juniper, Pinion, Jack Oak, and Sagebrush. Rough, steep roads in the summer months with six inches of alkali dust filling the air, and twelve inches of mud for miles and miles in every direction in the winter.

Union Carbide had mines all through that area. The first mine they put me in was the Paradox D, a shaft mine where the company tried out the new men to see if they really were miners. So down the shaft I went, in the cage, with part of the crew. When the cage stopped at the bottom level, which was all that there was in that mine, the shift boss led me to a raise, and we climbed a thirty foot raise ladder along side the ore bin. There was an old Ingersol ten horse electric slusher, and a Pacific slusher bucket which was resting on the grizzly above the bin. There was also a Cleveland jack-leg with air and water hoses, even a drill steel that was called a Swede steel, and a jug of machine oil. "Great!" All that was expected of me then was to set up and drill twenty, six foot holes and blast them at the end of the shift. "Piece of Cake!" I was drilled out by coffee break time two hours later. Setting the jack-leg and tools aside, I located the powder magazine, and the primer bench, and made up enough seven foot primers to shoot my holes. By lunch time I had the dynamite and the primers at the face. I could hear a jack-leg running next door somewhere, so I thought perhaps the machine man could use a little help from me. Now, there was this guy in carpenter's overalls, just drilling away. I found out that his name was Frank. He wasn't half done, and it was real easy to see why, when that man moved you would have to make a chalk mark to see if he was actually moving. Frank came late for lunch, and left early, he was the first to leave the lunch room to go back to work, because he was serious about getting his twenty hole round in time to blast at quitting time.

The shifter came around after lunch, and all he told me was to help Red empty the ore chutes and tram the muck to the dump pocket if I needed something to do. Red, that afternoon, was tramming muck to the dump pocket because he was also drilled out and ready to blast and needed something to do. Red came through the automatic air door, which opened automatically (sometimes), operating an old air trammer pushing four one ton mine cars. Now an air trammer, or air motor as most of us referred to it, is just an oversized air tank fastened above four mine car wheels, with a piston type air motor, a two-way valve to go forward or reverse, and a hand brake. So it was, fill the trammer, putt- putt, to the receiving tank, pull the squeaky hand brake, jump off, fill the trammer with high pressure hissing air, throw down the filler hose, jump back on the trammer, release the squeaky brake, putt-putt to the air door, slowing down waiting for the hissing doors to open, then putt-putt to the ore bins, and fill the four mine cars, then putt-putt to the doors, and watch the hissing doors open wide enough to get the train through. Putt-putt through the air doors, and make sure you hear the air doors hiss, closing off the drift, because if they don't close, you have to pull the squeaking hand brake, jump off, run back and kick the doors several times until they decide to hiss closed, then you run back, jump on the trammer, release the brake, and putt-putt into the dump pocket as fast as you can, because there are always air leaks somewhere in the trammers air tank. If the air pressure in the tank gets too low, then the mine cars must be unhooked and wedged to keep them from rolling away, and then the air trammer pushed to the receiving tank for more air.

At the dump pocket, you lock the brake, jump off and dump the four mine cars, jump back on the trammer, release the hand brake and putt-putt back to the receiving tank, fill up, go through the air doors to the bins, fill the cars, then back to the air doors, the receiving tank, the dump pocket, putt-putt-putt, squeak-squeak, and hissss until the bins are empty or the end of shift. It was nothing unusual, just everyday procedure. So it was that Red trammed and dumped the cars and I loaded them, and helped him as I could, and laughed at his comical mad antics until my sides hurt.

Later that afternoon, Red and I each loaded our rounds and were ready to blast. We checked on Frank, as he was running out of time, and helped him to clean up his tools, load his round, and wire in his round, just in time to blast. Frank had been working in this hole for more than three years and as he had a wife and family, the Company didn't have the heart to let him go. Frank was still working in the same mine when Union Carbide closed down their mines in that area two years later.

One day, Red saw me eating glazed donuts at lunch and I gave him one, and that led us to having donuts and other sweets each day on breaks. We ran into one small problem with this, the shifter caught on to our little tea party and we were expected to share our goodies with him, however he did furnish his own coffee. This went on for about a month. Red and I kept our end of the mine producing, and trammed our ore to the dump pocket. We still found time to make up primers for Frank, and carry his powder up the thirty foot raise ladder to his working area. We ground our own drill steel, Timken knockoff bits, as well as the Swede chisel bits. We repaired hoses, timbers, bad air and water lines, and still found time to get into trouble.

One afternoon we embarrassed another shifter's son so much when he was making a poor attempt to operate an electrical slusher and got so mad he kicked the Joy electrical cord plug into a puddle of dirty water...well, the electricity in that cable was four hundred and forty volts, three-phase and was hot stuff! Now, that was like a miner's Fourth of July fire works underground!

Working in this shaft mine, we had time to kill, so we began coming topside before the end of shift. The first day it was five minutes. The second day it was ten minutes early and then it became twenty minutes. We took turns shooting each other's rounds. But we got caught and were sent back underground, and I guess that I must have become more conscientious because I became the last miner to signal the hoist man to pull me up. If I was five minutes late the hoist man would yell down the intercom, "Damn is that you again, Bellm?" It was never more than five minutes.

Earl was the hoist man, and he was slowly dying of lung cancer as many did at that time, not realizing it. After all, most of us had some lung problems from breathing too much powder smoke and dust. This was just common to most miners of that time. So Earl was hoist man because he couldn't work underground any more, and he was a good steady, reliable man.

Earl became a good friend, even after Red and I caught a squirrel in the mine and slipped it into his pie can and he caught us in the act. Earl swore at us as he let the squirrel loose, wondering about the condition of his missing lunch. Nobody and I mean nobody, messes with another man's pie-can, especially underground. You might be able to take a drink from his Clorox bottle of drinking water, and he would share his coffee and his lunch, but to mess with another man's lunch could about get a man killed. Top side it wasn't quite so bad, and we had Earl's lunch wrapped up in a clean cloth, and both Red and I had added a couple of sweets. This was another case where one of my wife's raised donuts or peanut butter sweet rolls saved my life.

The next morning, and this was in the fall of year, I helped Earl place a section of mine rail across the collar of the shaft so he could set the cage down on it and check it's safety dogs. Then Earl went back in the hoist house and raised the cage. I pulled the mine rail back across the shaft and set it aside. It was a little early to go underground but it was cold, so I climbed on the cage and signaled with one finger in the air for him to drop me into the hole. Earl smiled at me through the open window of the cable hole, punched the electric button, took hold of the controller with one hand and released the hand brake and said, "Damn you, Bellm, I got you now!" He raised me thirty feet to the top of the tipple in the cold air, and my diggers were still damp from yesterday's drilling. Fifteen minutes later, with the shifter and part of the crew standing at the cage gate laughing at me shivering way up there in the air, he finally let me down. We all descended down the hole, cheerfully beginning another shift way down in the ground, where the sun never shines. It's sad to say that Earl died of lung cancer in Saint Mary's Hospital in Grand Junction, along with many of my fellow miners.

Anyway, Friday, at the close of shift, the shifter collared Red and myself and told us that we didn't belong in that hole and informed us that we were to report down to the Paradox 5&6 the following Monday afternoon for swing shift.

Incidentally poor old Frank thought that Red and I had done something pretty bad or were awfully poor miners to be transferred after our first thirty days. After all, he had been right there for several years. But then, there was the thought that the Pentecostal preacher at the 5&6 that was shifting at that time, just might be able to straighten out us poor wayward miners.

Uranium To Molybdenum
Back To Climax

Enough! Enough of this hot country, the tail end of creation, as it was referred to by us High Country people. Working in the bad air with a positive danger of lung cancer, and with the price of uranium dropping and no one to buy the vanadium ore, it was really past time to move back to what all of my family called "God's Country". Fresh cool clean air with ice cold snow water to drink, fishing and prospecting, black top road to the mine, proper health care for the entire family and wages that were almost double that which I was getting as a miner and lead man on the Colorado Plateau in the uranium mines.

Another definite incentive to leave was the number of sick and dying underground workers. Even my old friend at the Paradox D shaft died, and he never went underground as he was the hoist man. Strange, but the radon daughters managed to kill him anyway, and about the same time one of the shifters died after "exploratory" surgery was done on him. The doctors at St. Mary's were not absolutely sure what was causing these strange health problems. There seemed to be lots of cases of cancer that disabled and in the end killed many of the miners. Doctors back in the fifty's were well aware of the effects of radiation exposure from x-ray and were using radium to treat some problems. But the effects of mining this ore were still not understood.

In the years since, most of the mining men of that area and most of the uranium miners suffered and died way short of their expected life span. I don't scare easy, but it was time for the move, and the entire family was more than ready for the move "Back Home" as we all called it, to Leadville and the mine at Climax, on top of Fremont Pass, above eleven thousand feet.

I told my boss that I wouldn't be hauling any more dynamite or nitrate or miners to the far end of Bull Canyon and Wild Steer Mesa, over the many miles of rough, bad, pot-holed, poorly maintained cow trail that was then the main haulage road to the mines (and still is, more than fifty years later).

We had a 1950 Chevy Suburban with the little engine in it with only the dip system on the crankshaft, and it was mighty lacking in power. We mounted two good but well used off road tires on the rear of the Chevy, and loaded camping gear, a well used sheepherder's tent, groceries and clothes for a week and my three boys and I left for Leadville. I drove about four hundred miles and set up camp at the mouth of Buckeye Gulch, which is half way between Leadville and Climax.

Early the next morning I drove up to the mine and re-hired after being gone six years before when Climax went on strike (which I did not agree with or have a part of). I was hired just that fast, as my work record was top of the line and I still had the appearance of being able to move mountains. Climax always made use of any available experienced hard rock miner in reasonable health and they seemed to need miners like me at the time. So Monday, I hired out. Tuesday, I took the physical, and Wednesday, I went underground. Climax was about to set off one of the biggest explosive charges in the United States, at that time, in the Glory Hole that next Monday

I had to move our camp to the head waters of the Arkansas, a little farther up and across the stream. I was on the payroll and my credit was good at the Trading Post just across the highway from the mine. It was a pretty fun week with the boys roaming the mountains and catching all the fish we could eat. I located a trailer park on the road to the mine where we could park our trailer house when I brought it up. I had worked for two weeks and had one week of pay and it was a good time for me to take a couple of days off to make the move. We abandoned camp and headed back to the Colorado Plateau and Naturita as fast as that little six cylinder engine would go.

We loaded up everything we owned. Freda had our two youngest with her in our 56 Chevy car. The two oldest boys were with me in the suburban. I was pulling our fairly old thirty eight foot Nashua trailer house. We took off going down the canyon past Uravan, through the high winding narrow road, around the deep cut Delores River toward Gateway. One of the rear tires went flat but we were able to get off the highway and put another inner tube in the tire and took off again for Grand Junction, up over the pass on the North end of the range of mountains and down Nine Mile Hill, (where many vehicles lost their brakes and either went over the embankment or into the ditch on the upper side of the road, either of which was disastrous). There were for many years, the remains of ore trucks, trailer houses, cars and trucks that went over the hill, probably when coming down or going up on the icy winter road. We finally made it to the bottom. The hot brakes on the trailer house and the truck left a bad smell for many miles on down the road to Grand Junction.

We stopped in Grand Junction long enough to fuel up and get new tubes put in the rear truck tires. New tubes were necessary as the cold patches melted off when they got too hot and those rear tires stayed too hot to put a hand on until we got to Battle Mountain and started up that hill. It wasn't the speed that got the tires hot because we never traveled more that forty miles an hour anywhere on the entire trip. In fact, the State Patrol pulled me over to the side of the road just below Silt and he walked around the truck and the trailer two times and then shook his head and said that he could not find anything wrong, but he did ask that when we began to hold up traffic, that we pull over and let them by.

On up the road we found a wide spot to spend the night, after traveling about all of two hundred miles that entire day. Early the next morning we passed through Glenwood Canyon and stopped at Minturn for fuel and to check the tires. Then we started up the Battle Mountain road toward Gilman, in first gear all the way, stopping several times to cool the engine and fill up the radiator, until we reached the top of the hill. We could not have been going more than five or six miles an hour, but that little engine never hesitated, although we could hear the tappets and almost count the times that the engine fired. We went down another short grade to the high bridge below Red Cliff and then right back up Tennessee Pass, going by the now abandoned Camp Hale and upward to the turn off before Leadville, then on toward Climax to the trailer park which was our destination.

It took two long days, but we were back in the Colorado High Country in the cool Rocky Mountain air. Good schools for the kids, good wages and benefits for all of us, stores and a hospital if needed. There was fishing and prospecting. It was all there, and much more. Of course, we were younger then, and had much to learn, as we found out later in life, but this I will say, in behalf of us all, we loved the High Country and were able to cope with the intense cold of winter and the ten to twelve thousand foot elevation. We all still have fond memories of the many years we lived there.

NOTICE! WARNING!

DANGERS IN AND AROUND INACTIVE MINES

COLORADO DIVISION OF MINES

SHAFTS:

TUNNELS:

STAY OUT

RESCUE PROBLEMS

COLORADO STATUTE

PLEASE! DO NOT REMOVE

COLORADO HIGH COUNTRY
MINE EXPLOSION

The smell of smoke, the lack of machinery running, and then the sound of feet coming from the dark cross-cut, coming our direction and voices shouting our names is what received our undivided attention as George and I set up a slusher high in the stopes of the Climax Molybdenum Mine early one morning in 1964. Two miners stormed into our working place, which was more than three thousand feet back under the thirteen thousand foot mountain, where we were driving development drifts to open up new areas, which would be systematically allowed to cave in, crushing down into the draw points where the ore would be hauled to the crusher outside.

"You boys been playing with matches again, or did your partner fall asleep again and burn the bands off that slusher of yours?" I kidded Frank about Ken. "No, I already jumped Ken about that, just before he disappeared in the blanket of smoke." Frank said seriously.

We could hear a Lyner Drill (first designed by J. Geo. Lyner in about 1890) pounding away, down in the next dash, below us, and we knew the machine man was drilling in a pocket of compressed air created by his machine. A solid wall of smoke had him completely cut off from us and as soon as he shut down the machine, the compressed air quit holding back the smoke, he would suffocate in minutes. We dropped out of our pocket of clean air to the dash below us, sliding down the wet forty five percent grade, with its two right angles. This area was clear of smoke we ran to the draw hole and we climbed down to the haulage drift below us. We could see that one end of the drift was completely cut off with smoke flowing like dirty water, down out of the next draw hole. We ran again, this time to the opposite end of the drift and went around to the next haulage drift, only to see the suffocating smoke pouring out of the dash. Again, we heard the machine still drilling away. We couldn't get to the miner up there, and he couldn't hear us until he shut down. We yelled and he began screaming that he was trapped, and we told him to run for his life.

That young miner did just that, he ran through the smoke, falling over the three ton folding slusher bucket. He fought his way over and through the nose and the tail cables and the muck piles and fell head first nine feet down out of the draw hole to the track level. He made a complete flip and landed in a loose pile of mud right in the center of the haulage drift track where the rail and the ties had been removed. The two of us grabbed him by the arms and drug him backwards farther into the mine where the air was free from smoke. He was coughing and gagging and yelling for a respirator, thinking it would give him better air to breath. His eyes and mouth were filled with dusty smoke and dirt, but he was breathing air again. The two of us drug and pushed this miner back around the main haulage drift to the repair shack where men were standing around a water wagon in the last of the good air.

Suddenly there was a loud explosion, men and hard hats were flying through the air along with lunch buckets, water jugs and dust. All of us were deaf and half blind because of the noise and the dust that slowly began to change into that deadly liquid brown smoke. There was only about three feet of breathable air down next to the mine rails, and we crouched down into it and examined our options. Men were beginning to crawl around, looking for lights and hats and other possessions, but no one seemed to be hurt, so most of us began working our way down the tracks toward the inside dispatcher's station that was eighteen hundred feet inside the mine.

Communications were out to the surface and the air lines went dead. The radios in the locomotives that pulled the mine cars, all went dead, as the electricity went off. There were close to six hundred of us on the Stork Level trying to escape, not knowing just what was taking place. Our group was among the last to get out the portal, and all of us moving on our own power, but two men could not be accounted for, our pipe man, who was our crew's repair man, and another new hire that was on another crew at the time.

Men were sent back in as the air began to clear and the two missing men were finally located. The first man was brought out in a basket head first and that was a good sign, for we knew that he was still alive, but the second man came out feet first and the upper half of his body was covered with mine blankets that were arranged to cover up the injury. We knew it was Steve our pipe man, because we could see the new recap on his mine boots. It was a knobby design, the only one in the mine at the time.

I found out from the injured man that he and Steve realized that some of us were working close to the source of the smoke, and Steve opened a ventilation door made of sheet iron, in an attempt to check on us. Steve had a habit of taking short cuts through the vent shafts, but when he opened the door, he saw or felt that something was not right and tried to fasten the door back shut. However, the explosion that hit us at the repair room, hit Steve and his partner first, and the heavy metal door along with a large piece of concrete hit Steve in the face, actually severing his head from his lower jaw, which was why he was covered with blankets in the basket. His partner had a broken arm and collar bone and lots of cuts and bruises from the flying rock, but he recovered.

The explosion came from a large vent shaft, that furnished most of our fresh air and it had caught fire from the sparks of a welder that was doing repair work in the shaft the night before. It was an unavoidable accident. Although the vent shaft was water soaked, the sparks smoldered and then started to burn the next day and the thirteen thousand eight hundred volt electric line hanging down the shaft burned and shorted out igniting the dense smoke, causing the explosion that we thought was a powder magazine going off. There was no fire, just an explosion of enormous proportions. I remember seeing men, lunch bucket, hardhats and water jugs all in a pile on the far side of the track. I asked my partner George if he had been knocked down and he said no, but in the mine dry (where the men changed their clothes) I noticed bruises in the shape of boot prints on his back. All of us miners were off work for two weeks while the mine was being repaired and the smoke smell lingered on for months.

Climax actually had a very good safety record. For as many people they had working for them, there were very few accidents. My last hitch there was a little over ten years, but the altitude and the cold and the wet finally got the best of me and I had to quit and head down off the mountain for warmer country.

PART 4
COAL MINING

My Experience At Coal Mining Fifty Years Ago

There is a satisfied feeling of watching the outside coal chutes filling up and knowing that it was your sweat and labor that made it possible. I will always remember the sound of old coal cars, hooked together with short chains, clanking over the well used fish plates that bolted the thirty pound mine rail together, and the musty smell of old mine timbers and bad air and the pungent aroma of carbide lamps. Memories of the time I worked in the coal mine at Placita.

The hard coal that we were mining was used in smelting steel for the CF&I Smelter at Pueblo, Colorado and the mine was part of the old Placita Coal Mines that produced coal for the CR&SJ Railroad and the Colorado Steel Mills. The seams of coal extended far into the depths of the mountain and we were mining the one closest to the surface. The thirty eight inch seam of coal was inclined at almost thirty eight degrees and was broken out in sections fifty feet wide and a hundred feet in length. It was then loaded in a tin chute that was wedged between mine props that supported the back, or roof, of the coal seam, and then it was slid down to the inside coal bins. A two man crew cut out a fifty foot wide section, then left a twenty foot pillar to hold up the roof, along with vertical mine props spaced every four feet in all directions. George and I were partners, and we were pulling pillars, we stood props against the face of the pillar and began digging away at the bottom of the vein of coal. The weight of the mountain then began crushing the coal down in large lumps, which we then loaded on the tin to slide down to the inside bin. After we had loaded all the broken coal on the tin, we drilled holes in the pillar with a large coal auger in a big electric drill. These holes were loaded with thirty percent coal powder and a dummy or two, which were cylinders of clay wrapped in two pages from the Saturday Evening Post magazine, then well tamped with a mahogany tamping stick. All holes were shot with electric primers at the end of the shift after we were safely outside. The morning after, the mine was checked out for any methane gas and then we would load the broken coal in the tin chute, stand props and augur new holes for blasting, which was our daily routine. We were paid one dollar an hour with a ten cent a ton bonus to be split between us, that is after we moved the first eight ton of coal apiece. Some days we did make ten or twenty cents extra, but at that time the minimum wage was about thirty five cents and hour. That was in 1951.

George was the ""Real Miner"", and this was my first time at mining, but I was learning real fast. He was an old man with a crippled right ankle which was the result of a cave-in years before at another coal mine. We had to work on our hands and knees or sitting cross-legged, because of the low roof above us. We would drag several mine props at a time to our working place, many times a day, standing them up in place to keep the rock slabs off our heads. Some of these saucer shaped slabs were called "Widow Makers," a self explanatory name. There were times when we could hear hissing sounds, just like air being sucked in somewhere and also the sound of the roof crushing the coal down. If the hiss could be located, a stull or two was placed under the section that was coming loose, or we pried the bad sections down. Sometimes there were several sucking sounds at the same time and not always in the same place, so we would shut down and listen and would begin supporting the loose rock. This was an everyday all day experience, until the whole roof collapsed, but that part comes later in the story.

This was an interesting old mine. It overlooked the Crystal River Valley and what was left of the abandoned coal mine just below us. The tram cable hung on broken towers, with empty buckets, stretching over the river to a tipple at the town site of Placita. There were some old company houses there, still used as summer places and even an old garden where my wife gathered rhubarb and some other volunteer vegetables. There wasn't much activity in this beautiful setting, so the coal mine wasn't regarded as an eye sore.

One Monday morning we picked up our Edison mine lights and went up to the portal of the haulage drift and emptied our pockets of any matches, lighters and all smoking tobacco, and placed it on a shelf outside the mine. Methane gas is much like propane and can not be detected except with a safety lamp. Just across the canyon was mute evidence of this, as there were still fifteen miners buried underground, dead, because of an underground explosion caused by methane gas. There were eight of us working in this mine, two men drifting through the coal seam, two men lowering the loaded coal cars down the track with an electric tugger, George and I pulling pillars and the mine operator with his helper down on the track level advancing the haulage level ahead of the miners.

That Monday, George and I drug props up to our crumbling pillar and went to work. Soon we were out of tin for the chute, so I went down the incline to dig out a piece of tin that was buried under a fallen slab of rock. It was not too safe, but I hit the slab with a twelve pound hammer to break it up, and as I hit it for the third time, a big blast hit me and I was blown backwards down the incline with my head lower than my feet and my hard hat and lamp knocked off. It was a moment before I got right side up. The air was filled with dust and there was a light coming down the tin, with the sound of sliding rock and coal right behind it. As the light came closer, I could see that it was George with a ton of muck right behind him. As he saw me, he reached out with both hands and grabbed for a post, but he kept on going, knocking out several more posts before coming to an abrupt stop. The entire roof had fallen in at our working place, closing off the open area, but no one was hurt bad, and we went back to carefully pulling pillars.

This was my first time as a miner in a coal mine, but it was a beginning of a love of mines and mining that I still have to this day. This coal mine was a place of interest with; the rough timber of the black dusty coal bin, the big dump of shiny black-jack waste and the flashy Diamond Rio Truck hauling coal down the narrow steep mine road to the bin, the unusual loud noise of coal sliding down the chute to the bin and the squeal of mine car wheels on the iron rail. It was a real show place and "Real People" doing "Real Work".

COAL BASIN

Coal Basin goes way back into early Colorado history. It is located over the Mountains west of Aspen, below Marble and Crystal City. The road up to the basin starts just at Redstone, where the big mansion is still standing and the beautiful Redstone Inn is still open. There is number of coke ovens just out of town where the Coal Basin coal was made into coke for the mines of Leadville and Cripple Creek and such. Most of those ovens are still intact. That road up into the basin was the old narrow gauge railroad. This area was special hunting country for the Bellm Boys where they hunted both deer and elk.

The road went all the way up to the mines and the country is fantastically beautiful with the view of red sandstone mountains and tall snow capped peaks to the south and east. It was a special place to us back in the fall of 1950. I was supposed to meet up with the bunch and then we were going by Jeep and pack horses up the side of the mountain to the hunting country. This was just before Freda and I were married and I drove the 1941 Buick Special up to where we were to meet the rest of the hunting party which consisted of my boss, my father and my uncle. It was the day before hunting season opened. I drug the bottom of that old straight eight Buick several times getting it up the rough road and Freda claims she never drug bottom once on the way out and it was in the dark.

I think that I had food poisoning from eating at the cafeteria in Gunnison at the college where Freda was going to school and I was sick, but still determined to hunt! My boss gave me a cup of whiskey and a handful of aspirin and I hit the sack. Then early the next morning we started up the steep side road to Dexter Park. Dad drove the new big flat bed International truck and I handled the horses. My dad stuck the truck in the beaver dam and I had to get it out and I did, with the help of the Jeep and a lot of bad advice and swearing. After that we parked the truck in a wide spot and loaded up the Jeep and the horses with hunting and camp gear. We had about four miles more to go to our hunting camp.

When we began setting up camp digging out bedrolls, tents and food. There was one specific duffle bag there that we had to take special care of and then we found out why. My boss began digging gear out of that duffle bag, and there must have been a case of whiskey wrapped in clothes and such. And, yes, there was a bale of hay on that Jeep, too.

The next day I was still sick and my boss still gave me booze and aspirin and some soup this time. I stayed in camp and Dad and the rest of them went hunting elk. They managed to shoot a two point elk and hang it up in a tree.

Early the next morning I was to help, but two out of the three horses were gone. Mine came back after his morning oats, it never failed. My dad caught him, saddled up and climbed on board but I forgot to tell him that my horse, Comet, humped three times every cold morning just to feel his oats. Dad in his old G.I. low shoes kicked Comet in the ribs and away they went! Clear across the park and every time the horse humped. Dad kicked him in the ribs again and we laughed until we cried until they got out of sight, but he came back with all three horses and he was still riding. Now my dad's behind wasn't in the best of shape anyway as he had accidentally shot himself in the behind thirty years before with a Russian 44 Navy Revolver when it bounced out of his holster.

One of our horses was a spoiled pet belonging to a dude rancher. My uncle's horse was a tall old one-eyed mare and then there was my horse, Comet, and we got along quite well, even though he had a few quirks. The next morning we went after the elk. We began loading part of the elk on the spoiled pony and he didn't like it, but we did manage to load some of the larger single pieces on him. Next came Comet and he didn't like anything flapping on him. You cut a deer between the third and fourth ribs and hang the carcass off both sides of the saddle, then he was fine, but when my dad threw the elk hide over the top, Comet began to rear up, so I grabbed the halter and when he reared up again I raised up my knees and caught my dad under the chin and knocked him flying. So I tied that horse's head to the bottom of a big quakie tree and my dad finished the job and then tied the elk horns on behind the saddle, just out of spite. "Turn him loose!" Dad said, so I did! Comet looked us over, trotted out to the park and put his head down and began eating grass just like nothing had ever happened! My dad's next words were "I'll kill him! I'll kill that horse!!" It was later that we hauled the elk and a nice buck to the truck.

I'm sad to say that's the last hunting trip that I had with my father and uncle. This was a time when "Real People" did "Real Things" and I tried to raise my sons to be the same way. There are so any memories of those times past and the good time we had even with difficult situations.

CR & SJ RAILROAD STORY
ROY WHITBECK

Along the route of the old CR & SJ (Crystal River and San Juan) Railroad and above Bill Creek on the same side of the Crystal River is the old Whitbeck ranch that rambles along the bottom of big old Mt. Sopris. To the south there is a horse trail over a ridge to another small section of farm land. That is where my Uncle Roy Whitbeck had a few acres of potato fields along a small swift clear running stream that he used for irrigation and drinking water.

Seven days a week, morning and evening, he would ride his horse over to his parent's house to milk the cows and feed the livestock. His potato fields yielded a lot of spuds, but I also remember finding lots of arrowheads because the Shoshone and Ute Indians used to camp in that area. I also remember that if I was there on Friday night I got in line for a tablespoon of Epson Salts just like all the rest of the family, men, women and children and early the next morning there was a run on the outhouse. Women and kids got in the privy first and men and boys sometimes had to head to the brush.

They sure ate pretty good back then, that was in the 1930's. They had deer, elk, bear, grouse, and fish along with whatever vegetables they could raise and wild raspberries, strawberries and choke cherries. Most of the meat was shot with a 25/35 rifle but for the bigger game like bear and elk they used a thirty 30/30. Many still used the octagon barrel Winchester 45/90 and even the 38/40. I had a Navy Colt that size many years ago. Many deer were killed with just a 22 long rifle and even less powerful guns.

My Uncle Roy was a "Real Man" and his wife was quite a lady, a bit rough maybe, but hard working. I think she was Swiss and she was my mother's sister. She cooked and baked on a old coal range. She was lucky to have some hard coal to use in her stove and she gathered that from the train track where they would throw it off the train for her as they went by. Besides cooking and baking on the stove she had to heat all the water on top of the stove for bathing and washing clothes. She used a washboard and wrung the clothes all by hand. It was hard work, but nobody really complained, that's just the way things were done.

Around another ridge south of Avalanche Creek is a large deposit of silver and lead and just a few hundred yards from that is the remains of a natural hot springs. Roy had a saddle horse that got into the swampy area close by there and it was severely burned by the hot water and that horse had a whitish grey colored high water line on it for the rest of his life. At one time there was a bath house there and across the river were more hot springs. When I had a job working at Marble one summer in the 1950's Freda and the kids and I used to soak in the tubs that were there. There were two tubs lined with marble and enclosed. We'd go after work and sometimes it was after dark and we'd bath by candle light. It was sure nice, but they are all gone now and you can't do that anymore--makes me sad to think of it. Those days are all gone now, too, and I still miss them but I will remember them fondly as long as I live.

Going south following the railroad and the river is the old coal mining town of Redstone with the Redstone Inn and farther up the river is the famous Redstone Mansion with a story of its own. Across from Redstone are the old coke ovens that are still intact at the mouth of Coal Basin Valley. They are a tribute to the men that mined the coal back up the west valley near Dexter Park. We hunted deer and elk up there just after World War II.

Continuing up the Crystal River is the coal town of Placita where Freda and I parked our first little un-modern trailer which was half on the county and half on the Forest Service ground just to keep them all confused. I was working in a coal mine there pulling pillars. That's where I first learned to mine. It was the only coal mine working in that area at the time and it was closed down because of graft and politics. We hadn't been married very long at the time and money was tight. We ate grouse and ground hog and even porcupine once, and lots and lots of fish. Freda had found an old garden at an empty house up the road in the old town of Placita and she dug turnips, parsnips and carrots that had been left in the ground and there was rhubarb growing there too, so she made good use of it all. My lunches at the mine were sometimes just sardines and crackers and graham crackers with powered sugar frosting. Freda used to walk down to the store in Redstone and buy a few groceries and on the way there and back would look for fishing hooks and flies that had been snagged in the bushes and trees and left by fishermen and she kept me supplied with what I needed to fish with. Freda also gave me my first home hair cut with just scissors and a razor. It wasn't the best in the west, but she got better at it and I never went to a barber after that.

With our first paycheck in hand, I borrowed some diesel fuel as we were out of gasoline, and I put that in the car. We were driving a ten year old straight eight Buick. I primed it with Colman light gas and we smoked off to the big city of Glenwood Springs. Glenwood Springs had about three thousand people back then! These are all fond memories that bring us both laughter and tears.

Traveling further up the track there is an old slate mine and then the mill yard at Marble but maybe I'd best stop there because there is still the Yule and the Strauss quarries and the bridge we built to the quarries, Lizard Lake, Crystal City, the old Ghost Mill, La Knight Silver Mine and so much more. I'll have to leave those stories for another time.

POTATO BILL AND THE CR&SJ RAILROAD

There was a time when the Crystal River and San Juan Railroad ran between Carbondale and the end of the line at the mill at Marble, Colorado. It used a ten hundred steam locomotive, a small 2-4-0 as I remember. There was perhaps forty miles of track and it was used to move hundreds of tons of white marble from the quarry in Marble to the D&RG Rail Line that ran between Glenwood and Aspen. In fact, the Colorado Midland Railroad might have been involved at times too, as it stretched from Leadville up and through the Hagerman Tunnel to Lake Ivanhoe and down through Hell's Gate to Basalt, but for right now this is about the CR&SJ Railroad.

As this small train with it's flat cars, box cars and coal cars, plus a plush Pullman passenger car, climbed south up by the farms that were known for growing red McClure potatoes, it passed by Bill Creek. Now Bill Creek is on the east side of the Crystal River. My very old friend Rome Isler was the last conductor on that train and he told me that he would stop the locomotive and load and unload Potato Bill and his groceries, supplies every spring and fall and then continue on up the line

Bill lived in a small cabin up the creek that was named after him. He raised potatoes as his main staple in his diet. He also had a small gold deposit somewhere near his place on the west side of Mt. Sopris that he worked every summer and when the snow began to fall, he stopped the train and went to a warmer climate for the winter. Each fall he carried out a small bag of gold. This went on for many years Rome told me, but one year as the summer came to an end, there was no Bill to stop the train. Rome began to worry about him because back then most people had concern for their fellow man. They didn't butt into another man's affairs, but they were always there when needed.

Rome notified the local sheriff and on the next trip to Marble, the entire train was halted at Bill Creek and Rome and the engineer and the fireman waded the river and went up to the cabin where they found the old timer dead whether of natural causes or unnatural causes they couldn't say, but what about the bag of gold? Was it hidden somewhere? Rome said that they looked but didn't find it, however, Rome found what looked like a map that he thought might have been directions to the lode or a bar or maybe just a pocket of ore. The Sheriff was coming up the road in his Model T Ford with his deputy. Rome studied the map and then threw it into the wood stove. Rome was a railroad man and not a miner and not a mountain man so he never found the gold, but he told me about it years later.

Potato Bill was dead and Rome died in the later 1950's. There is a mobil home park right at the mouth of that creek and even a bridge across the river now. I believe that gold is still there yet and I drove by that place for close to sixty years and always remembered that story. I still think about trying to find it, but I am old and worn out but I can still dream can't I? I had an uncle that lived just up the river from there, but that is another story for another time.

Old Hard Rock Miners
"Real People"

Their tools at first were picks and muck sticks or banjoes (shovels) and Irish dump trucks (wheelbarrows) hand steel and single jacks and double jacks, candles or Miner's Sunshine oil lamps that dripped hot oil on everything and hard boiled hats (hats soaked in linseed oil to make them stiff). Then they had carbide lamps that made it necessary to carry a small bottle of water and a tobacco tin of carbide to keep it going. Explosives at first were black powder and there was the ever present danger of any spark or flame igniting it.

Working conditions would be from cold bad air with dripping water and unstable rock to intense heat and little or inadequate ventilation with the temperatures going to over a hundred degrees. I understand that Finlanders in Tabor's Matchless Mine spent an equal amount of time at the face of the drift and the same amount of time in a wooden tank of ice and water (used to cool them down) that was furnished at the start of each shift. Despite all this, the digging and mining didn't stop. The tools have improved and the mining still goes on.

I got my start in mining in 1951 at an early age. First I was hand steeling on the surface at a very old coal mine on the side of a hill above the Crystal River. I turned steel for Dick Pendergrass (sixty years old) and he never hit my hand with the eight pound hammer, but when he turned steel for me, that was a different story. We were trying to dig from the surface into a developing air course as another crew was digging to meet us from underground. The day started with Howard Holgate (the boss) putting a dozen number six blasting caps in the front of my bib overalls and filling one back pocket with eight inch sticks of coal blasting powder, then he handed me a small role of orange Aztec fuse and then we were handed hammer, steel shovels, picks and our Clorox bottle of water and were sent on our way up the hill. So it was drill, shoot and dig. We had moved up the slope several times, but after our last move and blasting, I was above our workings sitting down behind a tree when the underground crew's shots went off. They were just ten feet under me. It would lift me off the ground as each shot went off. So we finally joined up and after that I was put to work underground.

I used an Edison cap lamp (electric) and wore a gunnysack diaper and our job was to push wet clay down a tin chute with our feet and our behinds to clean out the new air course. The next job was pulling pillars (the blocks of coal left to hold up the roof of the mine) which required us to bring short timbers six hundred feet up a thirty eight degree slope, two at a time and to stand them upright every four feet. We hand picked a groove at the bottom of the coal vein and that allowed the overhead weight to break the lump coal out, then we would sit cross-legged and shovel the coal into the tin chute. The coal vein was thirty eight to forty inches high. An old weather proof wire was hung on the wet posts along the chute was the power for our big electric drill that we used to drill one inch holes in the coal vein. Toward the end of the shift we loaded the holes with two sticks of coal powder (thirty percent) and two dummies (clay wrapped in Saturday Evening Post magazine pages) because to use dummies made of waste coal (black jack) could cause a fire or a mine explosion as there is always the danger of methane in a coal mine which can kill slowly if you breath it too long or kill quickly when it explodes or catches fire. The mine was always cold because of the forced ventilation to blow the methane out and it was damp and musty but swinging a double jack, picking, shoveling or standing posts always worked up a sweat. You had to be careful not to hit yourself with that sharp pointed hand forged coal pick or you could end up with blood poisoning right quick.

Still, I have many fond memories of the sound of loaded coal cars being lowered out of the mine by cable, the sound of the wheels scraping along the rail and the click-click of wheels crossing the fish plates that joined the rails together. It was like music to me, even if my crippled up little partner and I were expected to slide eight tons each of coal down the chute every day and anything over that we got ten cents a ton to be divided between us, all for one dollar an hour plus the ten cent bonus. I can remember my-father-in law telling of working in the mines for four dollars a day, six days a week and ten hours a day. He hand trammed on wooden rails with a metal strip nailed on top. He used carbide lights and big hand lamps. He was an old hard rock miner, too.

At Leadville, Colorado in the late 1800's and the early 1900's there were three grave yards and five undertakers to handle the deaths in the mines and the deaths from sicknesses related from working in and around the mines that were at an altitude of ten to eleven thousand feet. Of course drinking played its part, too. There were no unions in those years to protect the less industrious ones and not much concern for the men that carried the bulk of the work. It was dangerous, but not always as dangerous as some jobs on the surface, you learned to be careful. Most hard rock miners were capable, reliable, cautious real men who had great concern for their fellow workers. It never took long to separate the men from the boys underground and when a young man desired to be a "Real Miner", assistance was always available. Mining requires a great variety of specific knowledge and practical experience and few men of this generation have the ambition or grit to become one.

PART 5
"REAL PEOPLE"

My Wife The Lady Cat Skinner

My word is my bond and if I give my hand on a matter, it is as good as done if it is humanly possible. Climax Molybdenum Mining Company had gone on strike, so four of us took a ten year contract to cut out several blocks of aspen trees for the Diamond Match Company that was operating out of Placerville, Colorado. When Climax started up again in the early fall, the other three went back to mining. As my word was given, I stayed and moved Freda and the four kids to Placerville. More cutters were hired and as the size of the block of timber was not as big as believed, it was cut out by late fall. So I took another cutting job in the mountains out of Norwood. I camped out in the snow a week at a time, coming in on the week ends.

After the first of the year, and not getting paid as promised, I quit. I was offered a contract in Placerville in the spring so, living on unemployment, the rest of the winter was spent on rebuilding an old worn out 35 Cat to use for a skid cat. That machine is a story in itself.

Then as the snow began melting, I cut and skid logs on Dallas Divide. As the days grew longer, the working hours increased from four in the morning until after dark at night, all the hours the weather would allow. Late one evening in the rain with lightning striking all around, I left the Cat on a run, and the charging system drained the battery. So the next morning, finding the battery dead, I went after the first help that I could think of which was my wife. We took the D4 to the top and started the 35. Fritz wanted to take the D4 back down to save me a trip. She could operate it okay and as the road was steep, I had her pull two big tree length logs, butt first, for drag, to help her steer going down hill.

I had just engaged the engine clutch on the ancient 35 Cat, pulling four tree length red spruce logs down the abandoned coal mine road near the top of Dallas Divide and I heard a piercing scream behind me. Looking back over my shoulder, there was my wife, pulling the two big spruce logs, and she was falling over the side of the narrow mountain road! Her Cat made a three quarter turn and lit against a small pinion tree. The tractor, still running while upside-down, was just barely hung in the tree, and she had disappeared down under the tractor and the logs.

Kicking my main clutch out, I jumped off and ran the length of my logs to the overturned machine, thankful that its tracks were not still turning. I could see one scraped ankle sticking out, her body was in under the Cat and the two big logs had slid up against her legs. The most precious, loving person of my life and now was she was crippled or dead or worse. There was hardly enough space for me to crawl under the still running machine, over the top of my unconscious wife and reach overhead to kill the engine.

After finding no evidence of a broken back or neck, which there could have been, I eased her out and tried to pick her up. She screamed again, the same piercing scream I heard when the Cat had gone over. She actually stumbled along, with me holding her up, to the car a hundred yards away. Holding her up with one arm, we dropped down out of the canyon and down the pass to the sawmill. We called a doctor in Telluride, who drove the eighteen miles down Keystone Hill and the narrow canyon road to Placerville, where we were living.

Freda's folks were there visiting and they helped me get her to bed and by then her head was swollen and there were bruised spots showing up. She was beginning to moan and move around a little. The doctor checked her over and could find nothing too serious except her swollen head. Her folks took her to the hospital in Montrose while I went back up the hill to shut down my Cat as it was still running. I stood under the overturned D4 and cut the pinion tree down and the Cat finished its roll and came to rest right side up on its tracks without much damage to it.

Then I looked and could see what had taken place to cause the accident. We had blasted out a tight turn near the bottom of the grade, and there was a slab of stone about the length of the left track. When Fritz pulled the right steering clutch, the left track, under power, kicked the stone out causing the Cat to fall about three feet and then roll. She hit her head on the canopy as it rolled and when it came to rest against the tree she fell out the back hitting the logs and falling back under the running Cat.

Apparently, she had her hand on the engine clutch and had disengaged it as she should have. Knowing what had happened did not make me feel any better, but then I realized that she probably saved my life because I was wearing a hard hat and would have tried to jump off and probably been killed. I won't make excuses, and I am thankful that we are both very much alive and still love each other after more than fifty nine years together. We still do what needs to be done.

I promised myself that this would never happen again and it did not. Later that same year on another contract, cutting and skidding, a big yellow pine had set back on my saw. As I was in the process of pulling the engine off the bar, I heard the old 35 Cat coming down the hill and on it was my wife, knowing I needed help. That is the kind of wife she was and still is, only more so now. We still work together as a team and there is no doubt that we always will.

Gus Hansen
One Of The "Real People"

Gus was my father in law and he was no saint, but he was a "Real Man" and there were really quite a number of them more than half a century ago. Gus was one of the many men back there in the early 1900's that grew up around hard rock mining areas, primarily in Arizona and Colorado. He raised his family of a wife and four girls during the Great Depression of the 1930's.

He was born in Canyon City, Colorado in March 1904. He died February 12, 1991 and he lived a very full and interesting life. He was married to Lois Murrell on July 17, 1924 in Bisbee, Arizona. His father was a miner in the Copper Queen Mine. Their first three girls were born in Bisbee, but his youngest girl was born in Miami, Arizona when he was working in a mine in that area. He tramped many mines, where ever there was work.

He was offered a job in Colorado near Grand Lake and had to leave his family in a walled tent in Naco, Arizona, on the American side. After several months he returned with a new pickup and seven hundred dollars which was really good because miner's wages were about three to four dollars a day. He then took his family to Cripple Creek, the "District" as it was known at the invitation of his older brother, John. He worked in the mines there except for one year during World War II he was too old for the service but he volunteered to do mining work constructing underground airplane hangers at Diamond Point, Hawaii. When he returned back to Cripple Creek he and his brother, John and another miner took a split lease on the Ruptured Duck gold mine. Gus told me later that they hit good gold and even having to give the Company their fifty percent and splitting the other fifty percent three ways, they all ended up with quite a large amount of money so Gus decided to get out of the mines and buy a fruit ranch near Hotchkiss, Colorado. He found out that running a fruit farm with just four girls for hands was just too much of a gamble for him. So after a few years he sold the ranch and moved into town and later went into a venture with three other friends from Cripple Creek. It was called Ranch Haven Industries and it was a logging operation with two seven thousand foot sawmills. The finish mill in town produced tongue and groove house logs. They were some of the first ever made. This job took Gus and his family to Glenwood Springs, Colorado. This is how I first became acquainted with Freda. We went to high school together.

After operating their logging business a few years they came to realize that they were only making four cents per one thousand board feet of finished product so the Company closed down. During the years that they were operating, I worked for Gus skidding logs with horses and later with a little T-20 International crawler tractor. At that time Gus had never operated a Cat nor had the desire. Later he got a job working for a local contractor near Minturn, Colorado blasting out a ditch line for a water works of some kind. The contractor liked Gus because he was such a hard worker and knowledgeable. He wanted Gus to run his equipment and he told him he'd train him. He was a natural on the equipment and he learned how to operate big dozers and even a rubber tired Le'Tourneau dozer. Gus got so good operating the equipment that he was in more demand on the jobs than his boss.

From that job Gus ended up back in Bisbee, Arizona, and he hired out as a truck driver, driving one of those huge haulage trucks out of the pit. P.D. (Phelps Dodge Company) liked his work so well that they had him alone hauling waste from a by-product plant, they nicknamed him the "Orphan Boy." Gus told me later that he had a supervisor drive his pick up in behind his big truck and he didn't see him and he backed into the truck. He could have gone right over the pickup and killed him and it really scared him. After that he got badly burned in a fire while he was on the job and he decided it was time to retire.

His wife died in 1964 and he was footloose for a while, but he married a nurse that he'd met in the Copper Queen Hospital when Lois was sick and then later she took care of him when he was in the hospital being treated for burns.

We came down from Aspen in the latter 1980's to evaluate and re-stake about thirty placer claims for a promoter living in Aspen. It worked out that Gus bought a small Airstream trailer and lived next to us. Gus then moved with us to Kanab pulling his own trailer along with us. That was some trip down the Salt River Canyon and up the other side, switchbacks and all. We went through the Navajo reservation and to the Colorado River at Marble Canyon and then up over the mountains and down into Kanab where our oldest son lived with his family.

My wife and I went up to Virginia City, Montana, to see about working a gold placer claim and we left Gus in Kanab with our son to keep track of him. We found out that he got out by himself and walked all over the town and ended up in bed because he'd over done the exercise. We returned to Kanab and my wife stayed there with Gus while I went back to Virginia City and began working the claim. I agreed to work the claim on a split-check arrangement. I furnished the equipment and did all the work and the owner got twenty five percent and the man he leased it to got twenty five percent and I got fifty percent and I could still make money. The gold was on a high bar with twenty feet of overburden. I was working on the steep side of the deposit and it was extremely dangerous digging it out. It was a case of dig and cave and cave and dig. In a short time Fritz and Gus drove up and we rented an ancient log cabin in Virginia City. It was located up two flights of stairs on a hill side. It had two bedrooms and inside plumbing. It was mighty rustic but livable. After risking my life and producing six and a half ounces of gold in two weeks and because of making it look too easy, I was politely but firmly kicked off the lease. The owner of the claim and his relatives thought that they would get rich working it when they got rid of me but they never produced a dimes worth of gold.

We stayed in Virginia City for a while and I found other areas where I could bring in gold bearing sand and we worked it at the cabin. Now we get back to Gus—he was hobbling around on crutches yelling at me for more gravel from my small gold recovery operation below our cabin. Leaning on one crutch he was spreading the waste gravel on the road to fill in the holes. "More gravel! More gravel!" Crutches or not he was sure pushing me and it was great to see him up and active, even pushy. Poor old crippled up Gus was told by his last ex-wife that he couldn't do this and couldn't do that and he was feeling worse with the inactivity and negative propaganda. She even told him that he couldn't play pinochle and he was beginning to believe her. We did play a lot of pinochle and three handed is a mean game and he won hand after hand and began to use his mind and became quite cagey playing cards. We also played poker rummy until the deck was worn out. I was going to shoot a hole through it with my 38 pistol because he wouldn't give up that old deck of cards but I never did and I still think I have that old worn out deck of cards.

While we were there the three of us drove the Dodge power wagon around the hills looking

267

at old mines and mills and we learned a lot about Virginia City's history. Gus began telling us stories about times back before he and his wife were married. One was about a dollar watch for instance—before Gus and Lois were married some loudmouthed miner made a bad remark about Lois. Gus hit him in the mouth with his fist, his very big fist, and the loudmouth flew up off the ground, backwards for some distance and landed on his back and his dollar watch jumped out of his pocket and flew up the drift and hit a mine rail and exploded into several pieces. If you can't believe that, you never really knew Gus. Another incident was in a mine. Gus swiped a burrito from a Mexican's pie can while eating lunch with him underground. Now that wasn't so terrible because he left that Mexican a peanut butter sandwich in exchange. He told me that his Mexican friend threatened to kill him for that stunt. Now the end of that story was that his Mexican friend ended up bringing extra burritos for him but he didn't want any peanut butter sandwiches in exchange. I know personally that Gus was willing to share his lunch with anyone because he did with me, it was a limburger and rye sandwich and it was my first one. I came to like them and still do.

Gus was much of a poor man's hero, big, strong, capable, willing to work and share with friends that worked with their hands. Gus would never take advantage of a poor man but big companies were fair game. Gus would not tolerate anyone abusing a woman in any way or a child or even a man. Fritz and I would kid about Gus that he would give a man the shirt off his back, but if he had reason to get angry at the same person, he'd say they stole it from him. He was different from the average man and that's what made him quite unique. I worked with him and for him and we fished in more lakes and streams than I could possible write about.

Now there are some stories that just need to be told. The limit on fish back then was all the fish you could catch without getting caught yourself. So it was that the old man and two of his brothers hiked into a string of high mountain lakes above the Woods Lake area on the Frying Pan side of Holy Cross Mountain and they all caught "their limit." Each man placed the proper amount of fish in their own fishing bag and the excess was wrapped up in Gus' hunting jacket and covered up way back in the trunk of the car. They did get checked and when the licenses were checked Gus realized his was in his hunting jacket with all the extra fish so when he opened the trunk he did his best to block the game warden's view. It was dark and the game warden was trying to shine his flash light into the trunk to help out. Well, it was like most of those old flashlights it blinked on and off all the time so Gus offered to fix it for him. Boy, did he "fix" that flashlight for the game warden. He twisted the top clear off of it and then used gopher matches to find his license. He missed getting caught that time!

Another time Gus and I were fly fishing on the North Fork of the Frying Pan River in a deep canyon called Hell's Gate. The stream was full of about seven inch trout and we were really catching them. It began raining and we were wading in ponds waist deep. I was catching them two at a time and Gus had on three flies and he was catching them three at a time. Late that night back at camp at Chapman Dam we began unloading our fishing bags and even our pockets. We ended up with about fifty five seven inch fish and used an old wash tub to clean them in. The next day Gus found a fish in the pocket of his bib overalls. There were never any fish wasted we always ate all the fish that we caught.

Another time when Gus and I were looking for the Old Vandyke Mine in the same area, we caught all the fish we could carry. Once when Fritz was on a trip with her mother, Gus and I caught nineteen big trout at the inlet of the Clear Creek Reservoir and had almost thirty pounds of High Country pink meat good eating fish. At that time we were fishing up to our armpits in a cold water lake at ten thousand feet.

Gus didn't smoke very much but in the later forties we were roofing a new cabin on the top of Basalt Mountain and he handed me a part of a carton of Chesterfields or maybe it was Philip Morris and a handful of cigars and told me he quit smoking after he read an article in the Reader's Digest. But we did make sure we had a Mississippi Crook or a Red Wolf when we went fly fishing to keep off the mosquitoes.

Truth and honesty are relative to the situation at hand and Gus did what needed to be done as honestly as possible. He had asked the Forest Service to please come up on the mountain and mark ten thousand feet of lodge pole pine needed for a bridge at Meeker, Colorado, and they promised several times and ignored their promises. Well, Gus made a promise, too, and when the time ran out. We went out into the woods at the lower camp and he chopped a slash on the butt cut and scribbled on the slash and I did the same on the stump. Then he produced a long cross cut ribbon saw and we went to work. He would pull and then I would pull and so it went and the sawdust flew! He was in his forties and I was eighteen and neither of us would give in to the other. We fell and limbed and bucked the poles in three days and had the order lying on the ground ready to go. As the poles were too heavy for the skid horses, he had me skid the logs with an old Galleon Maintainer with a

Studebaker engine in it. It had a single axel and was too awkward to get into the woods but using the team to drag the logs to the main trail, I pulled them the rest of the way with the struggling maintainer. Pulling as many as I could at one time and getting a run at the steep places, it got very interesting. When the logs dug in or got hung on a root or a rock, the machine came to a halt and the front end began climbing to the clouds. I would catch the clutch when it was about five feet off the ground and down it would come and bang and bounce up and hit again and one front wheel would go to the left and the other one to the right. Gus just told me to beat the tie-rod back into shape and keep moving timber! This happened several times before we got the job finished. We gained a lot of respect for each other on that job.

Another little incident that proves the point of honesty being relative to the situation was when Gus had me help him tear down a walk in freezer north of Glenwood Springs. A couple of young hot-shot Mormon boys made Gus a deal and then tried to "sock it to him." Now it wasn't that he didn't go the extra mile for them. I told him that it had to be my uncle and father that wired the building, He (that is we) loaded up all the wire and fixtures and most of the hardwood decking and hauled it to his place at diner time driving right through the entire length of Glenwood Springs. Most likely it would have been hauled to the dump anyway, perhaps. So those two boys showed up asking where the hardwood and the electrical material were and Gus looked them both in the eyes and said, "Ah, hell, you hired me to tear it down, not guard it at night!" And we went on to finish the job and it was well done.

Hard work and difficult times are not without its humorous side and more so when the work is demanding and dangerous. Back on Basalt Mountain we worked skid horses and they were well taken care of. Gus made sure that they were well fed and watered as they should be. Gus ran quite a few men off of the mountain for negligence and laziness. Some of them even took off walking to town twenty six miles away. One man's negligence caused Big Joe, one of the horses, to get a sharp wooden snag run into his side almost six inches, deep enough to keep him out of the woods for the rest of the season. When I began working him again, he would panic when tied onto a log and he would try to run away with it or take off when it was being hooked up. Before I got him settled down and cured of his fear, he managed to run me into a stob about the size of a lead pencil and it went into my leg about an inch and a half. Fritz helped me pack it with snow and then cut it out with a razor blade. Dick was another of the skid horses and he had been beaten about the head and worked with a collar that was way too small and it had damaged his neck. It took me about a week with a good collar and care and after that I could swing a pine bow at his head and he would just blink his eyes at me, that was Dick and he was small for a skid horse, but he would pull his heart out for me or go to his knees trying. Now Oscar was a big brute of a skid horse and not nearly as smart as Dick. When both horses were pulling together, little Dick would get the log moving then slack off and let Oscar do most of the work. Oscar found that if he deliberately stepped across one of the chain tugs, we would have to unhook and then re-hook him. Gus told me to just make Oscar pull that log a little way with the tug on the inside of his leg and I did and Oscar got his leg scraped. We let him pull this stunt and get his leg scraped about four times and he quit that stunt, but his leg needed cared for. We took him to the shed and Gus had me find a beer bottle and fill it half and half with turpentine and water. Well, just as Gus tried to pour the mixture on his open sore, Oscar kicked the bottle and that was one turpentined horse! He humped and kicked and backed out of the shed and ran around in circles, humping and bucking and squealing like a pig. I chased him around with a bucket of water to cool him down and finally got him cornered and got the turpentine washed off, but we sure all got a good laugh out of watching him. After that he never stepped across the tugs again. There are ever so many more stories to tell about Gus.

GUST AXELSON THE SWEDE
ONE OF THE REAL PEOPLE

"NO! by Gott vy should I? I got no respect for him alive; I should when he's dead?" That was the comment that I received when I ask Gust if he was going to shut down the sawmill and go to Alex Bowie's big funeral. Old man Bowie had been a good customer for years and he always paid cash for his lumber when he got it. Later, at lunch time, I found out why.

The story was that Alex came into the sawmill at Paonia to purchase cottonwood lagging for his mine cars and he asked Gust the price. Gust told him it was $45 per thousand board feet. Alex said he could buy it for $35 at another sawmill, so Gust said, "What the hell are you doing here? Go buy it there!"

The next day, Alex showed up and told Gust that they wouldn't sell to him for $35 and asked Gust to saw him ten thousand feet of mine car siding and then turned to leave when Gust said to him, "You didn't ask me the price." Alex replied, "It was $45 yesterday." Gust then told him, "Yes, but it is $50 today!" Alex stormed out the door saying that he would not pay that much.

The next day, Alex was back and told Gust he had to have the planks for the mine cars and again asked him cut them. As Alex turned to leave, Gust said, "You forgot to ask the price." Alex replied, "Well, you said yesterday that it was $50." As you may have guessed, Gust said, "Yes, but today it is $55." Alex turned in a rage to leave, but then Gust said to him. "It is $55 today and if you set foot out of here now, it is going to be $60 tomorrow." Finally, Alex agreed to take it and Gust told him he would have it ready for pick up in two days.

Several years later, when rough lumber sold at $75 a thousand, Gust still sold to Alex at $55 because he was a good customer. Gust still had no respect for Bowie even though Bowie owned a big coal mine and even had a town named after him.

Gust's sawmill was set up in an old fruit packing plant, so there was a roof over it, which was nice. It was a right angle mill where the logs were pulled inside with a little donkey engine and rolled onto the carriage that fed the logs into the saw where they were cut into lumber. The problem was that the sawed lumber had to be man handled as it came through the saw, then the boards had to be turned at a right angle and placed on a cut off table. They were then trimmed to their proper size and then stacked in piles according to width and length. All the cut-off pieces were used for fire wood or set aside for wedges or cap boards for the coal mines. All the slabs were cut for blocking the box car doors as they were filled with lump coal for shipping to the east. There was no edger, and lumber with bark on either side was stacked to be run through the saw again and then cut to size. Nothing was wasted at this mill, even short pieces of plank were placed on the carriage and cut for mine caps.

I sat straddling the main shaft, with my feet at each end of the mill saw, and my head sticking in the mill saw, so it felt, but with old Gust, it was reasonably safe. We cut many large timbers that weighed two hundred to six hundred pounds and we had to handle that rough heavy lumber by ourselves, trimming it and stacking it. We would get a fifteen minute break at ten in the morning and at three in the afternoon, but there was no stopping for anything else. No one smoked while they were working, they didn't run to the rest room, they didn't stop for a drink of water or a cup of coffee, and they didn't take off their gloves to scratch their nose. When we worked, we worked and when we rested, we rested, really rested.

Gust paid the average wage at that time and it was one dollar an hour and we worked a forty hour week. If for some reason we worked overtime we were paid accordingly.

Gust was about five feet, five inches tall and about forty four inches around the waist. He had two sons who were both over six feet tall, but they didn't back-talk the old man. Carl and Lennart didn't back off from any one or anything, but their father.

When Gust was a young man, he walked seven miles up to the Farmer's Coal Mine and loaded coal into coal cars at a dollar a ton and paid off three thousand dollars in debts. Walking fourteen miles round trip every day, rain or shine, snow or muddy road, six days a week, he kept at it. He had been a hard rock miner in Sweden, and at Leadville, working for H.A.W. Taber, and in Cripple Creek mines, too. He built fishing boats and fished, even made his own fishing nets. He operated a steam-run sawmill which he later regretted selling.

That old man treated me like one of his own sons, maybe it was because I did the work of two or three men. His sons could also do the work of two men and for him we all did it gladly because he was a man that wouldn't ask you to do anything he wouldn't do himself. There were times when I saw his boys break three inch hickory handles unloading logs and Gust would swear at them and tell them, "Leave it alone--me and Harvey will unload it!" And 'Me and Harvey' unloaded it and we broke no handles.

We had a slab runway to drag the logs into the mill. On one occasion, one of the logs had a knot that was about to snag on the run, so I rolled it over and the knot caught Gust on his big toe. Tears came to his eyes and he sat down on another log to check the damage. He said, "Don't do that some-more, Harvey, I tink that you got my last toe nail!" He had lost the other nine in the mines. The next day he came to work in slippers. He was just as happy in slippers and he was still singing in Swedish as he sawed the logs into lumber. Later he gave me those old work boots.

When the mill wasn't running, I was put to work hauling logs down to the sawmill. When winter was getting close, Gust laid off the old man that he had running the donkey hoist and helping him turn logs on the carriage. Lennert said to him, "Dad, I thought you were going to run the mill this winter, but you laid off the help." Gust's answer was, "By Gott! Harvey and me, ve will run the mill!" And 'By Gott, Harvey and me, ve ran the mill!' With me turning the logs and the both of us on the donkey hoist pulling in the logs. There was an old planing mill that we used that came into the country by ox cart. It had a top cutter and two exposed side cutters that Gust adjusted while the mill was running.

One day he hit his finger with a wrench, jerked back and stuck his left hand into one of the two-edged razor sharp cutters. It cut off the end of his first finger and routed out the rest of his fingers as well as his hand. The air around his head was filled with a spray of blood and flesh for a second. I shut down the mill and locked the doors and took him to town. A week later, he was back on the job sawing lumber, with his left hand wrapped with a cloth and with tears of pain in his eyes. His oldest son took over the sawing, but when he motioned for me to straddle the main shaft when he wanted to saw the small pieces; I shook my head, that was something that I would only do for the old man!

Gust and I went along with the boys when they built roads for a coal mine, once, to do the blasting. We had no crimpers and Gust tried to crimp the caps onto the fuse with his pocket knife on the powder box, but the knife would slide off because his bad hand wouldn't work right, so I went back to crimping caps with my teeth, not the safest way to do it, but a lot safer that what he was doing. "Safety" can be relative.

We were building a road around a mountain above a county road and there was a lady living close by that had a tin roof on her house and rocks sometimes landed on the roof, she moved to town until we were done. On that same job, the company's engineer came up and asked Gust how much powder he was using and Gust said that he always used seven sticks, but at times we used a half a stick and sometimes it was half a box. The engineer would say to us, "That sure didn't sound like seven sticks." Next time he might say, "That sure sounded loud for seven sticks." The joke was on him.

It was dangerous work but we realized our limitations, at least, most of the time. Gust would cut off three feet of fuse to shoot five different shots scattered over forty feet, and then spread a trail of dynamite in the wrapping paper for a fuse spitter, and then he would hand me the spitter and go hide behind the blade of the Cat while I spit the fuses. He never doubted my ability to light those fuses with that sputtering dynamite spitter while he peeked over the top of the Cat blade. At times I landed right on top of him when I dived over the cat blade just as the charges began going off. No one can escape the occasional injury working dangerous jobs, and I've had my share, but we tried to look out for each other's safety, even if it was at our own expense.

Well, Gust has passed away and I heard that Lennart lost an eye when a piece of steel shattered off a track pin when he was driving it back in and then later he had his back broken in a coal mine cave in. For me they will be remembered as some of the truly "Real People".

As the Swedes say, "Too soon old--too late smart!" Ya?

EARLY THOMASVILLE
ON THE FRYING PAN

One of the most remarkable people there was in that community was Nellie Irons, a stately old retired school teacher of close to ninety years of age and still living by herself for about seven months out of a year, snowbound in a small but comfortable log cabin on the North Fork of the Frying Pan.

She was a lady, tall and slender, with hair that reached the ground and she brushed it each day and put it into a tight bun on the back of her head. She always wore long dresses even when cutting hay or milking her goats. In the winter, she had to carry the water in buckets for the goats and herself. The goats had the run of an ancient two story barn that was once a stage station. I remember that in the later 1930's it was still filled with much of the equipment that was left behind. The loft was full of mountain hay, hand cut with scythes from the pastures around her place. As youngsters we played in the loft and even swam in the icy waters of the creek.

At nine thousand feet she raised a big garden with onions, lots of potatoes, turnips, carrots and anything else that would grow in the short growing season. The plot was watered by a small hand dug ditch that started close to two miles up the stream.

I know that she burned tons of wood each winter because I had to help saw it in proper lengths with her old wood saw, and split much of it, too.

Her cabin was of closely fit rough logs and lined inside with many hooked rugs that she made by the dozens each winter while she was snowbound. Besides making rugs, she would listen to her old hand cranked Victrola. She had records from around 1914 and World War I. There was an immense rosewood Steinway Baby Grand Piano in her living room and when she played it and sang with the windows and doors open, it could be heard for miles.

She lived thirty miles up the Frying Pan from Basalt and there were many fishermen of that time that became acquainted with her and would end up renting one of her five cabins, sometimes for weeks at a time in the summer. Her remote cabins were right on the road leading to the horse trail to the big Savage Lakes which were nine miles on up the road.

Each spring, my father hauled about fifty dollars worth of groceries up to her, fighting mud and snowdrifts, sometimes having to turn back and then try again in a week or so. A person would have to see it to believe it, but that is what we did.

Just before the Second World War, she came to live with us in Glenwood Springs. I think that she must have been close to ninety years old. She brought her big rosewood Steinway Baby Grand with her and she would play and sing for us. She began recounting many stories and told about the piano coming into the valley by ox cart. She told us stories about the Colorado Midland Railroad that climbed over and through Hagerman Mountain and about the seven mile tunnel on the route beginning above Hell's Gate. The train had to travel eight miles just to gain a half mile to the flats at Turquoise Lake near Leadville. She told of her boarding house at Thomasville where she provided room and board for the men working at the lime quarry. She also took in laundry that she washed in a little shed in the back. Her places were always homes for those in need.

Nellie, Mrs. Irons, that is, told one story of the powder man that forgot about a few sticks of dynamite that he left in his bib overalls. When he got to the boarding house, knowing Nellie wouldn't like it being around, he decided that he needed to hide it somewhere. He went to the laundry shack and stashed them in the oven of her wood stove. It was Friday night and she wouldn't use the stove until Monday, which was wash day. Well, come Monday, early in the morning, she fired up the stove to heat water and in a few minutes she was told that there was smoke coming out the door, bad smoke! It was rolling out the oven and there was a stream of amber syrup dripping down the stove legs to the floor. She opened the oven door and after seeing the fresh baked explosives, she evacuated the entire community. The lime quarry was just a little ways up the road and in a very short time the entire crew was assembled in her back yard. Most of them moved way, way back and the powder man had to apologize and beg forgiveness while the stove cooled down so he could clean up the mess. It did not ever happen twice. The smell remained for several days and nothing was washed that week.

Well, the quarries are shut down and have been for eighty years or so. The last sawmill closed down, it was a one-man operation run by old man Trump who was a sawyer on Basalt Mountain where I logged over fifty years ago. Billing's sawmill is now Billing's Springs and the high open parks where we watched herds of elk grazing are just a graveyard of Columbines and

Monk's Head and the grass doesn't come up to a horse's belly like it used to. There is even a big manmade lake there just below town. I had my fun around there more than sixty years ago. I can still see it in my mind and nothing can take away the fond memories. Sorry you missed it, I really am, but I have enough enjoyable memories for all of us for all time...

WHOA! WHOOA!! WHOOOA!!!

The heavy loaded semi was coming down an icy hill just slipping and sliding with the driver doing his best to stay ahead of his jack-knifing trailer. There he sat, fighting the steering wheel with his left hand, his left foot on and off the clutch, his right foot jumping back and forth from the brake to the foot feed and back again, time and time again. His right hand gripped the C.B. mike with one finger on the talk button and another finger snagged around the blasting air horn. His head was turning back and forth from the road ahead of him and then to the mike, then back to the road then back to the mike and pulling the air horn and screaming all at the same time, "WHOA! WHOOA!! WHOOOA!!! YOU SON OF A ₊₊₊₊₊!!! WHOA! WHOA!! WHOA!!!" At the bottom of the grade he hit his trailer brakes on a bare section of the road and finally got his rig stopped along the side of the road where we just happened to be parked. He jumped out of his truck and we told him that we had been listening to his ordeal on our C.B. When he was calmed down it all of a sudden became real humorous, the yelling, "Whoa, Whoa, Whoa!!" in the C.B. mike to stop a runaway truck coming down an ice covered hill. It did seem to work, or did it?

I heard a similar story told by Gust Axelson, who I had worked for several years earlier. It happened on Kebler Pass. Now Kebler Pass is way up the North Fork of the Gunnison River and is an extremely steep, rocky and narrow road. It is beautiful but dangerous and even downright deadly. One day Gust was riding shotgun with a young driver hauling a load of logs coming down the pass. He was in the lowest gear that old GMC truck had and was doing about three miles an hour with the ignition key in the "off" position. The truck was smoking a bit with the back pressure and the brakes were smoking about the same. Then because he couldn't speed up on the lesser grades, as the key was off, he began slipping the clutch just a little bit and then letting it out. Gust said to him, "You really shouldn't do that some more because..." and right about then the "because" happened, the clutch was gone. He sat hard on the brakes, and the two rear axels began smoking something fierce and the front axel just went, "poof" in a cloud of smoke and then the brakes were gone. They managed to get around the next curve but the next grade was long and straight and steep. Gust just sat there as he said all that could be said. Melvin, the young driver, was wide-eyed and yelling, "WHOA!

WHOOA!! WHOOOA!!! You durned old truck!"
I guess the truck had lost its hearing and just
went faster and faster down the hill and another
curve was ahead of them. If by chance they
could make it around that last curve, and get
across the bridge, it was possible they could at
least get out of this alive! Perhaps, maybe, but
as they came around the curve they could see
some kids fishing off the narrow bridge. Melvin
gritted his teeth and drove straight ahead, right
down the fence line and into an enormous lava
rock slide. Gust said there were cedar fence
posts and wire and lava rock flying all over the
cab. The windshield broke, tires exploded,
wheels were torn off and finally the old truck
came to a stop. It was right side up and still
had the load of logs on it. Melvin jumped out
and looked at the wreck with the ruined tires
and bent wheels and the fence posts and
tangled wire and he just collapsed alongside the
still upright junker. I am quite certain that old
Gust just sat there in the off seat and said,
"Melvin, DON'T DO THAT SOME MORE!"

On that same pass I was hauling a load of
logs on a long-bed single axel Mac truck. It was
all low gears and air brakes and lots of patience.
I ran up on an old Surplus G.I. 6x6 truck that
was stopped in the middle of the road with
smoking brakes. We were both headed to the
same location. The driver said that he had a
few too many logs and he was running with key

turned off and was riding the brakes. He asked if maybe I could tie on to him and help him off the hill with my rig. "We have done it before." he told me, like it was not unusual. I hooked on and helped him to the bottom of the hill and we took our loads to the sawmill. When Gust found out what I had done, he said, "How come you do a stunt like that?" So I said, "The other driver said that you told him that you had been doing that." So his reply was, "DON'T DO THAT SOME MORE, HARVEY!" You know that's what he told me the day I rolled a log over on the skid way and he ended up losing his last toenail. He said then, "Well, Harvey, that's the last one, the rest of them got smashed off loading lump coal in the cars at the mine, but, by Gott, Harvey, don't do that some more!" Old Gust was like a father to me and treated me like one of his boys. He was certainly a special friend of mine definitely one of the "Real People".

Just Two Uranium Miners During The 50's Boom

This story took place one cold, fall day around hunting season. I was working at a uranium mine out on the Colorado Plateau. We were staying in tar paper shacks furnished by Climax Uranium. We had a cook shack and an elderly widow woman for a cook and we even had lights in each shack. Oh, yes, we had a two holed outhouse way out on the end of the camp that hung over the valley and it played a part in the story that I'm going to tell about the two uranium miners, Beardsley and Hard Rock.

Larry Beardsley liked his beer and his bars and his bar women and that was where you could find him on his days off, in or around a bar in Naturita with a woman or two. He was very consistent. It seems that Larry was enjoying the company of a couple of the local girls while driving down through Paradox Valley and they were all drinking beer. They were all feeling good and having a good time when one of the gals pulled the keys out of the dash and dropped them on the floor amongst the empty beer cans. That didn't bother Larry; he just hit the clutch and coasted off to the side of the road, opened the door on that old Chevy pickup and lay across the legs of the two women and began searching for the keys. About that time a Colorado State Patrol came up behind them and saw the whole thing. He knew Larry and the girls and might of laughed it off except one of the three knocked over an open can of beer and it was running out the door. OH-OH, that did it. It wasn't funny any more and the Patrolman wrote Larry a ticket so he had to go before the judge in a J.P. court and pay a fine. The next week end he was back in the bar with the girls drinking beer as usual and he told the girls that he had parked the pickup and had a bicycle and he took off weaving back and forth going down the street. He told me that he wasn't that drunk, but was just showing off, but the law stopped him and smelled the beer and gave him another ticket and back he had to go to the judge and pay another fine. Larry told the judge that he wouldn't see him next week and the judge told him that if he was even caught walking down the street intoxicated next week end that he would see him again. Larry was just a typical hard working, hard drinking uranium miner.

Now Hard Rock was somewhat different, he was short, with a full beard (always tobacco stained) always wore dirty bib overalls and was about as deaf as a rock. When he ran the 12-B Overshot Emco Loader, he had one foot on the step and galloped along the ground with his other foot. He said his belly was too big to get both feet on the loader's step. We all had to yell in his good ear and when he talked to any of us, he put his face right up against ours and yelled right back, spitting tobacco juice right in our face. We couldn't yell back then because we would have our mouth as well as our eyes full. He was a good enough miner and he was Larry's partner, not mine. So that is the reason the following thing happened. Larry had a problem with his nose and he put mentholatum up it on a regular basis. His partner Hard Rock had a problem with his behind and he came back from the outhouse early one morning and sticks his finger in Larry's mentholatum jar and applies it to his tail end. Now that isn't so bad, but what took place was that first application of mentholatum felt so good that he did it again and Larry's nose was bothering him and Larry is looking at the open jar and at Hard Rock's finger and the party starts. It's a long trip to town after work and Hard Rock had no transportation and he continued to double dip in the jar and Larry needed to use it, too. I think that Larry talked the cook out of a clean jar of mentholatum for his nose and that one he kept hidden from Hard Rock. Then one morning Hard Rock came in for his usual two fingers of mentholatum, but such screaming and swearing you never heard before as Hard Rock streaked back to the outhouse, trying to drop his bibs and get into his long handles to do something to relieve the burning pain! Somebody, I can't say who, had put Vicks in the mentholatum jar and just one finger full of that was more that enough. Beardsley, in the meantime, had filled a bucket with ice cold water and eased around and down under the outhouse and threw the whole bucket of water right up Hard Rock's injured back side. The entire camp was watching as the old man came charging out the door with his pants down and the back of his underwear wide open, even the cook was there to watch the fun. When it was all over and the kidding died down, Hard Rock and Larry were still friends, but perhaps a little more cautious about taking advantage of friendships. Hard Rock said that he was getting too old for this nonsense and drew his time and went down the hill. To an easier life, I hope. All of us were really sorry, I guess, sort of because mining is a hard life, the older miners are a vanishing breed, not many of us left any more.

This story is just another one of life's lessons, another one is you don't mess with the cook and it's a good idea to keep you finger out of your partner's mentholatum jar, unless it is an emergency, but only put your finger in once.

HARD ROCK MINER
AND THE
LITTLE JAPANESE NURSE

There was a cry in the dark from clear across the lake, "Help, help us!" My mining partner could see car lights a quarter of a mile across the lake and could hardly hear the cries. So both of us with carbide lamps for light got in our little boat and rowed as fast as we could to the far side and there was a late model four door car stuck in the mud along side the lake. It was a man and a small Japanese woman, his wife, and a couple of small children. The woman looked and sounded somewhat familiar to me. So being a couple of "good old boys" Gene and I rowed back across the totally dark lake and loaded up the slabs that we'd brought for fire wood putting them crosswise on the boat, also with a jack and a shovel and back across we went.

We were able to get the car up out of the mud and on solid ground and they were so appreciative, but just about that time this little Japanese woman tells us that she was a nurse at the infirmary in Uravan. OH! Now I remembered her! She said something to Gene and her husband that you wouldn't believe but before I tell you what she said let me tell you how I met this woman.

I was a hard rock miner at the Nil Mine on Monogram Mesa. I hadn't even met Gene Hinkle at that time. Top miner I was there at two dollars and twenty seven cents per hour. I could run anything they had and did. Alice Chalmers diesel loaders, Emco loaders on rail, wheel loader outside on the dump, D6 loaders and any size slusher and air hammer they had. I even ran the trammers both diesel and electric hauling ore to the surface. I was hauling uranium ore in one and a half ton and three ton buggies to the dump pocket. They all had steel plow seats just like the farm equipment for the last hundred years. We hauled ore fast over rough underground roads down through the tunnels to the dump pocket, dodging air lines and water lines and other equipment. It was always rough, damp, cold and hard with a capitol HARD on our back sides. We couldn't stand up and drive and we got pounded all day long. The shifter kept crying for "more ore, more ore" and we gave it to him until he began complaining about roughing up the equipment by going too fast, but we didn't slow down one bit and hauled ore like good miners should and did. We paid for it as Harley, my partner, ran his buggy in the dump pocket. I began calling my buggy "the pile driver," and was having severe problems! Oh, well!

Some time later Freda and the kids and I went fishing at a little lake on Fall Creek near Telluride and as I was fly fishing across the lake on a big truck inner tube it felt like lightning struck down there where the sun doesn't shine. I had to roll over on my stomach and paddle back across the lake to our camp. There was no way that I could sit down in the car on the way home. On Monday morning Freda took me to town in the Chevy Suburban with four kids and me on a slanted seat more standing than sitting. We headed for Doctor Greenwood's in Montrose and I'm dying for sure. Doc Greenwood was a good old doctor but he was not very gentle. He said just as calm as you please for me to drop my pants and leaned me over the table and took a scalpel to me and slit me open. My eyes crossed and I bellowed like a mad bull. The doctor said, "I wanted to cut a little more, but I was afraid of what you would do to me!" I assured him that he was perfectly safe when I was in that position! He went on to say, "I will expect you in the hospital the first thing in the morning." "Fine, okay, great! I'm in no position to argue." Freda got me to her sister's place and she was such a great help she says to me, "Eat good tonight, Harvey, because you won't be able to eat for about a week." That sounded good to me because at that period in my young life I could work like a horse and eat like one. I was able to climb up a thirty foot raise ladder with a fifty pound box of dynamite on my shoulder and a roll of primers around my neck. So I took my sister-in-law's advice and ate and ate and ate while watching TV.

So the next day in the hospital a grey haired old lady had to give me five enemas to get me cleaned out and that little old lady caused me a great deal more pain than the doctor did with his knife and it was well that my sister-in-law didn't make an appearance, her life would have been in jeopardy. Then to add insult to injury they sent in what looked like a sweet little sixteen year old girl and between her and the grey haired lady they shaved every hair off of me from my waist to my knees front and back! It took better than an hour and I lost count of the razors. I was hurting too much to be embarrassed. The young girl was awfully quiet during this process, but the grey haired lady said, "If we have another one to do, I sure hope he isn't as hairy a bugger and this one!" Later after I got back to work at the mine, I was too embarrassed to strip down in the dry because I looked just like one of those "goons" in the Popeye Comic strip because the only hair I had was from the knees down and the waist up.

So there I was in the operating room lying on the operating table with my legs propped up the same way they do women when delivering babies. Much to my regret, I was still conscious. There I was with the bright lights and all and someone sticks a needle in my arm and I was out of it. Some time later I woke up in bed with a kotex belt on and quite undecided what my next move should be. When the doctor came to see how I was doing he asked me if I remembered what I told him during the operation. I didn't remember saying anything to him, but he said that I told him, "You are a good doctor but you are sure a pain in the butt to me!" The doctor said, "Give him a little more sodium pentothal, please!" That's one problem being an old miner, calling it like it is.

After the third day in the hospital and not even a cup of coffee and no solid food, Freda was sneaking me fried chicken and milk shakes and I was eager to get out of there. I had a big overfed male nurse that ignored me so I got my clothes on and eased out into the hall and the big fellow says, "Can I do something for you, sir?" "You sure can you can, get me the doctor because I'm going home!" "Oh, my god, you will have us all fired!" "That well may be, but I'm going home!" When Doctor Greenwood came in he said, "It looks like you are going home, so you might as well," and I did. I took off walking to Freda's sister's place with much difficulty, I might add.

We went back home to Naturita where we lived and before I could go back to work I had to go to the clinic and guess who I had to talk to, a cute little Japanese nurse and she wanted to know what my problem was. And thinking about all that I'd gone through with having five enemas, shaved bare bottom, wearing a Kotex. I wasn't about to tell her all that and didn't want to bear my bottom for her, so I told her loud and clear and very distinctly, "Oh, hell, I had a hysterectomy!" "Ya, ya, ya, wha, wha, wha, you couldn't have!" she stammered. We both laughed and I didn't have to pull my britches down.

So the end of the story is back to the lake and this was the Japanese nurse that I saw in the clinic and so she said to her husband, "Honey, I want you to meet the only hard rock miner that ever had a hysterectomy!' That was nearly fifty years ago and it's still laughable—at my expense, that is. OH, WELL!!

P.S. I had an infected fistula removed... just so you know what the problem was.

HINKLE

Clarence Eugene Hinkle was his full name and I met Gene and his family when I was mining on Beaver Mesa and he was a motor man. We hit it right off and so did our families. The biggest mistake that we made with them was teaching them to play pinochle because they wanted to play every night about half of the night. The second mistake was to tell Gene about the old Van Dyke Mine, but that's another story and a good one.

Gene was living back in Kansas somewhere and was a car spotter for a ring of car thieves and was quite good at it, this was during the war. Then he discovered that these same fellows were trying to set him up to take the blame in a drug deal and that was the end of that job. Next he boiler plated (bullet proofed) a big Packard and began running booze, that is until a good woman got hold of him. When they got married and it took a half pint of boot-leg to get him out of bed in the morning. She gave him reason to quit that habit also.

Gene was a master mechanic and when it came to making any broken-down vehicle or machine run, he could do it, but he became allergic to grease and oil and took a job on a ditch line with his brother-in-law. They were both broke, so at lunch time they began trying out used cars just to get home and back for lunch. He was pulled over by the law on several occasions for speeding and he would always use the excuse that his wife was "expecting" and he got away with it for a while and avoided a ticket, but on about the third time that he was stopped the law officer finally asked him just what was his wife expecting? "She is expecting me home for lunch!" he replied. He didn't even get a ticket. Why? Well, he was the most innocent looking person with his big blue eyes and soft talking voice. Always dressed like a poor person, but clean and polite, just a nice guy. Another time Gene went into a used car lot and wanted to try out a car and the dealer told him that he didn't think that he had a dime to his name (which was true). So Gene said, "Just what would you take for that last line of cars in the back of your lot, those that don't run and you can't sell?" "I'll take two hundred dollars in CASH!" The owner said. "Would you give me about twenty minutes to get the money?" Gene asked him. "Sure!" came the answer. Gene walked across the street to a loan outfit and told them the deal. The man there said he had been trying to get to that crooked car dealer for years and gave Gene the money and took titles for just two of the twelve cars in that back row and Gene was in the used car business for himself. Gene and his family were good friends and we sure enjoyed knowing them, but it was only for part of one year. The mine was shut down and we went our separate ways looking for jobs.

"Woody" Woodrow Simpson

"One hundred dollars and court costs!" Jack Frost, the J.P. told him. "I won't pay it!" said Woody. "You'll go to jail!" said Jack. "I'll eat lots of hamburgers," was Woody's reply. (That was the regular jail fare in Monticello, Utah.)

Now Woody was different, he claimed to be a Mormon, but came closer to being a Jack Mormon and a free thinker, but went along with the Mormon thing because it was easier and safer in Southeastern Utah. Woody had been on Coregador in the South Pacific during World War II, when our not so friendly scrap iron weapon makers (the Japanese) tried to take over soon after Pearl Harbor. Woody got hit with shell fragments in the stomach and laid there on his back in shock with his eyes open, looking up at the little bandy-legged killers stomping on him, more dead than alive. Later he was patched up and he survived, but the appearance of his belly in a t-shirt looked like a sack of pipe fittings, and he suffered with his stomach the rest of his life. Woody tells the story that when it happened, there were only three bullets per rifle for them.

After the war, when jobs were few on the west coast, he was loading lumber on a Chinese freighter, and the captain persuaded him to return to China with him, where he was given a job as messenger runner for one of the big shots because he couldn't read Chinese and could be trusted. He had enough of that quite quickly and headed home to Utah. That's enough about that, back to the story.

Well, let me explain. I bought an old winch truck from Woody and paid for it with mechanic work, hauling his backhoe and giving him a hand setting septic tanks that he made himself. Woody and I were on our way to Cortez, Colorado, to haul back a "little" diesel farm tractor on the winch truck, and we had to stop at the Port of Entry east of Monticello. The inspector asked, "What's wrong with that safety sticker, it's upside down, that seven looks like a hockey stick!" "Well, it keeps falling off, and I stick it back on," answered Woody. He was actually using it on his big truck, too. The inspector replied, "You can't do that, Woody, get a new one as soon as you get back." So we made it through okay and on to Cortez.

I folded back the gin-poles and drove the "little" farm tractor on the truck forward because the rear wheels were too wide for the poles and that placed too much weight behind the rear wheels. Next, I took down the poles and placed them between the wheels of the "little" tractor as we backed it on the truck. With the back of the "little" tractor against the winch and the cab, it still hung over all three side of the bed! We tied it down and headed for home. As we pulled into the Port of Entry this time, Woody said, "Stay away from the scales, and don't get close to them, stay back here where they can't see the 'little' tractor." We left the truck back a ways, out of the way of the big rigs and walked into the station. The officer took a look at us and peered out at the distant "little" farm tractor on the truck and said, "My God! Are you two here again? Get out of here!" and we did! Now, I couldn't see him smiling, can't say that he did.

Woody told me this story; he hand loaded about nine tons of mine rail on a single axel truck from a mine north of Monticello and the law stopped him because he was overloaded and made him unload about three ton of rail along side the road, then he and his truck with the six ton on it was escorted to the J.P. The J.P. said to him, "You know better than to move that much weight Woody that will be one hundred dollars and court costs." "That's too much, I won't pay it!" Woody answered. "You'll go to jail!" said the J.P. "I'll eat lots of hamburgers." "Well, will you pay seventy five dollars and court costs?" asked the J.P. "No! I won't pay seventy five dollars and court costs!" said Woody. "You'll go to jail!" "I'll eat lots of hamburgers!" About then, the J. P. got distracted with another situation and as he was distracted, Woody walked out of the door, got into his truck, returned to pick up his three ton of rail on top of his six ton and drove on down to his home in Bluff.

The next day about mid-morning a deputy drove into the yard and hauled Woody fifty miles back to the J.P. at Monticello. "How come you walked out of here yesterday? We weren't through!" said the J.P. "Well, you were talking to someone else and I figured we were through, so I just walked out and went home." said Woody. "Well, we weren't, Woody! You will have to pay fifty dollars and court costs." They continued to argue. "That's too much! I won't pay it!" "You will go to jail!" "I'll eat lots of hamburgers!" "Well, Woody, will you pay twenty five dollars?" Woody answered, "Sure, I'll pay twenty five dollars. I would have paid twenty five dollars yesterday!" Woody handed over the twenty five dollars and no court costs and then the deputy had to drive him fifty miles back to Bluff then return the fifty miles to Monticello. I just think that they didn't want Woody in their jail.

Another story about Woody was the one about the cannon ball that held his door open. When a nephew of his asked what it was, Woody said that it was the last of several kegs which he had dug up near Moab on the Colorado River by accident. Never got a clear story on that, but they were silver dorey (a combination of several minerals) poured into cannon ball shape, supposed to date back to the early Spanish. It would be interesting to know the rest of that story.

Woody and his wife tried to home stake (not homestead) a piece of ground near Grand Gulch on the high mesa above the San Juan River. They even had legal papers issued right from Washington D.C., but they were forced to give it up because his cattle were stolen, and his property destroyed by self righteous government vandals.

Another scheme Woody wanted to have me help him with was mining out a body of platinum in the Sinbad Basin at the head of Salt Creek on the Delores River east of the LaSalle Mountains. He suggested that my wife operate a boarding house for it. The Government was to furnish the expenses and the metal was to be used to cover the Space Shuttle. It sounded good but, and this was a big BUT, Woody's equipment had the tires slashed and the hydraulic hoses cut. The shaft was down about thirty feet and was subject to explosions from methane gas, which could also suffocate the miners.

Platinum has always been a byproduct. There is a low-grade vein of it that begins along the San Miguel River below Naturita and extends clear across the Uncompagre Range. There was no money in it. There was about ten thousand dollars worth of platinum recovered in a placer operation at one time and I got to see it building up on the riffles of the shaker table. That was the first and last time that I ever saw anything like that. Needless to say, we didn't get involved in that scheme and about ten years later I was told that it had been a completely dishonest deal. The only platinum worth mining was that which was "salted" into the liquor (mineral in liquid form) in the recovery process. Woody didn't even realize this as it was a deal set up by his brother at Moab.

Another job I did for Woody, after he had me wire on the bed of a Ford truck with number nine wire, was to help him move his septic tank mold and equipment down to Black Cannon City. That turned out to be a mistake for him as his concrete tanks were not large enough to meet the requirements of the area. One of the reasons for his move was because of a big old cab-over tandem axel dump truck that was parked on a lot near where Woody worked in Blanding and every time he looked at it, it reminded him of his old friend who was the owner and operator of the gravel truck. This guy went out to work on it one evening and his wife got tired and went to bed only to wake up to find that he never came back in the house. He was crushed under the dump bed, mashed into the transmission and frame when the bed apparently came down on him. The ancient truck sat there for many years and no one would buy it and no one would drive it. I could have had it for the price of getting rid of it, but I didn't want it either.

Woody's stomach and chest had always been a serious problem since the war. He carried a box of Arm & Hammer soda with him at all times and many times I saw him pour a hand full and put it in his mouth. There would be white on the stubble on his face, on his shirt and down his front and a look of pain on his face. He never said much about it, but it was a problem. Finally he went to the V.A. Hospital in Salt Lake and when the doctors weren't too busy delivering Indian babies, they examined him. While they were putting a probe down his throat, they tore something loose and then had to operate and try to patch up the hole. In the meantime, they put a hole through his ribs and gave him a tube and a funnel so he could eat, well, stay alive a little longer, but he didn't live much longer. When we heard of his situation, a friend of his, Harvey Butler and I went up to the hospital to see him. When he saw us, he began to cry. He was in a pitiful sad condition, laying there with his wife holding his hand. Skin and bones, his eyes sunk back in his head. Surely that wasn't Woody, but it was. Cancer, they said, and the end of Woody. "Ah, Fellows, I don't want you to see me like this!" That's all he said along with the tears on his face and there were tears in our eyes too. We left. We were too hurt and there was nothing to be done but try to remember him as he used to be, as he wanted us to remember him, a "Good Man" and a "Real Person." He was our friend and still is, always will be. We were proud to be his friend.

GARDNER AND THE
SUPER CRUISER

"There go my bedrooms!" Amy said, as she looked up into the clear High Country sky at the small orange and yellow Piper Cub with its oversized wings. "Gardner's flying in it. That was supposed to be the money for our new bedrooms." My wife and I were visiting Amy and she showed us the diggings under their house where those bedrooms were supposed to be. There was a set of twelve pound rail leading out from under the house to the side of the hill where an empty half ton mine car was setting. Gardner, Amy's husband, was a big, good natured, easy going electrical boss at the Climax Mine. He was quite exacting in all that he did, but not really very excitable or fast and he did good work and sooner or later, he got the job done. Everything was absolutely level and exactly square and he had been laying up cinder blocks for walls and it was sure pretty. It was about this time during the laying up of the blocks that Gardner asked one of his sons what he thought of his building work up to date and his son told him that he had been watching him and the wall surely did look good, but at the rate of construction, the job was going to take him ten years to finish!

I didn't help any either because I questioned Gardner about that High Country ridge on Independence Pass that I was looking for or he said that we should go and look for it in the plane. So I asked, "Okay, when?" His answer was, "How about right now?" And so we headed for the airport. That was the first time that I was ever close to his plane and truthfully, it looked better in the air than it did up close. He showed me the new weld on the tail wheel assembly and it was a good weld. Then he pointed to the new wing struts on the right wing. He told me he blew a tire landing and the wing had collapsed, but it looked real good. Next we walked under the wings and looking up I could see little pin holes of sunlight coming through and he said that he had to get a new paint job soon. Then he says, "Hold the tail up so the wings are level and I'll check the gas. It's got enough gas for the little trip we want to take, now get in the rear seat (which I did), that lever on the left is the throttle and when you are flying the plane, NEVER take your hand off of it." He told me all about the control stick and the seat belt and all the instruments on the dash, the foot pedals and brake and such and it was sure a thrill to understand a little about the plane. We went around to the front and with the ignition off, he explained how to spin the prop, because his battery was dead or the starter didn't work something like that. You stand close to the prop when you turn it or when it starts you may fall into it (but only once!). I practiced several times and even with the ignition off the engine compression was something to pay attention to. He gets in then and yells, "CONTACT!" and I spin the prop, somewhat like a little old lady, but after the look he gave me, I spun it hard enough to start it up. I crawled in the rear seat and fastened the seat belt as he closed the door and away we went!

He hadn't told me about the coffee can and the paper bags behind my seat in case I got air sick and I really wouldn't have needed it except that I forgot about the chew of Copenhagen tobacco that was still in my mouth and I swallowed it. I thought that I was going to be sick, but my stomach was in good shape back then and I was okay. As we left the ground and the valley fell away before us, I felt like Crocodile Dundee on his first flight in the jet and my comment was probably about the same. Gardner got us up to about eleven thousand feet. I might add here that Leadville, where we were at the time, is situated just at then ten thousand feet and the airport is the same altitude so when the plane leaves the ground, it is already at ten thousand feet above sea level. While crossing the frozen Twin Lakes, Gardner pointed to the ignition keys and it looked like someone was pulling them straight down. He had hit an updraft and it put us up almost two thousand feet, which he explained was a good thing as he was having trouble getting altitude. He flew up a valley at the upper end of the lakes and the mountains were still higher than the plane. He circled and gained just enough altitude so that I could see the country. I would be looking at the side of a hill or down into a valley and all of a sudden all I could see was blue sky and then brown and green and white snow and then back to blue again, "A little rough," Gardner would say. I think that I could have taken a few grab samples along the hill, he flew so close. That old man could really fly that little underpowered plane. Back down the valley we flew, down across the still frozen lakes then all too quick my stomach was up in my throat as we dropped a thousand feet straight down and the ignition keys were hanging upside down all the way. He tried to get me to fly the plane back to the airstrip and I did of sorts, but I could not get any feeling on that control stick. It was like a short broom stick in a bucket of water. I thought that I saw the ridge I was looking for with the old abandoned Manhattan Mine dumps. That old Cub was quite a plane and so was the pilot, and there is more to come about Gardner and his Super Cruiser.

This was my second flight in the Super Cruiser and it was educational to say the least. We had plenty of gas and the weather was fine that is, crisp and cold. "CONTACT" and I spun the prop and climbed in and up, up and away! Just ahead was big, blue Turquoise Lake and Hagerman Pass. Behind us was the thirteen thousand foot Mosquito Range and there was several thousand feet of open air all below us. I finally did get some feeling on the control stick with needed assistance from Gardner, and flew around in circles to the left and to the right and made a few shallow dives and pulled back out of them and I was feeling pretty cocky. Now he says to put the plane in a dive, and I didn't feel so secure, shall we say, because now we are in a dive and Gardner tells me to turn loose of the stick, which I did, and the prop was turning and we were headed for the ground. Then as the plane picked up speed in the dive, all by itself it began to level out and came out of the dive. AMAZING! I'm feeling pretty good again, good lesson to learn.

Gardner took over the controls and began a steep climb, up, up and up and then I saw his right hand held high in the air and he yelled, "Just watch!" The little piper just nosed down, made a swoop and leveled off, pretty neat! Then he did the same stunt several times. "This is called a 'stall', now you try it," he said. It looked quite simple and I began to climb, you know, with my left hand on the throttle and my right hand on the stick and I didn't have to turn or bank, just climb and turn loose of the stick. Then from the front of the plane he calmly tells me not to whip stall the plane. My eyes were really wide open then. A whip stall is when you climb too steep and lose your flying speed and the plane falls backwards. "So what happens then?" I asked. "Well, if the plane falls backwards, the wings fall off!" he said. "Well, shucks, Gardner! And there we were flying along with the nose of the plane some twenty degrees or so higher than the tail and I kept thinking, don't whip stall it because the wings will fall off!' Well, I flew that plane with its nose in the air for several miles and it didn't stall out, but no way was I going to risk the wings just falling off, they never did. "Maybe we can try that later," he said. We circled around and went up and down and I was the pilot, more or less. Then he told me to swing around and come down over the airfield like I was going to land. No problem, it real easy and smooth so after a few passes he asked me if I wanted to land the plane. My comment to that was, "WELL NOOO, Gardner!" I didn't want to pick asphalt out of my teeth. He wanted to make a licensed pilot out of me, and much as I would have liked to, it just wasn't reasonable at that time.

Gardner flew his plane into Utah some where and had the engine rebuilt. Then he and Amy flew to Las Vegas but the engine was running hot so they landed in the desert and while landing, blew a tire. He left Amy sitting under a wing and caught a ride to town packing the blown tire still mounted on the wheel. He found someone to bring him back with a new tire and they got back in the air and went on to Las Vegas for the week end. Now with a good rebuilt engine and new tires he decided to fly to Denver to have a new paint job. When the plane was ready, one of his sons drove him over from Leadville so he could bring back the newly painted little Piper, but on the east side of Loveland Pass, he lost all his oil pressure and down he went. He managed to miss the traffic on the road when he landed it on the Interstate while his son saw the whole thing from the car. No damage, other than the engine because the oil plug was missing. When it was painted, the oil was drained and the plane was turned up side down to paint the bottom. When the paint job was finished the oil was put back in, however the oil plug was not tightened and it fell out on the flight back home. So what now? Off comes the wings and the plane was hauled back to Denver and Gardner got a new engine put in at no cost to him.

Several years later after we moved away from Leadville to Utah, Gardner and Amy flew that same little orange and yellow Piper Cruiser with the oversized wings, clear to Blanding, Utah, to return some pint fruit jars they said. We took them out to Comb Ridge where I was quarrying stone and Gardner laid down on one slab of protruding sandstone and looked straight down about a thousand feet or so to the bottom of the canyon and he laid there for an hour or more just looking. After a time, he got up and said that in all his years of flying this was the first time that he could ever lay down and enjoy the scenery without one hand on the throttle and the other on the control stick.

This part of the story is about two of Gardner and Amy's kids. Gardner and Amy had taken the plane back east to visit relatives and the kids were left at home. They were old enough to take care of themselves and the family had just bought a new International four wheel drive Scout and the two of them decided to take it out for a spin in the country. Down out of Leadville, across the Arkansas River, around the Fish Hatchery loop and up the hi-line road that goes up over to the Hagerman Pass road just a few hundred feet away. Going up the road was no problem to speak of, but on the side hill, the new Scout slid down off the road and it almost rolled over. They were much like their dad and started walking back down to the Hatchery in low shoes with no jackets. There was snow, slush and mud ankle deep and it was four miles to the nearest phone. They called us for help and we loaded up clothes and food for them and we took shovels and axes and picks and a five foot timber saw, chain saw, chains and cables and all else we might need and started out. The people at the Hatchery laughed at us in the old 1950 two wheel drive Chevy Suburban. We were going to rescue a four wheel drive in that old thing? We did and you know it wasn't easy, didn't figure it to be. With my three boys and Gardner's two and incidentally one of those kids was a girl. We went around by Turquoise Lake and up the abandoned Colorado Midland Railroad bed that was now a road, up through the mud and snow within seeing distance of the new Scout that had less than a thousand miles on it. Those two kids were so scared, and their parents were somewhere in the air traveling back east.

We shoveled and chopped ice and frozen snow, we cut big blocks of frozen snow with the timber saw and slid them over the bank. I rammed into the snow on the road and the crew shoveled it out of the trench. It was getting late and getting cold but we stayed warm and by then all of us were wet with snow and sweat, but we were only about fifteen feet from the Scout. We dug out the front of the Scout, made a trench up to the road and piled all the snow we could move on the lower side of the Scout so it couldn't roll over. My son, Gus, fired up the Scout and hung out the open door on the upper side while the other four kids hung on the door on the upper side and we gave a little jerk on the chain and then did it again and again until the old Chevy began to move backward. We chopped a trench in the frozen mud for the upper wheels and jerked some more. Gus had to be very careful that he didn't slip the wheels and slide farther down and finish rolling the Scout. Jerk and dig and chop mud and jerk some more and I was moving back and Gus was chewing his way up onto the road and he was slinging mud and snow ten feet behind him, finally out it came. Everybody was screaming and jumping up and down and shouting until they were hoarse. There wasn't a mark on the Scout except for the mud and snow.

We loaded up and came down off the mountain, each to our own homes, wet, tired and muddy, but well pleased things turned out as well as they did. It could have been so easy to have rolled that Scout, but we didn't. Later that evening that same Scout showed up in our yard with two now clean and warm kids with two gallons of ice cream and all sorts of cookies and their no-ending gratitude. Were we well paid for that rescue job? Yes, we thought we were and we know that old saying is true, "What goes around comes around." or better yet, "Do unto others."

THE LAST WHISKEY STILL
IN LAKE COUNTY

It was a raid! Two Federal Officers from A.T.&F. knocked on the door of the Earl Shane residence, introduced themselves, produced a warrant and then the party started. One George Demengue had made a complaint that Earl was running a whiskey still and the booze poisoned him. George drank some of it, got sick, went to the hospital, the local law was notified and they called in the Feds. After all, this was big news-- BIG NEWS in the small city of Leadville, Colorado, the highest incorporated city in the United States, ten thousand feet above sea level.

Leadville is a mining town with a fantastic history, surviving in the later years on the Climax Molybdenum Mine which was on the top of Fremont Pass and was fifteen hundred feet further up than Leadville, on the north end of the Mosquito Mountain Range. Leadville is cold country and mining country and miners are known to consume a great amount of alcohol. Now that's not to say all miners are drunks, but if you have ever dug for old bottles, mining camps beat all for quantity of old liquor bottles found.

George and Earl both were drinkers, in fact a lot of us on the stope crew made good use of alcohol. Earl paid me to haul him to the mine and back and he would buy us both a quart of beer at the Trading Post after we got off shift. A cold beer sure relieves a powder headache, which is similar to a migraine head ache, but is caused by the nitroglycerin in the explosive that miners use. Earl was one of the best mining partners ever, and we made a good pair for getting the most footage in the least amount of time. We worked together as partners for several years underground. After swing shift we almost always stopped in at the Scarlet Inn for a couple of draft beers and a visit with the owner who used to be on the track crew at the mine.

Earl bought a Polaris snowmobile and had me weld roof bolt rods down the skis to make it handle better in the snow. I did, but that didn't keep him from ending up in a shallow snow covered mine shaft. Come to think about it, it didn't keep him from hitting that pine tree either, but there was a quart of beer blocking his view when that happened, and he was more concerned about the broken bottle than he was with the snowmobile. As I repaired the machine, he still had a bottle of beer in his face.

The reason that Earl had left Illinois and came to Colorado was because of a little too much beer and a little mishap with a local law officer. There were hard feelings between them and one night Earl seeing the officer's patrol car rammed it with his Scout. That felt so good that he did it again and then again and then again! Earl went up before the Judge, who was a pretty good, understanding fellow who liked Earl and his wife but this time the Judge explained to Earl, was the last straw. He gave Earl twenty four hours to get out of the state, or he could figure on looking at the sun through iron bars for several years. So back there in Illinois Earl told the judge that he didn't think that he needed the full twenty four hours, and he didn't, he was gone. Oh, Earl still had a driver's license, but he was safer riding with me.

So what was a beer drinker doing with a still? It was just one of those things. Earl was recovering from a badly broken leg and had too much time on his hands. He needed something to do and of course, he might have had some outside encouragement.

Earl was my partner when he had the accident. It was day shift and we were lowering hoses and machines out of our stope, as we had finished developing it. We were lowering our equipment down the forty five degree angle slope to another one at a right angle and then down another one, just as steep, made of concrete, to the slusher drift. The muddy coiled air hoses, stopper, jack-leg and a ten horse slusher began to roll end over end landing on its side in the wet muck in the drift. I then heard Earl yell that he thought it was broke and I yelled back, "I think you're right, it sure looks broke. Next time you should tie a rope on it." "NO...Not the slusher, it's my leg that's broke!" he said. Even with a full wet suit on over coveralls and long handles, it was broken, badly broken.

Rounding up help from the neighboring stope, I took off leaving him hanging on the muddy rope in the mud and water, twenty feet up the slope on the cold slick concrete. I climbed down to the haulage drift and called the One Switch Dispatcher for a trammer. The dispatcher called the guard shack and the infirmary and in just a few minutes, we had Earl tied down in basket, and lowered him down to the slusher drift. By then, he was in a lot of pain from loading and moving him. A thirty ton trammer stopped under the draw-hole and we lowered Earl down on the back of it. Two of us laid down with a leg and an arm under the basket and tried to hold it from bouncing around. With the main line open for the emergency, the trammer was going as fast as it could and all three of us on the back took a beating, but it was Earl that was suffering the most.

Half a mile to the surface and we loaded him into a guard's vehicle and up the hill to the infirmary. We got him inside and his wet suit off and on to the table. Helping the nurses, we skinned him like a rabbit. With his boots cut off, and his leg now on display, it didn't look too bad but the x-ray showed a three inch section of bone broken loose. They decided to send Earl to Denver. The mine safety man hauled him close to a hundred miles with his body firmly secured but left the broken leg loose and it moved around, grinding chips and slivers off the bone ends.

Earl returned home to Leadville, he ended up on his back in a bed in his living room for several weeks. When he was able to move around some and sit up, his wife complained that he made a grab for her every time she went by him, so she most likely suggested that he needed to hobble out to the garage and find something to do. So, something to do became a whiskey still and when George came for a visit, he drank too much of that one hundred fifty proof White Lightning and got sick. That's what led up to the local law and then the Feds being called in from Denver. The still was cold, there was no mash cooking. All they found was a hard rock miner with a big cast on his leg, but because they had to make the two hundred mile drive, and all the fuss about it, they told Earl that they had to fine him and destroy the still.

This was about the greatest thing to hit the town since the Tenth Mountain Division Ski Troops had to pull out of Camp Hale more than thirty years ago. The Rocky Mountain News and the local paper made a big story out of it. All of Lake County and the surrounding towns, from Climax to Salida clear to Denver and beyond, talked about it for a long time.

What about Earl? Well, he was fined all of fifty dollars and agreed not to make any more boot-leg booze and went back to drinking beer which was his preference anyway...and he didn't have to buy much of it himself for a long time afterwards as his friends at the Scarlet Inn wouldn't let him pay for anything. So when Earl got too frisky at home, his wife most likely told him to find something to do, like to go down to the Scarlet Inn and have a few beers. Which I'm sure he gladly did.

STORIES ON THE
ALCAN HIGHWAY

My Uncle, Leo Bellm, worked on the lead gang of the surveying crew for the Alcan Highway, all the way through Canada to Alaska, and here are some of the stories that he told about that time.

The first one that comes to mind is about the guys on the crew stealing sweets from the cook shack. The cook baked rolls and cookies and cakes in his tin sheepherder's oven on top of the wood stove at times when he wasn't cooking meals. It was hard to have an excess of sweets and they were rationed out, one piece at a time.

This crew worked seven days a week surveying the road that was being built to bring military supplies to Alaska to protect this country from a Japanese attack. It was a hard cold wet job most of the time and the crew was always sweet hungry, even with the usual three pound bucket of jelly that was on the tables--they were still sweet hungry. "Yust like der Sveeds, dey had to have der yams and yellies and sveets."

Most likely each tent had a coffee pot and it's sure nice to have something sweet with the coffee. So the thievery began, but NOBODY messes with the cook, nobody! He is really the boss of the camp, take my word for it, "Don't try it!" The cook decided that he was going to put a stop to the midnight thievery so one night he slipped up to the kitchen tent with a flashlight and waited until he heard the thief making noise--stealing his 'goodies' and he flipped on his light and yelled, "HA!! I GOTCHA!! OOOOH, My GOSH!!!" There pinned in the light was a big bear. The bear backed up into the hot wood stove, he let out a roar and swung around slapping the stove and hit the stove pipe and the pots and pans hanging close by and then turned around and charged the light in the cook's hand. The cook dropped the light and ran away from the tent screaming. The bear charged into the partition separating the cooking area from the tables and benches in the dining area. The partition was a series of shelves containing the dishes, utensils and supplies (it was also where the cookies and cakes were set aside for the next day). The bear, with his burned behind and terrified by the noise from the falling stove pipe and pots and pans and the screaming cook, charged straight ahead through the end of the cook tent, tearing it down. Still scared and mad, the bear charged right down through the line of tents where the crew lived and slept. Tents were flattened and clothes and possessions were scattered. The entire camp was laid flat. There were a few minor injuries, nothing too serious, but they had to sort out their things and set the camp back up the best they could. What a terrible mess over a few sweets. He was a good natured cook and scared of bears, but he still made an agreement to try to have more sweets and no more late night raids.

My Uncle Leo said that few of the animals up there had ever even seen a man and many of them were curious and some became a nuisance that had to be contended with. He said that he made a hook out of a wire, used a lid off a can for a spinner and could catch enough fish for the whole crew.

When the first trucks began coming through over the rough terrain and broke down, they were pushed off the road and used for parts. Sometimes the men would pull out the inner tubes and make beanies to kill grouse.

There were landing strips of a sort about every twenty miles or a lake close enough to land float planes on and the planes brought in most of the supplies and the mail. These small float planes were also used to hunt moose for camp meat. They would locate the moose and use the plane to herd it into the water where it was easier to shoot. It would then be towed to the bank to be butchered and flown to the camps. One time a plane with a load of meat couldn't get off the water so they unloaded part of the load and still couldn't get air born so on closer inspection they found the pontoons both had punctures in them, which was not unusual. They drained the tanks and patched the holes and went back to hauling meat. In one area the road building cats cut into a frozen bank and found a frozen Mammoth and the flesh was in such good condition that they cut pieces off of it and actually cooked it and ate it.

Kerosene oil, pine tar, bear and goose grease and hard liquor were just part of the things used for medicine. If a man had a bad tooth, it was pulled with a pair of pliers while someone held him down and it is rumored that they didn't always get the right tooth the first try. A serious injury or sickness was flown out to the nearest Canadian town. So you had to be a real tough man or you didn't make it on that job.

My Uncle Leo stayed with the lead crew to the end and came home with ten thousand dollars for about a year's work and that was when the average man made less than one thousand dollars a year. It didn't take him long to go through it. He drank a lot of it up but he earned it the hard way and it was his to spend. He never stopped talking about Canada, Alaska and the Alcan Highway and I was one of his captive audiences any and every time he spoke about it. He has been dead and gone for many years, but his once-in-a-lifetime stories live on in a few of us.

CRAIG POINT

Big Jim Kaywood was supposed to have killed off the last of the little grey wolves in the Colorado Rockies, just when, I can't really say, but there were wolves on Hoosier Mountain. Hoosier Mountain was next to Basalt Mountain where we were logging for Ranch Haven Industries. Just ask my wife, Freda, they sure spooked her one late fall night just at the bottom of the eighteen percent grade access road, as we called it, that topped out on Basalt Mountain. I knew them to be little grey wolves and harmless unless cornered, but with my wife sitting in a truck with a baby in a basket in the dark and hearing the wolves howling nearby on Mount Hoosier, she was terrified.

She had forgotten to fill the fuel tank on the old truck and had a full fifty five gallon drum of gas in the back and a load of hay for the skid horses. The truck was a 1940 Army Surplus weapons carrier with a Chevy cab welded on the front. Hearing the wolves she wasn't about to get out of the truck especially with the baby.

It was long after dark and I realized that something was wrong, she should have been back at least by dark. So I strapped on my Colt Woodsman and walked about three quarters of a mile across the mountain and down the steep road through the lava slide and there she was. She left our young daughter in her basket in the front seat and while I held the fifty five gallon drum above the gas spout she removed the cap and we managed to get enough gas in the tank to get back up to camp. She somehow got the plug back in and I got the drum set back up on the tail gate. Now this might be hard to believe that anyone could do that, but you just ask my wife, she doesn't lie or exaggerate.

At this same time Big Jim Kaywood's wife was camp cook and that's how we knew about him killing off the wolves. She also told us about her son's accident sliding off the road on Norwood Hill. That doesn't sound so bad, but he was found down over the bank dead the next day. Norwood Hill was on the west side of the San Miguel River and it had two right angle curves at the top and the bottom where it crossed the river. It was extremely steep and always icy in the winter.

It was about 1958-1959 that I logged across the valley in that same area called Craig's Point. I did it all myself—cut the trees, skidded and hauled the logs. I had a Mac 10 thirty six inch chain saw and a 1935 Caterpillar tractor with a little six cylinder engine in it. Now don't laugh—with a Chevy four speed and the old Cat five speed it was almost impossible to stop. This was gasoline powered and had two

335

foot feeds, one on each side and a buckeye blade on the front. The blade was hoisted by a cut-down model A Ford rear end hooked to the PTO on the rear end. It was just my kind of machine, heavy, well, I guess so, the Empson Brothers hauled it up that winding mountain road with an old army 6x6 and it was a load!!

Some logging had been done there fifty years before and there was even an old saw pit there that dated back into the 1800's. Freda and I and our four small children set up camp up there in a pole building covered with number fifteen black felt tar paper. We had a place to sleep and cook and running water a mile away. We were right on the edge of Craig's Point and we could see Norwood Hill and the San Miguel River far below us, what a view!

I was cutting and skidding logs when the timing gear went out of our car. I tore the car down and carried the cam shaft down the mountain and caught a ride to the sawmill at Placerville. I had to carry the whole cam shaft because I couldn't get the gear off with the tools I had, so we found another cam shaft with a gear on it in the junk yard and I got a ride back to the bottom of the hill and I climbed back up the mountain and put it back together. Freda pulled me with the 35 Cat and I finally got the car started.

The logs were piling up and the Empson brothers wouldn't pay me until the logs were in the mill yard at Placerville and they were deliberately not hauling them so they wouldn't have to pay me. I went ahead and hired my own log hauler from Montrose by the name of Ed Whistle. After loading the truck, I had to pull him up the steep places with the Cat, and we began moving the saw logs to the mill down off the mountain and up the river. The Empsons paid the trucker but still stalled paying me. The wind was blowing in gusts and I was laying the trees down like match sticks until the wind stopped and set the tree back on the bar of the saw. Freda had been watching and she's one in a million, and here she came on the old 35 Cat. This was not long after she had rolled the D4 Cat and I was still having bad dreams about that incident. I took the Cat and charged up to that big Engelman tree that had my saw pinned intending to push it over, but the pin came out of the main clutch and I could not disengage it so I cut the tree right off with the blade and the tree started falling right back over me and the cat so I left it in a hurry. I must have been at least a hundred feet away when the tree fell back across the radiator and the fuel tank and then I had to climb up on the tree and cut it up to get it off the tractor. About that time I got to thinking, "I'm tired of not taking care of my family as I should and the Empson boys still refuse to pay me." So we drove down off the mountain with all our possessions and left them at our house in Placerville. I went out to the sawmill and backed all four of the Empson boys in a corner of the store and told them I wanted my money, and only old blind Charley would stand up to me. He said, "Well, you can whip me if you want to, Harvey." but I said, "No, Charley, I just want my money!" And Charley replied, "But we never had to pay any other loggers before." "Well, I know, you starved them all out, but not me!" The end result was that I got my money, but they got the last word in. "Well, Harvey, if we get another good tract of timber close by, would you please come and cut timber for us again?" So I went to work in the Uranium mines on the Colorado Plateau. Like my old German friend said, "Too soon olt and too late schmart." And that goes for working in the Uranium mine, too.

At the bottom of the hill on our side was the old Empson spread, the parents of the four boys that I was cutting timber for. Lydia, their mother, reminded you of Ma Yoakum in Lil' Abner and Ed, the father, was somewhat like Jed on Beverly Hillbillies. When Lydia was a young woman she hauled logs off that mountain on a wagon frame with four horses. We all became good friends although the boys were something else at times. I used to read the Bible to Charlie the oldest of the boys, because he was born with the equivalent of two pupils in each eye. His eyes couldn't distinguish valleys from flat surfaces, it all looked the same to him. But despite this problem, he taught me how to run a big metal machine lathe to cut parts for the tractor. He was the best of the boys.

Lydia, the mother, when she was in her eighties, used to drive a small Farm All Cub tractor with a small trailer on behind some three or four miles to the highway at the bottom of Norwood hill. She would wait there and hitch a ride to Montrose eighty miles away, summer and winter to buy supplies for her and her husband, Charlie. She was there in the rain, snow, cold and heat, but she was well known and so usually didn't have much trouble catching rides. Even we took our turn hauling her home a time or two when we lived in the Placerville area which was twenty miles up the San Miguel River from her place. Sometimes it was late at night after we had been to a meeting in Montrose. As it got colder she would just add more layers of clothing. She was a lady and always wore long skirts so she added more skirts, more scarves and more head coverings and big oversized men's overshoes with several pairs of socks.

Late one night we picked her up after a meeting and loaded her, my wife, our four kids, her groceries and our's and started home in our 1941 Chevy four door. We were on Dallas Divide and the transmission wouldn't shift into high gear so I had to drive thirty five miles an hour clear to her ranch. I dropped my wife and kids at the house in Placerville and then drove Lydia all the way to her house. I'd guess it was twenty five miles from Placerville and by then it was about 1:30 a.m. and I had to leave the house at Placerville to go to work that day and that was a three hour drive. Getting her unloaded at the house she asked "Coffee?" "You bet, I sure need some!" She made me one cup and she poured it through a tea strainer. It looked like molasses! She told me that the two of them used a pound and a half of coffee a week and they only drank one cup each in the morning! I drove back home and went to bed and lay there with my eyes wide open. "OH, Well, I have to get up in and hour or so I might as well just get up and go, I'm not going to get any sleep!" I might add that I was working eight to twelve hours a day cutting logs and living in the back of a flat bed pickup with a tent top.

MY GIRL FRIEND

She was just another one of my special girl friends—one of the real western ladies and a Lady she was. She wasn't a hundred pounds wringing wet and always wore Levis and sneakers with a somewhat mannish hair cut under a baseball cap.

Her name was Virginia Hinderlighter and she was probably in her seventies when I met her. She lived on a ranch on the Frying Pan River on a side creek just five miles from Basalt, Colorado. It was a nice place just off the road with a metal homesteader's entrance with the big letters "Hinderlighter" in the center.

I was inquiring about some flagstone and I heard she had some on her place. It was on a bench way up above her place, actually right under the Public Service electric highline.

She really impressed me the first time we met. She was nice looking, clean and neat and orderly for a ranch gal. We talked back and forth for a while and then she asked me to go out to a large shed with her and she began cutting up an old piece of equipment with a hacksaw. I looked around and noticed that she had a cutting torch set up and asked her why she didn't use that and she said that it was too messy, so I volunteered to help her with the hacksaw and she looked me straight in the eye (she was just about as tall as me and I could have picked her up with one hand) and handed me the hacksaw to see how well that I could use it. She watched me make a cut and then she would make a cut and back and forth we went until we had it done. Cutting pipe freehand with no vice is very difficult and it's easy to break the blade, but I broke no blade and she broke no blade. I guessed that it was a test and I passed her test. We jigged the cut pieces on the concrete floor and she set up the two hundred amp AC Lincoln welder and set the hood on her head and I said, "I'd be glad to do that for you, Virginia." We were to first names by then and she just gave me a little smile and told me to watch my eyes and she struck an ark. I was just the helper, you know, so I helped her turn the project over and handed her rods until she said, "That's enough!! Let's go to the house."

I guess that she figured that I was okay and so she would let me quarry stone on her property and asked me to be there early the next morning. "I will be here when it gets light," I told her. I was there about four thirty a.m. the next morning drinking coffee in her kitchen, Hinderlighter coffee I came to call it. She made one pot in the morning and then drank it all day long hot, warm or cold however it came out of the pot. Well, it wasn't the coffee, it was the company. She was so interesting to talk to. One of the "Real People."

Then she took me up to the quarry, such as it was. She wanted fifty dollars a ton and she would weigh it on her bathroom scales, but I needed about eight tons so I told her that I knew a better way to figure the tonnage that was a lot easier. If it's stacked tightly and measured by the cubic feet, a ton is about four by five by one foot, give or take a few pounds. "Do you trust me?" There was that straight forward look right in my eyes and then she said, "Yes, I believe I do!" So we went back to ranch house and she took out a cold hot dog from the refrigerator and placed it on a bun along with some mustard and she asked me if I was hungry. "Well, not just now!" I answered. "Thanks, anyhow."

I took my Chinook back up to the quarry and started working out the stone that I wanted. Soon I had the boys down from Aspen to start hauling it. We had her check the measurements and she watched those boys like a hawk. She agreed to the measurements and the boys headed for Aspen with the first load. I stayed and drank more of that coffee. It kind of grew on me, after a while that is. We really became friends, more like family, really. It's nice to have a relationship like that especially in this generation.

She was such an interesting and capable lady. She ran her ranch all by herself and did her own branding and dehorning and all else that it takes to raise a small herd of whiteface cows. She went out and cut her own fire wood to burn and her corral poles using a chain saw. She cut her own hay and baled and stacked it in the barn and then did all the feeding in the winter.

As we became better friends, she showed me most of her house. She slept on a cot and once I saw it when it wasn't made up and I noticed that she slept between blankets and in the winter, I imagine that she slept in her long johns. I saw some hay in that bed but that was in haying season and I imagine that she was too tired when she was haying to worry about a little hay on her. Now, I don't say that she was dirty, she wasn't and she always smelled nice, like clean hay or sometimes vanilla or even medicinal and her house was clean and in good order.

She was something of an artist and had wood carvings of horses. One that I remember was a stallion rearing and it was a beautiful piece of work. I remember seeing rabbits and hand carved picture frames. She had tried her hand at painting and did some silhouettes out of copper made from flattened copper pipe. it all showed a lot of talent. She had pictures of old friends and family and lots of books, some

French and German and others. She never spoke of her past and I could feel her reluctance and aloofness and never pressed her about it.

With most people I have become friends with, I bang on their door and if it's unlocked, I open it up and yell to them and walk right in and I expect my friends to do the same at my house. I happen to catch her in the bath tub once, but of course the door was closed and it didn't bother her. She just yelled for me to check the coffee and help myself. It didn't embarrass either one of us and that's the way that it should be.

Well I quarried and hauled flagstone over several weeks, working by myself mostly. Then one day I came by her place and she was backing up a flat bed trailer full of baled hay along a baling string line to an electric conveyer. She would follow the string line with the tractor tire until she hit the log stop. Then plug in the conveyer and load the bales until the conveyer was full. Then shut it off and climb up to the loft in the barn and stack the bales six to eight feet high all by her self. Then she would go back down and fill the conveyer again and so on until she had it all unloaded and in the loft. Well, I was my own boss sort of, so I just HAD to offer her a hand and she really seem to appreciate it. Later I volunteered the two boys hauling stone for me to help her and after we were through and sitting over a cup of her famous coffee she said to me, "Those boys sure don't know much about handling hay, do they?"

I got the stone all quarried and hauled and went back to my regular work in Aspen and then I got loaned out to another Aspen millionaire to do some cleanup on a river bottom. About that time I caught my left arm in a piece of equipment after dark and really tore a chunk out of my arm. I could see both bones and a big blood vessel and had to go to the hospital. I ended up having a skin graft, but maybe that's another story better left for another time.

I ended up driving drift in the John Wayne Tunnel after that and was so busy that I hadn't been able to take any time to go see Virginia. One day I had to go to Basalt to the hardware store to get hinges for the new powder magazine and I'd be going close enough and it was late in the day so I picked up some doughnuts and went out to see Virginia.

When I got there she didn't seem to be at the house and so I called and she was up on the hill and said for me to wait right there. She came running to the house and put her arms around me and gave me a hug and I will have to tell you, honestly, and with great respect, her breast felt like two steel points against my chest, it took me by surprise. Anyhow, she was done for the day and we just sat down together and had doughnuts with her famous

Hinderlighter coffee and had a good visit. She wanted to know all about Freda and the job and how my arm was and what was going on and time got away and so she said would I please stay and eat supper with her, so I said. "Okay!" "Do you like venison?" she asked me. I'd been raised on it most of my life so that was just fine with me. Then she put on her overshoes and went over to trap door there in the kitchen floor to the cellar. I wondered why the overshoes. She explained to me that there were several inches of water in the cellar. Up she came with some potatoes and began cooking supper. The potatoes were cooked in the micro wave and she greased the skillet with butter and seared the inch thick buckskin steaks in the hot skillet and turned them a couple of times. Then she put them on the plate with two halves of potato with much fanfare and dinner was served. If it was cow, it would have gone moo, but I can't remember what a deer steak would say. Beautiful steaks seared to perfection on the out side, but inside all they needed was a little resuscitation.

It really was getting late and I didn't want the neighbors to get the wrong idea, besides I hadn't locked the door on the explosives at the mine so I excused myself and went back to Aspen. Sorry to say that was the last time I saw Virginia. Both my wife and I had a lot of love and respect for Virginia and we regret that we did not get to spend more time with her.

In some of my conversations with Virginia, she had confided in me that when she ever got to the point when she could no longer care for herself that she would not become a burden on anyone and she didn't seem to have any close relatives and not too many close friends. I just didn't pay enough attention. My job at that time took me to Arizona in the winter and then back to Aspen in the summer. So the next summer when I came back to Colorado, I finally took the time to drive up to the Hinderlighter ranch and something was very much wrong. Things were missing, there were no cattle and the house was cold and my friend was not there nor had she been there for some time. I drove back to Basalt and went to the police to check on her and they didn't want to talk to me. I drove up to Thomasville to talk to some friends up there and they gave me a funny look and told me a sad story. Sometime that winter, Virginia called the law and told them to come and get her because she was killing herself. I guess that's just what she did.

Makes us wonder if we could have done more for her. We will never forget her. I can still see her and hear her voice, "Come in and have some coffee, Harvey!"

CHET ROACH THE OLD STINKER
AND HIS BLACK AND WHITE TRUCKS

Chet was an old stinker and a first class one, for sure. He had a small fleet of tank trucks in Montezuma Creek, Utah, in the Anneth Oil Field, also known as the "Oil Patch". They were painted solid black with white skunk stripes the length of the tanks. Granted, he was a truck driver and he bragged that he could truck from the west coast to Kansas City and never have to stop at a Port of Entry. I'm sure he could, and did, until it got too hot for him. With his wife's money he bought a used White Auto car and began hauling crude oil and salt water from and around the Oil Patch. He was one of those few that were never happy with anybody or anything, not even his wife.

My wife used to visit with Chet's wife and that's how I became acquainted with him. I ended up through devious and uncertain circumstances driving his big green ten-wheeler tank truck up to a Texaco pipe line. Chet followed in his pickup and I helped him hook up and bleed air and salt water from a low spot in the line and after having several drinks with him back at his trailer in Montezuma Creek, I agreed to help him out just to fill in till he could locate his drunk Navajo driver and get him back on the job. With the Navajo it was a case of when I'm out of money and whisky, then I need to work, I will work until I have money again and not work again until it is all gone.

So that next Monday morning I was down in Montezuma Creek at six thirty a.m. ready to give him a hand. They offered me breakfast and coffee, which I refused. They seemed to be a really nice friendly couple. I took a truck right back up to Texaco to a low spot in the line and Chet left me to the job. About six hours later, he showed up with a big sandwich, an apple and a quart jar of Vodka and orange juice. Nice people, those folks. He still hadn't located his driver, so he left me working and drove back to the Creek. Later he came back over the hill and said to unhook the hose and come on in. I have to admit that I did like that big old tank truck and it was something new to me and a lot easier than working in the quarries digging, cutting and hauling stone, moving five to ten tons of stone a day. I parked the truck and they invited me in. They had another big mixed drink and a big sandwich waiting for me. Ham and cheese with lettuce, pickles and lots of mayonnaise. Those were the nicest folks!

It was twenty five miles back home to Blanding, and then the same twenty five miles back to work at the Creek. I was out hooking up to the pipe line at daylight which was five a.m. in the morning. Oh, did I forget to say that the day before when he came back to see me the second time, that I had been hooked up to that pipe line for at least twelve hours? Chet came by about noon that day with Vodka and tomato juice and another sandwich, not as nice as the one the night before. It looked like he had made the drink and the sandwich himself this time. He began contacting me about every two or three hours on the C.B. radio and everything was going smooth so he never came back again that day. About eight p.m. that evening, I got a call from Chet and I told him everything was going just fine so he told me to come on in. Well, that night after a couple of drinks, I excused myself and drove home so I could be back and hooked up at Texaco by five a.m. that next morning. I decided that twenty seven hours at five dollars an hour was a lot more than I was making in the stone quarrying business at the time, and much, much easier.

I always believed that days were just twenty four hours long until I took that job. Most of the days were ten to fourteen hours long with no days off. One of those twenty four hour days extended up to a thirty six hour day and twenty four hour days were not unusual. I would get a few hours sleep and then I would be right back on the job. Oh, there were still lots of Vodka drinks and occasionally he'd hand me a fifty dollar bill on the side, but no overtime pay, just straight wages and push, push, push!

The Navajo driver was back and he was driving the Auto Car and I had a 1950 B18 Oilfield built Mac with an eighty barrel tank and a worn out small Cummings engine in it. I had to carry at least two extra gallons of fifty/fifty motor oil and STP at all times. It took most of a quarter of a mile just to be able to slow it down to make a stop. I couldn't always stop. I spent more time shifting up and down than I did driving. And smoke? It smoked so bad that when I passed people walking on the road, they just disappeared. I liked that old solid welded piece of junk. I could relate to it, just like an old skid horse.

I ended up working for Chet five years or so and never could get the time off to go get me another chauffeur's license but I was lucky, I was never checked in all that time. Days and days, and long hours and not even a decent shop to work in and Chet was buying more trucks and hiring more drivers. I was keeping up the trucks and driving the bad dirt roads with the Mac, still working ten to twelve hours a day with few days off. I got old Chet back, though, and a good laugh at the same time.

Here's what happened after a very long day in December after eight p.m. at night. Chet came in the shop with his wife's Pontiac and told me he had a small hole in the gas tank and that he and his wife had to be in Denver early Monday morning. He asked me to repair it that night. He had run over a rod and it punched a hole in the tank. He had it repaired in Cortez but it still leaked, so he told the mechanic there that he would take it back to his own shop and have me repair it. There was really nothing to do the job with but my propane torch. I had to lay on the cold concrete and jack the car up, disconnect wires and hoses and the two tank hangers then drop it out. I finished emptying the gas out and then stood it on end in the little cold bathroom because that was the only place I had to fill it with water. So, I filled it with water to the leak and plugged the filler hose with wet greasy rags and I began soldering clean pennies over the other patch job. It was a good patch and didn't seem to leak so I put just a little more solder on it just to make sure. It was almost ten p.m. by then and I was cold and hungry and mighty tired. The patch was almost done, but (I hate those "buts" and this was the biggest "but" that ever happened to me, back then, anyway) what I didn't know was that my rag plug in the filler was leaking (just a little, mind you) but enough to create a small gassy air pocket under my "real good patch job" and with no water up against the solder, I had burned a very small hole through the melted metal. I saw it happen, and pulled the flame away but it was too late! That hole began to suck in air, and the pressure of the burning gas fumes began forcing the water out of the tank.

The tank began to expand and was blowing up just like a balloon (a tin balloon), crackling and popping and the hissing kept getting louder and louder. Then the rag plug in the filler blew out as the tank expanded to its limit. I was pinned between the toilet and the wash basin and the wall and the half closed door. I just knew that it was the end for me. I had my hands and arms up over my face, but the tank was pushing against my stomach, there was nothing I could do! Then with a louder hiss and a "whoosh" of sorts, and then a big sigh, it stopped. No explosion, no fire, just deadly silence, except for the pounding of my heart and a big sigh from me. The tank hadn't blown up! Well, I never was a quitter in matters such as this, so I filled the tank again with water and very carefully finished patching the hole. I drained the water out of it and had it setting on the floor behind the car when Freda came in to check on me. She looked at the poor misshapen tank laying there on the floor and said, "What on earth are you going to do now?"

I looked at her and said, "I am wet, and cold and hungry and tired and enough is enough!" I picked up a three foot four by four piece of wood and started beating the tar out of that puffed up tank until it looked like it might fit back under the car. Using a floor jack, I jacked it up where it was supposed to go, and beat around on that tank until it went in place more or less. I had to weld on longer hanger bolts, but I got it up there and when the tank was filled with gas, it did not leak! We Bellms do good work! So they say.

I checked the oil and the tires and cleaned the windshield, and it was ready for the trip to Denver. So the boss man and his wife were off early the next morning and I saw them off, glad to see them go, really. I went back to work in the oil field and put the whole thing out of my mind.

Chet got to Cortez and the car was acting up. A mechanic told him that he needed a new fuel pump and put one on. The car ran good for a hundred miles or so and began acting up again. At another garage they were sold a new carburetor as the fuel pump was new and had just been replaced. Away, they went for another hundred miles or so and had the same problem again. This time they are told that it must be the gas tank as it only seemed to run on the top part of the gas in the tank, but they had to get to Denver, so they got two extra five gallon cans filled with gas so they could keep the top of the tank full and they were on the road again. Then they had battery trouble and had to get a new battery, but before they were through they had a new alternator and a starter put on it. They finally made it to Denver and took care of their business. Then they took the car to have a new gas tank put on it and they found that the stand pipe inside the tank had about two inches broken off and that was why it would only run about a hundred miles, but the tank wasn't leaking!

When they finally got back to Montezuma Creek, we got to hear all about their problems with the car. Chet said, "My land, I never in my life saw such a beat up gas tank!" My wife and I had a hard time keeping our faces straight, but we didn't say a thing. My patch didn't leak and the car ran fine when they left, so we didn't think they needed to know how that tank got so beat up. We just smiled and told them that we were glad things turned alright and they got home alright.

I told that story to many people that knew Chet, and every one of them had a good laugh and said that it served him right. He had it coming and more. Well, he just never changed and I will always remember him as the "Old Stinker" with the skunk-striped oil field trucks. I finally had enough and I quit.

RAY HOKE

Solomon said that he had never seen the faithful begging bread—NEVER. He had begun serving Jehovah as a youth and in all his years Jehovah had never forsaken him. I might add to this Hebrews 6:10, "God is not unjust; he will not forget your work and the love that you have shown him as you have helped his people and continue to help them." Our names need not be mentioned for this story is really about the outworking of Jehovah's Spirit, as you will see.

We were nineteen, my wife and I, new in the Truth, eager, strong, and willing, but we were lacking in many of the qualities that can only be gained by years of association, study and personal prayer to Jehovah. Now, like Solomon, we are old, always tired, and infirm in body and slow in mind at times, but Jehovah has never ceased to provide more than we were in need of spiritually and materially, even when we were forced into a wilderness for a time, so on with the story.

This was in 1951 and we began studying with Jehovah's Witnesses and within about three months we were baptized and going in the service. Then in just a few more months we found ourselves a part of a very small congregation of just four sisters, Healy, Heaton,

Heady, and Mom Hosea, in Minturn, Colorado. No, this is not a funny story, it is the truth. One of the sisters had a young son and I was the only other brother to care for all the male responsibilities. I managed to make do but not without many tactful suggestions from Mom Hosea, who was acting overseer for lack of brothers. It was a healthy, loving congregation, however, but one day a letter came saying we were to have a visit from the Circuit Overseer, a Brother Mickey. Those four sisters would have thrown ashes on their heads if it had been bible times. Brother Mickey had visited there before and their description of him wasn't good, it sounded like he must have been one of those few that Will Rogers had never met. But it turned out to be a different Brother Mickey and the other, older Brother Mickey was assigned to the back hills of some southern state, later to become a District Overseer and much loved in the North West.

We, that is, my pregnant wife and I, agreed to care for Brother Mickey because all the rest refused to keep him. We lived about seven miles from the small railroad town of Minturn. We had a two-room cabin with only a little bathroom, but no tub or shower and our heat was from an old oil stove. Ours was one cabin of several that made up a makeshift motel and so we rented one of cabins next to us for the Circuit Overseer to stay in while he was visiting.

I need to add that we were having one of the worst winters in many years and there was about four feet of snow on the level. Sunday afternoon, late, a big black 1948 Pontiac came to rest in a snow bank near our little 1950 yellow Crosley. It was the Circuit Overseer, Brother Mickey, alright, but he was a nephew of the other Brother Mickey and soon, really within a few minutes, this became the most important incident that ever happened to us both since we were first contacted by Jehovah's Witnesses. This Brother Mickey was young and had his lovely young wife with him. That very theocratic young couple ate every meal with us. We had lots of pinto beans and venison because that's what we had. The rest of the sisters in the congregation helped out with food when they could. The Mickeys never complained about accommodations or food or the fact that we had to carry our little Crosley out to the road through the snow as many as three times a day to get to meetings and out in service.

We went out in the service with them all that week and even did street work in ten degree weather by working minutes at a time and then ten minutes to warm up, but we were giving a witness! The week ended all too soon for us and on the last day Brother Mickey came in and said, "There is something special that I'd really like for you to fix for us to eat." Well, we were running out of things and payday was a ways off so we didn't know how we were going to fix anything special, but we said, "Sure, what do you want?" He said, "Well, we never get just plain bean soup, so would you just add water to those beans and make us bean soup?" That meal was the best one of the entire week for all of us.

We dug out their cold Pontiac with its heavy oil, and got it started. Then we pushed and struggled and of course petitioned Jehovah, until it was out to the highway. Then Brother Mickey said, "We haven't enough gas to make it to the next congregation." All that we had was a jar of change and a lot of that was copper, but it was enough to get them there. "So we will be seeing you at the circuit assembly!" Brother Mickey said in parting, but I said, "No, we might not be able to make it." Then they left and we were sad and yet happy because it had been a wonderful week of theocratic activity.

The following week we got a telephone call from Don Price (the Prices were like parents, spiritual parents, to us) telling us very firmly that we will be in Glenwood Springs by noon Friday or we would all be late getting to the assembly because they would drive up to get us if we couldn't drive there. We got enough gas to make it there, arriving with book bags and little else, we were fed and on our way, Don, his wife, Louise, and their three small black haired girls and us. Three hours later at Grand Junction,

Don took the money they had for their rooms and got us all accommodations in a hotel, but it turned out to be pretty sleazy with blankets on the windows and towels that were cut up pieces of a chenille bedspread. They got their money back and we ended up staying at an elder's house sleeping on the living room floor. The next morning at the Assembly Hall, while Don was getting all of us meal tickets, a brother tapped me on the shoulder and handed me two folded up dollar bills very discreetly. Then like manna from heaven, brothers and sisters both began putting small amounts of money in our pockets or our book bags. Some told us, "The Mickeys were telling us about you two kids, here take this as from Jehovah!" It was evidence to us of Jehovah's spirit acting on our behalf, and how thankful we were. We were able to pay for the last meal for both our families and to pay for a tank of gas to get us back to Glenwood Springs.

The Mickeys went on to serve in other circuits and we lost track of them, but about seventeen years later in a round-about way we heard from them and I'd like to tell you about that. We were living in Leadville, Colorado, then and by that time we had six children. We were at the Sunday meeting and I was the Watchtower reader that day and I saw a longhaired "hippy" looking young man come in late and sit at the back of the Hall. He had a bible and a Billy Graham book in his lap. I talked to him after the meeting and invited him to eat with us. There was always room for one more at our table. He wasn't in very good shape and didn't seem to be able to eat very much, but we got into a bible discussion with him and he felt that he had already been in Hell, and he looked like it too with his long hair and beard and sunken eyes. We witnessed to him until late that evening and he went back into town, but the next morning early he was back and we talked again. Then on the third day he came back but he was clean, hair cut and the beard gone and clothes clean and neat and he told us, "Thank you, I'm on my way to California to see my uncle, he is a witness." It was about seven months later, my wife asked me if I remembered Ray Hoke, and I didn't recognize the name so she told me that he was the hippie that we talked to before, and he wrote us a letter from California. The letter said, "Dear Brother and Sister, thank you again for those three days that I spent with you, they changed my life. I am now a baptized, dedicated brother going into the pioneer ranks. Oh, by the way, Brother and Sister Mickey both send you their Love!"

We are both in our seventies now and our health is not so good, but Jehovah is still blessing us, maybe more so now.

DAVE HASTY

Dave Hasty just after taking this stand for the Truth was threatened by his family, especially his brother who was a lawyer. He said to Dave, "I will take you to court and prove you to be completely crazy!" Dave calmly replied, "That's just fine by me because I will show the court that I am the craziest Jehovah's Witness in all of Wichita, Kansas and I will make sure that they all know you are closely related to me." That was the end of the confrontation.

Dave and his wife, Pauline, were the ones who taught us Truth. We always loved hearing the stories of the things that happened to them in the earlier years, so I wanted to share some of them.

Dave told us that their first few years in the ministry became very interesting as the brothers were carrying the big signs and placards on the main streets that said in bold print: "Religion is a snare and a racket!" He and the other brothers spent much time rolling in the gutters. He looked back and laughed about it.

In the latter forties, at one of the conventions, there were rioters pounding on the doors, and one in particular was screaming to get at the brothers, "Let me at them! Let me at them!" So the brothers at the door opened the door and pulled him in and told him that every one inside was friendly. He could have a seat or he would have to leave and he left, that seemed to quiet the situation outside.

At a convention in Meeker, Colorado, impending mob action threatened the meetings. A select few of the brothers were assigned to guard the rear doors. They all wore red ties and they were cut about half way through in the back. "Why, you ask?" Well, back in Kansas some of the brothers were almost strangled by the mob grabbing their ties. Those were exciting times.

They had so many interesting stories to tell. Dave and his wife knew many of the brothers and sisters that were released from the concentration camps in Germany. They were aware of their need of clothing and personal things. In the door to door work they found an old store that had been closed since 1918 with a lot of the stock still on the shelves and they got permission to clean out all of the old stock (my wife and I helped them do that) there were pants, dresses, shirts, all brand new but all the old styles of that day, button shoes, celluloid collars, anything that could be used by the German brothers and sisters was boxed up and mailed. Can you just imagine them in all those vintage clothes? Men in striped shirts with celluloid collars and dark pants and the women in 1900's dresses with their high button shoes going in service and to the meetings, what a sight! I am sure our God Jehovah smiled.

PART 6
SOUTHEASTERN UTAH

A Gentile In South East Utah

As I recollect, it was in the early 1980's that a Mormon Bishop in Monticello told an old Mexican man, "There are no good Mexicans!" "Yes there are!" was the instant reply by the little dried up old man. "Name just one then!" the haughty Bishop told him. "Poncho Villa!" came back the quick response. "Why, Poncho Villa was nothing more than a Mexican Bandito," said the Bishop. "Just what makes him a good Mexican?" "Well, he ran all the Mormons out of Northern Mexico!" And that was the end of that conversation and the little old Mexican went on to probably hoeing weeds in one of the Mormon's bean fields and the Bishop went back to his Bishop Prick and what ever Mormon bishops do in a Mormon Bishop Prick.

Now, it is a fact of history that that Mexican revolutionary bandito did chase the Mormons and their cattle out of Mexico. Many of them came north and settled in the small border town of Bluff on the north bank of the San Juan River under the red sandstone bluffs. The party that settled in Bluff crossed the Navajo Reservation at Comb Ridge, fording the river and literally fighting an impossible road up the lower end of the ridge and forcing horses and wagons and the cattle up the mountain side to gain access to the east side. From there they had fairly easy traveling to the top of the bluffs above what came to be known as Bluff, Utah.

The biggest problem then encountered was, just how to get the wagons and the cattle back down off the cliffs to the river bottom. The divine inspired conclusion was to rough-lock the wagon wheels by placing a pole through the spokes of both rear wheels and dragging them down the tight little wash in what is now known as Cow Canyon. The wagon wheel trenches are still there, two parallel ruts deep in the sandstone in the bottom of the wash.

After fording the San Juan River, it took two weeks of hard labor to cut out the road up San Juan Hill as they called it. It was at the expense of horses going down on their knees and bloodying their legs on the rocks, and men, women and children pulling and pushing to force the wagons up through the rocks. That wicked road can still be seen on the west side of the ridge just above the river.

The old Mormon pioneer man that showed me this unbelievable trail had tears in his eyes as he again envisioned the agony of man and beast alike going up the mountain. "Divine Inspiration?" hardly, because the settlement of Bluff was only several miles up river from the river crossing. They finally made it and they built large sandstone houses with walls three feet thick and many of them two stories high with outside access to the upper rooms where a, how do I put it? The "Aunt" or "sister-in-law" as they called them, the second wives, lived up stairs. Bluff became the place where the extra wives and their children were kept.

Zane Grey lived in Bluff for a short time and part of his home is still there, but he was not too well accepted as many of his books were about the local area and he described the ways of life of those people at that time. His books were banned until just not too long ago, about the time L'Amour's stories became a big thing.

Bluff became well known in the area for its melon patches, and it was quite common for the melon growers to run the Indians out with shot guns. It is also true that some of the Mormon men began to hunt the old Indian Pottery and at that time it wasn't against the law. There were hundreds of pots found and sold for as little as twenty five cents a pot and they made good money at that. In their search for pots these men found stone quarries, and uranium and vanadium and developed them into profitable businesses.

Bluff had its share of characters and one I must mention here is "Billy." Billy was a real jewel, but he just wasn't quite right. Everyone liked Billy even though he was a little strange. He wore an old straw cowboy hat and a brace of toy cap pistols that looked like the real thing and a toy tin sheriff's badge. He had a habit of pushing an old iron tired wheelbarrow around town and one day one of the guys said to Billy, "You got a license for that wheelbarrow? You have to have a license for it, you know!" "Oh, no! I don't want to go to jail! What am I going to do?" Billy was all upset. So they found one for him and it wired on the wheelbarrow. "See there, I got a license on my wheelbarrow, I don't have to go to jail!" He pushed his wheelbarrow all over town to show everyone that he had a license now.

Billy was really quite harmless and old enough to go in the local beer joint, which only served beer at the time. Oil wells were being drilled in the general area and the bar always had a few of the oil workers hanging out in there. Most of them were of a pretty rough nature and the one in this next incident had just been in a mean fist fight and had shoved a man's head right through the grill on a parked car. Most of those men were tough guys, but this one in particular was sitting on a stool in the bar drinking a beer and looking for trouble, when Billy walked in. This skinny little kid clapped his hand on the driller's big shoulder and said, "You son of a bitch, we have been looking for you!" In the half light of the bar, Billy's tin badge and two cap pistols looked like the real thing and it scared that big mean oil field worker so bad that he jumped off his stool and ran out the door and was never seen again in Bluff. Some said that he never even waited for his pay check, he was that afraid.

Oh, that's not all, Billy was helping out at the Cow Canyon gas station at times and one particular time, he was helping put the new license plates on a lady's car. He was doing a proper job and proud of his work, the rear plate was right in place, bolted on and looking real good, for Billy, that is. Billy then went around to the front to attach the front plate on the bumper. He was almost through and the station owner walked up and looked over Billy's shoulder and said, "Well, Billy, you did a real nice job on the rear license plate but you have put this one on upside down!" Billy thought about a while and then looked him in the eye and said, "Well, you son of a bitch, it's NEW!" That was Billy's kind of logic.

Well, enough at this time. The twelve years we spent in the four corners area were enjoyable and quite entertaining, too.

BLUFF UTAH AND THE GOLD

Just a few miles up the San Juan River from Bluff is Recapture Creek where Cortez was believed to have recaptured Chief Montezuma, and there certainly are many stories, both factual to an extent and some that are only conjectures. Now, I have heard many stories about Montezuma and his gold and have even looked into the facts that were available at the time.

Kanab, Utah, has its share of stories with one telling of gold sunk in a mysterious underwater cave in one of the local water reservoirs and another about gold stashed in a sandstone cave in the mountains east of Kanab. That cave is there and my family and I checked it out, mostly out of curiosity. The cave is up on the side of a sandstone cliff. We went all through it except for a hand made shaft that was too deep and we didn't have any ropes with us. When we were entering one of the natural caves, we found hundreds of thousands of daddy long leg spiders swarming on the roof of the cave. It looked like they were several inches thick and when we shined a light on them they began to drop to the floor of the cave. We kept the light directed on the sandy spider covered floor and we ducked down and ran under the swarming mass above us. We quickly checked out the back of the cave and then back out. Once was more than enough of that for all of us. There was evidence of a great amount of time and effort spent in digging through the caves in the surrounding cliffs. Well, then again, those people spent unbelievable time and effort in endeavors that are hard for me to understand.

So, now, back to Montezuma Creek and some first hand stories with a measure of truth. On the side of the canyon wall near the entrance of Recapture Creek, there are engraved images of animals with packs on their backs, many of them in a string and all pointed in one direction, into the canyon. Dorey bars (bars of mixed melted metals) have been found in several places on the canyon floor and it is not certain just how they came to be there. All of this area is subject to severe flash floods, so who can say?

Several of the older residents of the area have told of an old white man bringing in pieces of or at least parts of Dorey bars and trading them for groceries at the local stores. Some of these same old timers told me that two cowboys found enough of these to start their own ranch. This was at a time when the Scorp Summerville Cattle Company controlled all the grazing rights from Moab on the Colorado River to the San Juan River to the south. All of this country is referred to as the "Oil Patch" which comprises most of the Four Corners area and is known to most as the Anneth Oil Field.

So now we look down river from Bluff to the mouth of Comb Ridge and right down in the river bottom of the San Juan. A Navajo family was moving a fence to enlarge their corn field and found a cash of placer gold in a container under a post in the old fence line. There was said to be several such "withdrawals" from post-hole banks in that old fence line. That is altogether possible, because just across the river on the Navajo Reservation, gold is still found in the mouth of the wash.

While talking to one Navajo man about it, he said, "Oh, Yes, that is where they find the little pieces, (and he rubbed his thumb and forefinger together as if he had a grain of rice or wheat between them) many of them!" He did not seem too eager to tell me of the exact location, but indicated that it was across the river on the reservation. With just that much direction, I took a small rubber boat across the river in the cold month of December and checked around the best I could, without loosing what little hair was still on my head, if you know what I mean. I found very good indications of gold as well as foot prints of someone in moccasins about size thirteen and a half. I found the prints but whoever it was didn't find me, because I am still here to tell the story!

There was much fine gold in the sand bars all along the San Juan River from Bluff to Mexican Hat and there has been enough recovered to authenticate it. The problem was that it is just too fine and was not concentrated in large enough deposits to make it profitable. There is likely fine gold spread out clear to the Colorado River and under Lake Powel.

Small amounts of gold have been recovered in upper Recapture Gulch and above a reservoir just north of Blanding. I found an old monitor used in washing gold, clear up on the side of the Abajo Mountains west of Monticello.

A little off the subject, a friend of mine who happened to be an old Ute Indian who lived on the Ute reservation in that area was talking about the way the white people do things, he said, and I have to agree, "Those people stand around all day looking up into the sky, looking for their god for help and they don't find him, but we look around us and see our god in everything, the mountains, the plants and the animals, in everything we see and touch. We see our god all the time, everywhere." You might call them "Dumb Indians", but they don't have to die to get their reward from their religion sometime in the distant future, they have it now. Makes you wonder who won? Us or the Indians?

CRIME & PUNISHMENT?
NO CRIME...NO WRONG!

Who is to say? After all, everything is relative to each different situation. I have found that I know nothing, and all I can do is the best that I can do, relative to the immediate circumstances. You understand that? And after all, there is a statute of limitations or you wouldn't be hearing this story from me.

I had just finished the story about Woody and the J.P. court in Monticello and it reminded me that not long after we hauled that "little" tractor through the Revenue Station with the safety sticker upside down, that another similar situation occurred. Same winch truck, same Port of Entry, and I had agreed to haul a load of mine rail from one uranium mine to the Betty Mine way back up behind the Blue Mountains, west of Monticello. Well...I had gone through the Port enough to know just about what I could get away with, me being a Gentile in Mormon land. So, I decided not to go through it. You might call me insane, but you can't call me stupid. I had crooked and bent rail in ten to twenty foot sections. The short ones went on the bottom, in under and around the good sized thirty five ton winch with the gin poles. The longer ones of various lengths went along inside the poles and some of then laid across the side mirror on the right side. What a mess! With the winch line still through the chiv-block, I wrapped the cable around the load and sucked it together. It looked better, but there were still several long rails hanging down to the ground. No worry, I tied the bundle together with a chain and wrapped my winch line around the tail-draggers and sucked them up, and then sucked them up higher so someone coming up behind me wouldn't get harpooned. No red flag! So I took off my shirt and wired it on the end of the rails.

Well, it was hot and I was hungry and my drinking water was hot and stale and there I was going down the blacktop just waiting for the siren and the flashing red lights. Fifty miles an hour, and the front end was much too light, but it did still steer okay. It was forty, fifty miles to Monticello and no way was I going to loop by the Port. I drove that odd looking load right through the length of town and up the other side in second gear and then in a few miles, down again to the bottom of Verdure Gulch and up the other side in second gear. Then there was Devil's Canyon, and I went down in second riding the brakes, then up the other side, trying for all the speed I could get. After Devil's Canyon, it was first gear on one grade, but then it was down hill, too steep for high gear going down to the bottom of Recapture Canyon. It was second and first gear all the way, never shift to forth because it was all uphill and then downhill again in second gear to home. I was looking back more than ahead expecting the red flashing lights just anytime, but there was no State Patrol, no Sheriff, no city cops from Monticello, no red lights! It looked like I made it! When daylight came the next morning, I was thirty miles west of Blanding, climbing the switch backs to the Betty mine. Well, did I commit a crime? I did the best I could under the circumstances.

One thing leads to another and speaking of the Port of Entry I'm reminded of a situation that happened back in about 1953. Remember I mentioned the statute of limitations? I still don't tell this story around Monticello. We moved into the area in 1974 and lived there for almost twelve years. One time I mentioned to one of the old timers, "Say, wasn't there a stretch of concrete road out there by the Port of Entry?" The old man said, "How did you know that? It's been covered up for fifteen or twenty years!" So I told him the story. Back in 1953 I was hired to stake Uranium claims in Red Canyon, down along the Colorado River below the now submerged old town of Hite. There were three of us riding in my old Army Surplus weapon's carrier. We were coming back through Monticello, heading for Grand Junction, and we were almost at the area where the Port of Entry is now. My old weapon's carrier was piled high with camping gear, water cans, gas cans (both full and empty) and there was a certain amount of questionably safe dynamite in the load, when, right in front of us, a semi gas tanker suddenly hit his brakes. His last two axels were bouncing up and down and his tires were smoking and skidding and when I hit my brakes, about twenty feet behind him, I said, "I'm going to hit him! I can't stop in time! We are all going to die!" Then out of my right eye there was an opening and I thought that I could maybe get around him. I jerked the steering wheel to the right and we avoided sudden death. But, we were still going about thirty miles an hour right up the center of a new patch of freshly poured concrete road that was about ten inches deep and there were men on both sides that were leveling and finishing. So there we were going right up the middle. Did we stop? Hell no! I knew these Mormon people and we were Gentiles, Outsiders. I then said, "Well, if I'm going to jail there better be a reason, we got nothing to lose!" Kicking the old Dodge into four-wheel drive, I glanced back through the mirrors; there were the screaming concrete covered men and the splattered tanker and everything else. I put the petal to the metal and away we went. There was nothing to lose. There was wet concrete sprayed out both sides of the forms. It must have been ten to fifteen feet out each side for thirty or forty feet (we didn't stop to measure it) and we didn't go back and say, "GOLLY, GEE WHIZ, WE'RE SURE SORRY FELLAS!" Just try to tell twenty or more cement covered screaming men (and all Mormons to boot), "After all, we DID save your lives!" I'm not kidding, we heard those men screaming and swearing (and Mormons do swear) for at least a mile on down the road. Stop? Hell, no! We didn't stop at Dove Creek just across the border into Colorado, no, we went north to drop down Slick Rock Hill and to the Dolores River and we didn't stop until we got to Big Gypsum Valley and then we hid out way off the road. We laughed until we cried and were scared to death, too. We drove the last hundred miles or so in the dark to Grand Junction. Then I found out that our whole job was just a scheme to sell stock, just a get-rich-quick scheme, but instead of getting rich, all I would probably have gotten was five to ten years in the pen. I was only about twenty years old at the time and it sounded good, too good to be true! But after staking out more than two hundred claims in both Colorado and Utah, I could see that it was a big hoax and I was right in the center of it. I got out and it wasn't long before the F.B.I. came in and put a stop to it.

One more story about crime and punishment and the statutes of limitations. We were living in Paonia, Colorado, and I was driving a big tandem axel dump truck, hauling gravel on a road job between Crawford and Hotchkiss. I was working a four a.m. to noon shift when this incident took place. One morning on a return trip to the gravel pit, on a side street in the little town of Crawford about daylight, a car ran a stop sign right in front of me. I hit the brakes, the truck did have good brakes, and I missed him. He kept going and I kept going, but at the next intersection there was an enormous "POP" and I could see poles waving back and forth through the rear vision mirrors along with quite a number of hanging wires. Apparently, when I hit the brakes, the P.T.O. (power take-off) lever flipped ahead and the hoist lever went into the "up" position so the bed on the truck had come up. I had torn down a guy-cable between two poles on opposite sides of the street and destroyed all the telephone lines in town as well as those leading out of town. I dropped the bed and kept right on hauling! What to do? Being sorry wouldn't have solved anything or trying to explain just what happened wouldn't have helped either. It was certainly circumstances completely beyond my control. I had a wife and two kids to take care of and had not even gotten my last paycheck from those Grand Junction promoters. Jobs were hard to find and I had found this one at three thirty a.m. in the morning and we were just getting by. It seemed the only thing to do at the time and no one got hurt.

It was years later that this incident came to light. We had four kids by then, so it was several years later. I met a fellow that said that his family used to own and operate the telephone system in Crawford and the surrounding country. I casually asked him, "Did you ever find out who it was that tore down all your telephone lines back in 1953!" He just looked at me and broke out in a big smile and said, "Was that YOU?" "Yes, it was." I told him and then explained just how it happened. "Water under the bridge." he said. "We never knew, but Ma Bell owns it all now, so it's not my problem." So, I bought him a Pepsi and we called it square. And that, my friend, is the end of that!

Joe Smith & The Last Indian Uprising In Southeastern Utah

There was poor old Joe Smith hobbling down the street to the Blue Mountain Café for his morning cup of coffee. He was eighty five years old with arthritis, crippled feet, hardly able to walk, but still going right down the center of the street, a common sight in the town of Blanding, Utah.

"Say, Joe, wouldn't it be easier to get your wife to make you a cup of coffee at home?" asked Harvey Butler, who was not one of the Mormons, or Later Day Saints as they were called, it being the predominating religion in the area. Since the Mormon Church prohibited the drinking of coffee, Joe's answer was, "Oh, no, Harv, it is a LOT easier to go down town to the café!" Especially since his wife was one of those staunch believers in the dictates of the Mormon Church. Joe was a Mormon, through and through, but he'd never lost his coffee habit.

My wife and I got acquainted with Joe and his wife when we were trying to buy a piece of land to live on in the Blanding area. We found out that the church frowned on letting us

"Gentiles" (as they called us) get too permanent in their state. This elderly couple was real nice and hospitable and although they didn't offer us a cup of coffee, we had a very nice educational visit. They had lived in Blanding and Bluff since the Turn of the Century and had seen many incidents take place around there. Joe said that he and a friend had been involved in the last Ute uprising down on White Mesa in the early 1930's. As Joe began relating stories of his past, he told us the story of his involvement with the Ute Indians. His words were, "Chief Posey and a bunch of his tribe came at us down there on White Mesa with their rifles and began shooting at us." He went on to say, "They couldn't get a bullet in me or my partner because we were hunkered down in the rocks so far they couldn't find us. That's when old Posey got shot by one of our group while they were trying to escape to Comb Ridge."

Joe didn't tell the complete story of WHY Posey and his followers were so riled up but later we heard "the rest of the story," as was told by both Mormons and "Gentiles." The story was that the local Mormons had rounded up most of the Ute women and children and had them confined under guard in a corral just south of Blanding. This was just part of the effort put forth by local Mormons to push the Utes out of the Cottonwood Canyon area and take over their grazing lands. When the Bucks came home to find their wives and children kidnapped by the local Militia, they started out to rescue them with loaded rifles. They didn't get far because the Mormons were coming after them and they all came together on the north end of the reservation.

The war started and the only man mentioned being shot, was Chief Posey. It set the wheels in motion for the women and children to escape. It was about this time that the Government sent in troops, not to put down the Indians, but to stop the Mormons from taking what was not theirs. The Army at that time ran the Mormons back out of Allen Canyon, and later had to do it again, several times, until the Army laid down the law stating, "The next time we find you (Mormons) in here after driving the Utes and their flocks out with guns, we have orders to shoot to kill! This is to be the last warning!" There was so much violence and rebellion on the part of the local Mormons that in the end, the Army shot the door open at the bank and confiscated all the money and took it to Denver.

Now back to the Utes. Chief Posey was badly wounded and yet he was able to organize and lead his tribe, with women, children and their flocks of sheep, down over the vertical cliffs of Comb Ridge to the west of Blanding. There was a hidden trail used only by the Utes and kept secret. It was Comb Ridge that stopped the Mormon inroad into Southern Utah at that time. Chief Posey died of his wound after leading his people down over the cliff. Some say that he was buried in Snow Cave on the west side of the valley.

I made friends with an old Navajo man living with the Utes on White Mesa. He said that he knew Posey. He and his brother-in-law had rifles shoved into their hands and were expected to fight the Mormons. He said that he threw his rifle down but his brother-in-law did fight and was killed. Pete Phillips was the old man's name and when I asked his age, he told me, "I'm about one hundred and four, I think. We have no naltose (the Navajo word for paper or records in this case) but I remember when the Mormons came into this country. They pulled their carts by hand and had steel on their shoes like the horses. Men and women both pulled the carts and all they had for food was flour, beans and coffee. "Coffee?" I asked. "Oh, Yes!" he said. We guess that it was still allowed at that time.

I had many very interesting visits with Pete, but he really wasn't quite one hundred and four years old and perhaps the Mormons that he had seen were the bunch that Poncho Villa ran out of Old Mexico and that settled in Bluff. My wife used to send down biscuits and rolls and jelly and things for him as he lived alone at the time, and he really loosened up and told me stories. When I asked if he ever drove, he said, "Oh, yes, I had a pickup (chidee in Navajo) but when I go down the hill off the mesa, all the time I have no brakes." Then he struck his open left hand with his right fist to emphasize that he always hit something with the pickup. Well, sad to say, he's dead and gone now and his little house was burned as is the Indian way if someone dies in a house.

That reminds me of another Indian, a Navajo named Shorty. I picked him up several times in the ancient Mac truck that I drove hauling oil out of the Anneth Oil Field, also referred to as the "Oil Patch" at Montezuma Creek. I would see him crippling down the road just after his check came in and heading for the Trading Post just off the reservation, going after beer. He would crawl up in the cab and with a nod of "thank you," pat both of his legs and say, "Knees no good for walking, family went off and left me behind, they get to trading post before me." Sometimes we managed to get there first and he would have a beer in hand when his family got there. That sure made his day and was fun for me, too. Shorty is dead and gone, so I was told. He was drunk on beer late one night and hobbling back to his hogan. He stumbled and fell over a cliff and was found sometime later, dead. He had lived a full life, I'm sure, but my regret is that he never told me much about his early life on the reservation. It is all left to my imagination now, and I am certain he had a very interesting life.

Things have changed, as always, but don't let the past be forgotten, whether it's good or bad, because there are way too many stories that need to be brought back to mind and put in writing.

THE SPECIAL LADY
LIVING AT THE DOORWAY TO THE VALLEY OF THE GODS

Mulley Point, John's Canyon, Mexican Hat, Monument Valley, Gouldings—they all do exist and are and were important locations in many people's lives. The country is always dry, all year long, dry and hot and cold, many times all in a single day. There is a beautiful mystic and even very dangerous aspect to all this high desert country. To see it just once is never enough. This area has a special attraction to those of a quiet nature such as the Navaho people and others of the same mind.

North of Monument Valley and the Trading Post at Gouldings across the San Juan River is the small town of Mexican Hat. Up river just a few miles is a road that leads right to the bottom of enormous sandstone cliffs. The Goose Necks of the San Juan are to the left some miles out and the road down river close by leads to John's Canyon. There at the base of that great wall of cliffs, really just under it, is a rambling one story stone house of many rooms. It was there that my wife and I met and came to know a very kind and loving elderly lady. We knew her as Connie Cartwright. That was the name she took for herself, it wasn't her real name. Some years before, she had been subjected too much mental and physical abuse by her husband and she had to escape from that life threatening situation by finding a quiet, peaceful place to live and begin life all over again. She soon became well known among all the local people, the Navajo in particular.

She was called Sister Connie or Sister Cartwright as she was known and for very good reasons because her house was open to everyone who came her way. She treated everyone like a family member. Her home was a living room with many adjoining bedrooms. It had been build about the Turn of the Century with the idea of it being a dude ranch. Each room had a stone fireplace. The roof was constructed of many great timbers that had been salvaged from the very old abandoned oil rigs near there. There was a large water tank behind the kitchen that the Mexican Hat Fire Department filled for her as she had the only water tank for many miles around. When the house was first built, we found out that their source of firewood was cedar and pinion from the mesa above. They had set up a cable from the top down to the bottom and stapled the wood to the cable and send it down to the bottom. On impact at the bottom the wood would come off the cable and some times be shattered into pieces and not have to be cut. Of course at the time Connie lived there, all the fuel they had was brush and roots that could be scrounged on the valley floor. We would try to take her loads of pine that we cut in the mountains around Blanding as often as we could.

In the cold winter months there would always be several families sleeping on the floor close to the open fire places. Her house was always open to all in need and she would share what food she had and she always had tea of some sort. The Navajos taught Connie many things about their religion and she in turn explained many bible principles to them. They have appreciation for all that has been created from the sun and moon to the trees and all that is on the earth. We were told once by an Indian, "The white man stands all day long looking into the sky for their god, and don't find him, but we look all around us here at the trees, the earth, the sky and our god is everywhere." The Indians have great respect for the sanctity of life and one of their expressions is "go in beauty" as they try to be in harmony with nature.

One cold winter the Indians found Connie very sick and the house was cold. There was not enough fuel and the house was hard to heat. So a group of them dug out a stone lined cellar that they knew was there that had blown full of sand. They cleaned it out and set up a small stove and a bed and put her things in there and moved her in and nursed her back to health. Connie, Sister Connie, Sister Cartwright has long since passed away. The Navajos and her son, who we met later, wanted to set up a stone monument in front of her house with an inscription in her memory, but it never came to pass. It was not really needed because her memory is still in the minds and heart of the many, many people that she gave her love to.

PART 7
A FEW MORE STORIES

MARBLE, COLORADO

A MOST FANTASTIC TOWN

It has been all but forgotten now, even Nellie Iron's boarding house. The Crystal River and San Juan Railroad extended from Satank just north of Carbondale and up the beautiful Crystal River, just west of Mount Sopris. The railroad crossed Avalanche Creek and extended on beyond two hot springs and what is now the town of Redstone, Colorado, and the access road up Coal Basin. I can still envision the red sandstone up on the hillside east of town and the old coke ovens that are still there across the river. The Redstone Inn is still there and up the river is the Redstone Mansion.

I remember when I was quite young my father and my uncle hunted and fished within walking distance at the river along side the town and we all caught Rainbow trout. Back then nothing was wasted not even the undersized fish that were caught. At a meal my father placed a very undersized fish on the game warden's plate along with some that were a little larger. The Rainbow trout back then were only about seven or eight inches long, the legal limit was seven inches. Either my dad or Uncle Ray shot a four point buck right through the heart, way back up the valley across the river.

That buck actually ran about a hundred yards into a rocky tight little wash before it died. They dressed it out, cut it up and carried it back to town. I was only about twelve years old and I was given all the rifles to carry. It took parts of two days for us to get that deer out and I remember that we ate the heart and liver with onions at our first meal.

There are so many true stories such as the little train (a little ten one hundred steam locomotive) that ran many years until the Second World War. The Superintendent of Marble Mill often drove his Model T right up the tracks and at times had to be pushed into the mill by the steam locomotive. The locomotive was called "Sage brush Annie" when it traveled between Aspen and Glenwood Springs.

So now back up the river to Marble and the Yule Quarry. In 1953 we constructed a large bridge across the Crystal River using the biggest spruce logs available. The Yule Quarry was several miles up the valley and mostly on a side hill. A special built street car that had a controller on each end and a flat bed was used to haul the marble blocks to the mill. I was told that a large steam powered crane got away and was lost over the steep hill.

The big block of marble that was used for the tomb of the Unknown Soldier was placed on the track on brass skids and then drug down to the mill. The last time I saw the underground

MARBLE, COLORADO A MOST FANTASTIC TOWN

quarry the bottom was covered with ice and it remained there most of the year. Big marble blocks were cut and hoisted to the top of the quarry and moved outside to be hauled to the mill. There were many big blocks of marble outside that had been stained various colors from minerals. There were actually seven or eight different colors of stone, each known by a specific name. There are just so many beautiful things if we just open our eyes and hearts and take notice.

Just up above the quarry there are multicolored crystals in formation. Across the valley the mountain is called White House or Treasure Mountain where there is a silver mine containing many quartz crystals and silver ore.

In 1953 Basic Chemical somehow acquired the quarry property and the mill. The primary use for the marble was for the lime content. Bellm Electric had wired in the conveyer and the jaw crusher and I was hired as part of the crew to get the marble crushed down to about one and a half inch size. There were three of us that loaded blocks small enough to crush with a truck mounted crane. We had a half-track truck with a tall tower and a three hundred foot drop ball that we used to break up the larger pieces. We also had a big English four wheel drive dump truck with single tires of enormous size that we used to hauled pieces to the crusher. At that time there was a large retaining wall by the Crystal River next to the mill and it had been used to stop the snow slides from covering the mill. Years before more than one slide had nearly wiped out the mill. While tearing down the wall, we found headstones, statues, rolling pins and all sorts of interesting things that had been made from the marble. They all ended up in the crusher. There was also a large Buda powered electric generator and a Ford industrial engine that powered the crusher motors. The drive wheel on the crusher weighed close to a ton and it broke twice. We actually pounded tons of marble into the ground with the drop ball until the ground became solid enough to make it possible break the marble pieces down to a size that the crusher could handle. We hand fed that crusher and wore out six or seven pairs of gloves a week. We even put them on backwards until we found heavy plastic gloves to use.

The boom truck operator would swing me into places on the retaining wall where I would place dynamite charges in the seams and cracks and after I spit the fuse, he would swing me around the other side of the wall. He gave me some wild rides hanging on that cable. We also loaded blocks of marble for certain sculptors to use. Another thing I remember is losing a brand new double bitted axe into the fast running icy stream. It took three dives to get that axe back! I did it to prove that I could do it.

The air was pure and the water was clean and clear. Just across the river there was a large hillside of wild raspberries that the bears seemed to think belonged to them and we didn't contest that. We ate lots of fish and venison and found time to get into water fights. Freda and I had an eighteen foot trailer and two children, Gus and Lois and for a while we had Freda's sister's three kids and a friend of theirs from California. The older kids slept in an old army squad tent and it was a wonderful summer. We had salvaged an old one-hole out house to use and we fixed a fenced in patio of marble slabs and a nice outside fireplace.

Our transportation was an old 1949 Desoto. One weekend with six kids inside the car and Dan and Irene riding on the rear bumper bouncing up and down we headed up Daniel's Hill which was a steep solid rock ledge to Lizard Lake to go fishing. I lost the plug out of the oil pan, so we had to go back to the mill yard for our Dodge weapons carrier and I braised the oil plug and put it back on and we still went fishing.

We kept our deer meat way back in a mine tunnel behind the lake. The lake and the mine tunnel were on the way to the abandoned town of Crystal City where the famous picture of the Ghost Mill was taken. Some distance below the town of Crystal City, up on a ragged cliff there is still a deposit of silver ore where three brothers were working and one fell and was killed and they gave it up. There is a lot more to tell, but that's enough for this story. That was our summer at Marble, Colorado

I Know About You!!
Maclure Pass

Two thousand feet back underground an electrician that I had never seen before said to me, "I know YOU! You're the guy that fixed the Jeep up on the top of McClure Pass." "Well, I haven't been over that pass in the last ten years!" I told him. "It was you and your wife, and it was a long time ago, he said. You fixed the steering on a Jeep with a piece of a rifle barrel."

Sure enough! I remembered that we had found two young couples standing alongside a Jeep that was nosed into the hillside. They were just college kids on a break. They had just bought a used Jeep and lost the steering on top of the pass. They were stranded with not much money, and no tools to boot.

"Let's see if we can fix it, at least enough to get you down the mountain," I said. It was easy to see what was wrong; it was a broken centering pin in the steering mechanism. It was a slightly tapered pin about three or four inches long, broken in half.

"I'm pretty sure I can fix it," I said. They looked at me and shook their heads and said, "Are you sure." I was more prepared than they thought. I had a piece of 30.06 gun barrel in my junk box that I had used for a bar, a roller and a cheater at times. I had to cut it down to size using an old worn out hacksaw. It was just the right size and fit just like a new part. Then I filed a notch in the top for the retaining bolt and poured a little motor oil over the works and it worked as good as new. They thought that maybe it was even better than when they bought it. It was good enough for them to go on their way, but they felt bad because they couldn't pay me anything for fixing it. "Don't worry about it, what goes around comes around. You don't owe us a thing," I said. The two girls brought out a small box of hand made earrings that they had made in school. They were copper with a baked ceramic finish on them, really pretty, and they let Freda pick out a couple of pairs of them. That was even better than money. It sure meant more to us. That is one of our many memories of McClure pass.

Another time Freda and I were heading over the same pass from the Muddy Creek side and we were almost to the top when we saw a pickup with a camper loaded with supplies. They had slid over the bank two days before and both rear wheels were hanging over the side of the bank. They said the mud was too deep to walk out. Both men were sick and one said that he had been shot in the stomach not too long ago and he was hurting. So we turned the car around and loaded the guys in and fought our way back down the pass on to Hotchkiss and then on up to Crawford where the wounded man lived with his school teacher wife. Then we found out "The rest of the Story!" These guys were not "sick" but were stuck and had drunk all the booze they had and the real emergency was that all their bottles were empty and they were suffering.

The story of the man with the stomach wound was an interesting one. He was skinning Cat for the Forest Service and had rolled a D7 Cat over the hill and although he jumped off, a rock about the size of a wash tub hit him in the face and he had never been quite the same since. The bullet wound happened when he borrowed ten dollars from an old age pensioner at the bar in town and refused to pay it back. Most likely both men were drinking at the bar when the old man wanted his money back and he chewed out and embarrassed the guy in front of friends. Later that same evening, the ex-cat skinner walked up on the old man's porch and began cussing him out right through the screen door. The old pensioner grabbed his "Saturday Night Special" which was on the stand by his chair and shot the other fellow dead center right thought the screen door. The ambulance came to the house and hauled off the wounded man who was screaming his head off and the local law gave the old man hell for shooting the guy, but after looking closely at the belly wound, they had a good laugh because the bullet was so old that the slug barely got through the screen door and only put a terrible big ugly bruise on that guy. Later the law came back with a new box of bullets for that gun and said his drinking buddy might come back and they thought that he needed some fresh bullets for the occasion.

Some time after we rescued that character, he talked me into climbing down the Black Canyon after some "good gold." After spending a night down there, we came back empty handed. I only went once with him and once was enough. It was a beautiful climb, but what a climb!

Just a couple of interesting side notes about McClure Pass; I understand that a man took an old wooden spoke touring car up there to try to prove that it was possible to go over the top and he was forced to leave the car somewhere up there. I looked for it but didn't find it. Also, Thomas Edison made one of the first motion pictures on the west side of the pass and the old cabin he used was still there in the 1950's. The picture had something to do with Grizzly bears, I think. It is interesting country and worth seeing if you have never been there.

Norwood Trip

We were living in Paonia, Colorado in 1957 in a little two room shanty with a covered porch on the side and an outhouse in the back, but we had running water! I was working three jobs and hardly made forty dollars a week and we had three kids with one due in the summer. One of the ladies in our congregation, Cora, a very slender widow lady, with two kids, came to me to ask a favor. She had a son-in-law that worked in Norwood and the job had run out and they had a little trailer that they were living in and they needed someone to move it for them. They were just kids and didn't have a car of their own at the time. How could I refuse?

There were a lot of needy families in our congregation that winter in the Paonia Valley on the North Fork of the Gunnison River. We all tried to help each other out as best we could and none of us ever went hungry. King Solomon said, "A young man I used to be and now I have grown old and never have I seen the servant of the living GOD begging bread."

I had an old 1940 Dodge weapons carrier that had just been repaired. I was hauling coal to some old folks and had to leave the truck set and it was cold that year. I couldn't afford Prestone for the radiator and had tried to drain the water, but didn't get the petcock opened far enough so it froze and broke the block. With that repaired, I agreed to move their trailer. With money tight both of the kid's mothers chipped in what money they could for expenses.

With Paul, his wife and myself, off we went with no side windows and a small inadequate heater. It was twenty miles to Delta then up through Montrose and up the Uncompagre River almost to Ouray. Then north up over Dallas Divide and down Leopard Creek through Placerville, down the San Miguel River canyon to Norwood Hill then up the steep winding, snowy hill to Norwood and on the other side of the town there sat that small old single axel trailer. It was dark by time we got to the trailer. We had lights of a sort, but no brakes on the trailer. We got on our way, eating cold sandwiches and lukewarm coffee from a thermos. It was dark and cold with lots of stars in the sky.

We stopped at the top of Norwood Hill and put Clorox on all the tires for traction on the snow and I eased down that steep Norwood Hill. I was relieved to find that it had been sanded because at the very bottom of that hill there is a right angle to turn to go across the bridge and then another sharp angle on the other side. Those corners caused a lot of accidents. Going up the canyon we found the road snow packed all the way to Placerville. Just above Placerville

I spun out, four wheel drive and all. The chains I had were too short so I had to find some wire to lengthen them and the handiest thing I could find was a fence along the road. It was barbed wire and I had to take it apart and take the barbs off to use it. We were finally our way again and it was COLD. I didn't have a thermostat so I used cardboard to block off the radiator going down hill and then had to take it off going up hill.

We saw flashing red lights ahead and there were vehicles off the road, but we kept going, easing by the mix up, we finally made it to the top of Dallas Divide in low range. We stopped at the top and ate what food we had left and finished the cold coffee. We could see lights shining up against the clouds forty miles away in the direction of Montrose. Down the hill we went at ten miles an hour with no heat except from our huddling together with a blanket over us. We had stocking caps and scarves and heavy wool socks for mittens, but it was still cold.

At the bottom of the pass we took off the chains and then we could speed up to thirty five or forty miles an hour in places and we finally got to Montrose. We stopped for gas and had just enough money for three hamburgers and three cups of coffee and a chance to warm up. It was on to Delta and then Hotchkiss. We were leaving the trailer in Hotchkiss at one of their mother's houses but half a dozen miles before town, we had a flat tire and the safety rim came off and went over the bank. Nothing to do but unload and change the tire and by then it must have been about two a.m. in the morning and the temperature was about ten degrees. We got the trailer parked and almost had to carry Paul's poor wife to the house and then I still had to drive the rest of the way to Paonia and to my house. To make things worse the radiator froze up and I had to find water and get it thawed out and when I got about a hundred yards from the house, I ran out of gas!

I would probably do it again, even now in my old age because you do what you can to help your fellow believers, Like the Bible says, "Do to others as you would want them to do to you." Freda and I have always had help when we needed it so we know that it works.

THE LITTLE LOG HOUSE
ON THE BONANZA PLACER

"Eleven thousand eight hundred plus cement blocks in the foundation alone?" was the question. "Well, yes, but a few of them were only eight inches wide instead of twelve." I answered. These blocks were cold stacked eleven feet high and filled with concrete to support a Finland style log building, a full two stories high. So to start at the beginning my friend and boss went to an auction just south of Basalt, Colorado, just a little north of Aspen. "There is a log house under construction over there," my boss said to me. I understood later that it was being built for Goldie Hawn in Steamboat Springs Colorado. "What am I bid for that log house?" said an auctioneer. Well, Ed said that he had thirty thousand dollars in his pocket so he said, "I bid thirty thousand!" Bang! "SOLD to Ed Smart for thirty thousand dollars!" And the logs and the house had to be moved from the property in thirty days. "Okay, Harvey." Ed told me. I hired my friend, Joe, to level off the south end of the Bonanza Placer claim which was a short distance above Castle Creek on the back side of Aspen Mountain. Then I hired three big logging trucks to begin moving all the loose stacked logs to the building site. It took two or three weeks and then I located a large Army Surplus boom truck from Glenwood Springs to begin taking down the existing building. It was raining most of the time. We did it with the help of my youngest son and his partner.

A contractor was hired to lay out the enormous pad of concrete and begin laying up the blocks on the perimeter and supports for the inside walls. Then the contractor hired a crane with a one hundred forty foot reach and began laying up the logs. The expense of that rig was astronomical and it was hired for four months or more. After finding out this piece of ignorance, I told the crane operator ten days and told the contractor the same thing. "We can't do it, what about the water and the electricity and the drain pipes?" they asked. "We will run it up around the door frames and window frames as much as possible," I replied. It wasn't easy, but we laid up all the pre-cut logs in eight days. There was no chinking but fiberglass between the logs and all of it out of sight. There were still the second story roof logs to put up and the enormous gable above the living room.

Soon the snow was there and we decided not to put down the sub-floor until spring, but the contractor started to do it anyway trying to force us to let him work all winter. I was told to lay off the whole bunch until spring. We covered the top logs and left for Arizona to re-stake placer claims and test for gold.

In early spring we went back to Aspen with our small Airstream trailer. Joe tied it on the blade of his Cat and pulled it to the site in the snow. We set up just below the house. First we shoveled all the snow out of the building and then removed the plastic sheeting on the logs on the house. Countless thousands of staples were left in the logs as we tore the plastic off. It wasn't long until the contractor had the sub-floor done.

Unable to locate a piece of equipment to place the thirty to forty foot logs on the first floor roof, we did it by hand. They were placed cross ways at heights of twenty to thirty feet by using a hand powered cable come along, and overall it was faster and less expensive and even less dangerous. There was a large center log support that had to be stood up at the far end of the living room. The log was nearly twenty foot long and three foot wide at the base. My wife and I put the log up by ourselves on the weekend just to prove a point. We drug the log to the building site with my old Jeep. We rolled it up on poles and placed it on the living room floor and then raised it up with two fifteen dollar cable hoists and pried it in place with a big steel bar. It could not have been accomplished without my wife standing back and making sure that I didn't get careless. Sure it took us several hours and a great deal of effort but we did it. Four of us put logs in place and my son, through trial and error, with a chain saw did what the other contractors couldn't do. We finished it by hand.

We also built outside stairs from logs and they met the specifications of the County to the inch. From the ground to the apex of the building was thirty five feet. The contractor got an estimate on a metal roof for forty thousand dollars but my wife located a roofing contractor that was much more honest at a price of eighteen thousand dollars. All of the inside walls were of logs and according to the blueprint there were three rooms missing. We began measuring and took a chain saw to the inside walls and sure enough found two more bedrooms. We doubled the size of Ed's bedroom and bathroom with a chain saw.

We were asked to locate the chandelier that was used in "Gone with the Wind." Ed had bought it and it was left in an old Catholic Church in old Bisbee that Ed had sold to an artist. When we finally found it, it was nothing but a great many gold painted pipe fittings fitted with electric candles, typical Hollywood movie junk. An old steering wheel from a steam boat from a Mississippi river ship showed up. It was a Hollywood prop used in the picture "Around the world in Eighty days," I was told. I was asked if I would like to live in that house. I replied, "Sure, I'll park my little Airstream in the basement and be quite comfortable!" There was plenty of room for it.

I had to bring the big air compressor down from the John Wayne Tunnel and set a jack leg drill on the grill of my Jeep pickup to drill through the cement filled concrete block so as to get propane into the kitchen. Flagstone was needed for outside work and I found beautiful red sandstone down on the Frying Pan River. I quarried out and hauled ten to fifteen tons to the building site.

My son and I felled many hundreds of aspen trees to clear the property and cut it into fireplace lengths and couldn't even give it away so we ended up burning tons of it. We build a log fence on two sides of the property and set up a decorative entrance way of logs with a big sign saying, "Ed Smarts Bonanza Placer." It stood for ten years and then the logs rotted and it all fell to the ground.

A humorous incident occurred at the open house on the Forth of July. I'd agreed to climb up on the ridge up the creek across from the house and at a signal begin tossing dynamite down the hill. So using just half sticks and a short fuse, I did make a lot of noise lying under a tree sipping wide mouth Mickey's Ale and reading a Louis L'Amour's book. After ten or fifteen blasts, I tossed a live stick of dynamite in a close tree and that's the fastest I'd moved all day. I placed all the rest of the explosives in a crevice around the hill and set it off. The blast was heard for miles. Down at the house there was a horse tank filled with snow and beer and pop. Some party crashers showed up and starting causing problems so I made a big snow ball and hit one of them in the back of the neck and then looked back to see who threw it and the war was on! So I put a contract on the boss's secretary, four bits to anyone who could hit her. She was sitting up on the porch in front of the big front room windows. I had to raise it to six bits and then she really caught it along with her mother and we ended up with a window.

I was told that three contractors had declared bankruptcy over this project already, but I didn't have four years of college, only a forty five minute introduction to "Higher Education," my education came at great cost. I've left blood and sweat and not a small portion of one arm at the mines in Colorado, Arizona, New Mexico, Utah and even a gold mine in Northern Nevada.   I've had ribs broken, a crushed chest, and a ruptured esophagus that bled into my stomach and I'm still able to function.   Sure I'm bragging, blowing my horn, because I was there and I did it.   I have survived being buried alive alone and trapped under ground by a great explosion that killed one of my mining partners. His head was torn off just above his lower jaw by a block of concrete. He lost his life attempting to get back to three of us in the dense poisonous smoke.

My point in this is that there are very few of us "Real People" left. We didn't do our mining or logging or bridge building or anything else in a bar where most of these stories come from. We made do and are better men because of it. That log house was just another project and I have pictures to prove it.   Much of my knowledge came from older men that have been up the creek and over the mountain.   I'm not that smart or overly intelligent or I wouldn't have all these health problems and scars. Moving earth, handling explosive, handling great weights, falling timber and building and yes even destroying and tearing down what was needed to get the job done, and I did it.

My son and I were told that we saved the man one and a half million dollars and we hardly got a "Thank You." We did the job to completion along with many others and this is just another true story of "Real People."

A Clothesline For Our Wives

First of all Eve didn't pressure Adam for a clothes line at least not at first, but for us today, we all like clean clothes or at least most of us do. I remember an old fellow that operated a truck line near Delta many years ago. He had a stroke and they took him to the hospital. One of the first things that they did at the hospital was to literally cut his long red underwear off of him because his body hair was growing out through the material. When conscious he complained that there were still several years of good use in them if they hadn't skinned him out like a dead rabbit! Phew! So let's get back on the subject of "A Clothesline for our Wives." I had a very special friend who was being pressured to put up an outside clothes line for his wife. She wanted it primarily for bed sheets, blankets and such. Now that's reasonable isn't it? However, that required the gathering and buying of the materials for it and that turned out to be difficult. It doesn't sound like it should be difficult though does it? But you have to decide just how you want it made.

We have all seen clothes hanging on barb wire fences and lines attached between everything and anything that seemed likely to support them. Why even at Crested Butte in the Colorado High Country, clothes lines are attached from the back porch to a pulley fifteen to twenty feet up to a wooden power pole because the snow gets too deep for a regular clothes line. Up there most every old house had a two-story out house because the snow got too deep and that's the truth.

Our wives would hang their stockings and underwear all over the bathroom, on the shower, towel racks, sink and bathtub and even manage to get a hook or two in the living room walls and manage some sort of line and don't forget the back porch, too. Our Navajo friends used the sheep pasture barbwire fences and even the beds on their pickup trucks if they didn't already have pieces of melons or something else already drying there.

But let's get back to deciding just what to use for clothes lines and how to make them. Using salvaged pipe was, or could have been good, that is if you had a hack saw or better yet, a cutting torch and then a welder was a necessity, too, of course. So with two, three inch diameter pipes and something for cross arms, you will still need two girts (diagonals) to hold the cross arms. As a matter of course most used material like this is zinc coated and is not conducive for good or attractive welding, so a coating of paint is always needed. You also have to determine the length of the pipe (pole), the length of the cross arms and the over all size. Another thing I've run into around this part of the country is that it's hard to find much used material available anywhere within miles of the Mexican Border. It seems to have all been salvaged and sold to provide money for beans and tortillas by the hard working Mexicans.

Using wood for construction seems the logical solution to me in this area. Four by four inch posts work well and treated ones are available but they are really very heavy. The tools needed for wood would be a saw, a framing square, an electric drill and a blue print (would help). Two ten foot four by fours are needed and two by four inch for diagonals and cross arms. Screws work better than nails. After you get the poles ready, there are still the holes to be dug and concrete mix to set the poles in. Yes, don't forget the paint! I might add a suggestion here, if many separate lines are wanted a four post construction method should be used. You also have to decide how far apart to set the poles and dig the holes in the right places. Then you have to decide how many lines you want (don't forget to figure how many feet of line you will need) and what you want to use for the lines. How are you going to attach the lines so that they can be periodically tightened? You might need eye bolts, turnbuckles and props for holding up the ever-sagging lines. So a simple clothesline for our wives turns into quite a project!

Now the lines are up and don't forget, a place is needed to set the heavy baskets of wet laundry while hanging. Then when they are all dry, you will have to fold them and carry them back in the house. It's sure a lot of work.

In my time I've put up a lot of different clothes lines for my wife, may Jehovah God bless her, she washed clothes and bedding regularly for all eight of us summer and winter for more than ten years at the altitude of ten thousand feet where we lived in Leadville, Colorado. She had to use a wringer washer for a while and with no dryer she had to hang the clothes outside where they would freeze dry in the winter time along with her fingers. We always had clean clothes. She did the best she could with what she had. That woman is still a very special woman to me. So I say that if any wife today that wants and needs a clothes line, I think that her husband should love her enough to put forth the extra effort that it takes to do it for her. They deserve all the assistance and praise we can offer.

There Is No Santa Claus!

"There is not a Santa Claus!" Well that is what my step mother told her school mate some ninety years ago, as the story goes. They were two young girls who lived many miles up the Frying Pan River and they were riding in the cab of a little narrow gauge steam engine of the Colorado Midland Railroad. The engineer would stop the train on occasion and pick the two girls up on their way to school down the river at Thomasville. Christmas was a big thing back then, and Ginger was looking forward to it, perhaps expecting a new dress or a new coat and perhaps some candy and an orange and such. It was true of the last Christmas and all the years that she could remember and that was a terrible thing for Loraine to say. So Ginger's answer to her was, "That might be true that there is no Santa Claus...for people like you!" Well, sad to say, my step mother was like that. She must have been one of the people that Will Rogers never met for he always said, "I've never met a person I did not like." I do admit that she did have her good points, but she had very few friends, real friends that is.

The point of this story is that all of us know the truth about Christmas and the jolly old character in the baggy red suit and the younger ones really know, too, that the gifts that they receive come from parents and friends. But I tell you for a fact, good things do happen to people who put their trust in good hearted people and beyond that those that put their trust in the Grand Creator and work toward righteous goals are provided for. Now don't get me wrong, there do seem to be miracles at times but there is more to it than is apparent. Prayers are answered, but we might not want to accept the answer that we get, for example the little girl who prayed for a pony for her birthday was ridiculed because she didn't get it. Her friends taunting her saying "See there, God didn't answer your prayer did he? You didn't get a pony!" "Oh, yes, he did answer my prayer, he just said 'No," she replied.

THE SILVER MINE TOUR
AND THE FOURTH GRADE

"Is this what they call strip mining, Mr. Bellm"? "No Mam, strip mining is much more like what they have done on that ski slope over there on the other side of the valley. We can see it from the mine here. They remove all of the trees and most of the vegetation and also cut dirt roads up the slopes to haul men and material all around." This was the innocent question asked by a fourth grade school teacher on a field trip with part of her fourth grade class. It was my job to explain just what we were doing and how we would mine through the mountain into the rich ore deposit of silver and then make it into pure silver ingots and coins.

I explained to this small group and to three more small groups of interested children and adults, that this mine is a show place and that we have to meet very rigid requirements enforced by the Bureau of Land Management, the local Forest Service, the State and various county officials. There are also radical groups and other individuals that feel it is their personal duty and privilege to stop any activity, however legal, just to enforce their individual ideas and that of their own little group.

I appreciated the honest question that this pretty young teacher asked in behalf of her class, children that were just beginning to learn what real life is all about. These groups were thrilled to actually visit a real silver mine in operation. I went on to explain that most small mine operators, even without all of the interference and opposition of the non-productive people, must maintain safe, clean mining practices just to be able to operate. I explained that we only disturbed a very small portion of the surface ground and this was continuously maintained so that we as miners could work safely and productively. However; if many of these ski slops are examined closely it becomes evident that they are governed in an entirely different manner. The destruction that is done on ski slopes for the pleasure and profit of some people is overlooked and covered up by political power and enormous amounts of money.

The "Real Environmentalists" are the "Real People" that work to keep the areas where they work and live beautiful and productive for everyone. We can do this to the lasting benefit of all the "Honest People" that are truly concerned. There is no honest way to explain why small mine operators are crowded out and others are allowed to do as they choose.

I am just a broken down old hard rock miner and it isn't my intention to single out any one group, but I really have a love for that which is beautiful and good for all of us and I very much dislike the dishonest practices of some to achieve their ends by any means. I know from over fifty years of personal experience in many mines, from the small ones to the largest ones, that especially small mines should and can be operated in a proper manner. That is why I could honestly state to the school children and the teacher, "No, Mam! Strip mining is more like what they have done on the ski slopes over there on the other side of the valley!"

YES, YOU WOULD HAVE TO SAY THAT I AM ENVIRONMENTALLY CONCERNED

Now, a lady, just the other day, asked me that question. As I opened my mouth to reply, being polite as I am, I had to stop a moment and think before I replied. You see, she knew that I prospected and dug gold bearing gravel and carried it home to concentrate. I do have to dig into gravel banks and at times remove plants and cactus from the immediate area where I am digging. And I do become acquainted with some of God's creations, such as rattle snakes, scorpions, tarantulas and all sorts of spiders and ants that sting and bite, as well as wasps, biting flies and gnats.

I can honestly reply that, yes, I am deliberately environmentally inclined. I would never think of deliberately killing or destroying some cute little creepy or crawly critter or spiny plant that someone else might enjoy. Why, they might be an endangered species! So, when I move a rock when I am down on my knees, and one of these very likely endangered species such as a scorpion runs out and charges between my legs, I always make a great effort to examine them closely to see if it is a black one that has a sting that will kill me outright, or if it is one of the less deadly ones that will only make me wish that I were dead. This can become a problem, so I take my digging tool and do my best to examine the little bugger being careful not to injure it with my bare hands.

This does entail some effort on my part because I'm getting on in years and not very steady when something nasty charges me. Besides, I can't see as well as I used to. So, sometimes I do get a little excited, or careless, and smash the hell out of the poor little things and for this I apologize. Of course I have tried to shoo them away, but with my shoes being a size nine, it is very difficult to shoo away one of those cute little six legged hypodermic needles. I guess that I do get a little rough on them, but never with malicious intent you understand, because the cute little critter needs to be left alive and fed and nourished so it can slip into someone's warm boot, or up some child's pants leg and kill them.

I do realize that if too many of them are accidentally exterminated, they will become an endangered species, and the government might have to pay some college graduates to begin breeding them in captivity and that would be just terrible. Besides, if I am caught in this terrible act, I could be fined and have to go to jail.

Now, rattle snakes are different and should be handled in a different manner, especially when you are down on your knees and come face to face with one of them. You see him and he sees you and he raises his head a little higher and hisses "hello" as he shakes his tail in rhythm to get your undivided attention. Many environmentalists and government officials will tell you that very few people die of snake bites here in the south west, and that if you carefully leave them alone, then they are not aggressive and will try to make up to you. This is absolutely true, because I personally don't know of any government expert being bitten and dying while sitting behind his desk in the big city thinking up these very intelligent facts based upon almost total lack of first hand observation.

There is a word of caution though, the rattle snake with the greenish cast to it's skin, and the beautiful prairie rattler may decide that they don't like you as well as you think they should. These two fine examples of God's creation may come right up to you quite quickly, to make your acquaintance, of course. The passionate kiss of either of these beauties could well cause you to lie down and rest in peace forever more. It would be well to avoid these endangered species and be sure to remember that the earth was created for rattle snakes and not for men, women and little children.

I personally have had only one green one try to get acquainted with me, but there have been several of the ordinary variety of rattle snakes that really have made an effort to make my day. Perhaps I became a little indignant with them in trying to get them to go away, maybe feeling a bit inhospitable that day, old age, I guess. There is one problem with these beauties down here next to the Old Mexican border, and that is.....they don't seem to understand the King's English. So, at a certain point in their advances, I have pulled out my 38 Smith and Wesson and assured them that my intentions are serious and that I don't wish to cultivate a further relationship.

But then again, being of advanced age, and with poor eye sight, when I attempt to shoot just under them, to warn them off, I do miss sometimes, and blow their heads off or the lead hits some gravel and rips their delicate little bodies to shreds or sorely injures these endangered species. And for this weakness on my part, I do apologize. I realize that these are God's creation and we should let them multiply and increase so our small children, our livestock and our wives, who may quietly back into a shaded bush and squat down to relieve themselves might painfully meet one of these most beautiful and endangered species. Yes, you will have to admit, I am environmentally concerned.

DEATH OF AN ENVIRONMENTALIST

This tragic incident that lead to death took place in the not too distant past on the Navaho Indian Reservation in south east Utah. It was on a Texaco oil lease at a sludge pond north of the town of Montezuma Creek. A young lad, recently hired by the Texaco Oil Company, in the presence of two regular workmen, discovered a large bird trapped in the oily salt water in a pond and immediately pulled on his hip boots to attempt its rescue. The pond under discussion was lined with neoprene and was completely enclosed with a stock fence to keep the sheep out and also had wire strung across it in a close pattern with colored tape attached to it to scare birds away. The pond was about two and a half feet deep and extremely slippery under foot. This boy waded out in the pond, stooping under the wires that were only about two feet above the stinking slimy mixture. His face came within inches of contact with the oil as he slipped and slid toward the struggling bird, while trying to steady himself by grasping the overhead wires that were spaced every few feet. He was in great danger of falling in the mixture and ending up just like the oil saturated bird.

It brought to mind an incident told to me by an uncle of mine while he was employed at a gold mine in California. It was told that he was caught high-grading too much gold, so they put him to mucking out the sump at the bottom of the shaft that had about three feet of mud and oily water in it. He said it was bad when it filled his rubber boots, but when he bent over to shovel, the soup ran down inside the front of his bib overalls, and that was something else. Now that was humorous, but in this instance, with crude oil and its dangerous fumes, it was a very bad situation. Not only could the bird die, but the young boy could also get his head under and he to might very well pay for his misguided endeavor to save a bird by endangering his own life.

Well, the big bird was about dead when the lad took hold of its wings and began struggling back to the bank, dragging it through the oil while he ducked under the wires. By then he had crude oil all over his hands and his shirt. When he finally did get the bird up on the bank and began wiping it off with rags, he found it to be a big Sand Crane. In the fresh air with the oil cleaned from its head, the crane soon recovered and began struggling to get away and finally did, but it headed right back to the pond and both boy and bird were back inside the fence. He jumped on the bird and it began flapping it's wings and striking at him with its long sharp beak. As he couldn't keep a hold of the slick wings with his slippery hands, he took hold of both of the bird's feet and held it at arms length, upside down, and then it DID take to flapping and squawking and flinging oil everywhere. The boy hung on and became completely saturated with wet, black crude oil, until he looked like something out of "Uncle Tom's Cabin." Now, that was a big bird, getting stronger and meaner by the second and the boy's arms were giving out. The bird began to strike out with its long beak until it latched on to the boy's leg just below his right rear pant's pocket and that big bird did take a big bite!

The boy let out a scream and a few very descriptive choice four letter works describing that ungrateful Sand Crane and gathered up his strength and swung that said creature up over his head and slammed it on the ground. He didn't turn it loose either. He swung it in the air over his head and pounded it on the ground again and again, in a figure eight-like motion. All this time he was cursing dumb birds and all of us were laughing at him and his earnest endeavor to show his personal concern for a poor creature that the coyotes would soon make a meal of anyway.

That was the day a young boy came face to face with reality, with the REAL facts of life.

THAT WAS THE DAY THAT BROUGHT DEATH TO AN ENVIRONMENTALIST...

As The Saying Goes,
"You Can Take The
Miner Out Of The
Mines
But You Can't Take
The Mines Out Of The
Miner."

Made in the USA
San Bernardino, CA
23 January 2015